2 Vols 25/-
18/6

gold gold 35 lly x35

THE EMPEROR CHARLES V.

MACMILLAN AND CO., Limited
LONDON · BOMBAY · CALCUTTA
MELBOURNE

THE MACMILLAN COMPANY
NEW YORK · BOSTON · CHICAGO
ATLANTA · SAN FRANCISCO

THE MACMILLAN CO. OF CANADA, Ltd.
TORONTO

THE
EMPEROR CHARLES V.

BY

EDWARD ARMSTRONG, M.A., F.B.A.

FELLOW OF QUEEN'S COLLEGE, OXFORD

AUTHOR OF 'ELIZABETH FARNESE,' 'THE FRENCH WARS OF RELIGION,'
'LORENZO DE' MEDICI

IN TWO VOLUMES

VOL. I

MACMILLAN AND CO., LIMITED
ST. MARTIN'S STREET, LONDON

1910

First Edition 1901.
Second Edition 1910.

PREFACE

THE preface to a biography of Charles V. necessarily resolves itself into an apology for its method. It is a comparatively easy task, if there be no stint of time or space, to write the life of any man, great or little, detailing year by year all that he did and suffered. Yet if the hero's interests or tasks are widely divergent, it may be doubted whether this is the most illuminative process of presentation. After all, in the everyday life of the most ordinary person there are compartments, intellectual, athletic, amorous, religious. Between these his own memory draws vertical rather than horizontal lines. Any fact which he may recall in any one of them has a closer relation to those which precede and follow than to the synchronous events in the other series, although it is true enough that the several groups are rarely without some trace of interaction.

In the history of Charles V. the method of strict chronological sequence would be peculiarly perplexing, because the vertical bars between the several sections of his interests are singularly thick, although not thick enough to produce total isolation. The condition of the Spanish-American colonies, for example, did really affect the Emperor's fortunes in relation to the duchy of Milan;

campaigns in North Africa did actually modify the current of events in Germany. Yet it would be confusing if contemporary incidents in these four countries were perpetually brought together in succeeding paragraphs. Hence it is that by way of compromise I have treated the main occurrences of Charles V.'s life more or less in the order of time, but have relegated to separate chapters the more outlying spheres of policy or action.

The causes which produce this peculiar difficulty of method are responsible also for the change in the character of the biography since its first inception. It was originally intended for the series of *Foreign Statesmen*. I found, however, that the inevitable limitation of space would entail, in the case of Charles V., one of two undesirable alternatives. Either the Emperor's life must reduce itself to an unpalatable compendium of facts and dates, or else it must take the form of allusive essays, crediting the general reader with a somewhat ideal knowledge of European history. It was therefore decided to detach the story of Charles from the series, and to give it the wider range accorded by these two volumes.

The very difficulty of sketching the life of Charles on the same scale as that accorded to other statesmen, equally great or greater, throws some light upon his character and career. It certainly is not due to the pre-eminence of his personality, nor entirely to the vast stretch of his dominions. Had Charles been as Napoleon, the task would have been more simple. The genius born gives to fluid circumstances the mould of his own conception. However multifarious the events, there is a certain unity of design. The initiative is his, and upon this the policy of friends or enemies is in the main contingent. The biographer has less need to rush from one European capital to another; he has but to follow in his hero's train with the certainty that the actions and characters of the other prominent personages in his story will fall into their place in the procession as the hero passes.

If Charles had been a greater man, it would have been easier to write a smaller book. He was no genius born, and he ruled several distinct nations in no one of which was he ever absolute master of his policy or actions. He was not great enough to give unity to circumstances of extraordinary complexity. Far from taking the lead he was from first to last put upon the defensive. It is his enemies who concoct the plans which it is the irksome duty of the Emperor to thwart. The history of Charles is that of the manner in which he met difficulties which were forced upon him by others, and which he would fain have avoided. Hence, therefore, the biographer must be constantly prying into the camp or the study of his hero's opponents. All this means space, and, moreover, the multiplicity of Charles's territories does materially add to the number of his historian's pages. His rule over Spain and Italy, over the Netherlands and Germany, over North Africa and America, has in each case characteristics essentially distinct, and no real idea of the infinite difficulty of his task can be obtained, unless these are to some extent set forth.

Even with the larger space at my disposal I have

found it necessary to make selection, and to abandon complete uniformity of scale or treatment. This book does not profess to be a history of the reign but of the man, and therefore prominence has been given to the events in which the Emperor's personality is most apparent, while others, perhaps of equal importance in themselves, have been consigned to the background. The relations of Charles to England have been lightly treated, partly for the practical reason that they can be studied in books easily accessible to the English reader, but chiefly because I do not believe them to have taken any considerable place in his calculations, except at three distinct moments. Henry VIII. was for two short periods his ally, and on the death of Edward VI. Charles eagerly sought compensation for recent disappointments in Mary's marriage with his own son. During a great part of the reign England was unfriendly, but her government caused annoyance rather than material injury. It was enough for Charles if he could keep his uncle-in-law on the further side of the Channel.

For a different reason the advance of the Turk in Eastern Europe has been made the subject of merely occasional reference. The importance of this advance to Charles was very real, because it perpetually hampered his freedom of action against the King of France and the Lutherans. Solyman himself was the greatest and most dangerous of all his enemies. But from the time when the Emperor granted to his brother the Austrian possessions of his house, upon Ferdinand devolved the direct responsibility of stemming the flood-tide of the Turk ; only once did Charles personally oppose a barrier

to its rush up the Danube towards Vienna. This subject, therefore, although the difficulties produced by it
should constantly be present to the reader, belongs more
immediately to the biography of Ferdinand than to that
of Charles. On the other hand, liberal space has been
given to the operations in North Africa, because in
these, though perhaps of less intrinsic importance, the
Emperor in person played a leading part.

The internal history of the Spanish kingdoms is,
apart from the revolutionary movements of Charles's
first few years, lacking in striking incidents. In Castile
there is, perhaps, a progress towards a more monarchical
order of government, but even this is hard to trace with
precision. The problems here are rather social and
economic than political. Yet, in view of the fact that
Charles spent in Spain a large portion of the period
which lies between his first visit in 1517 and his
departure for Germany in 1543, I have thought it
expedient to give some general idea of the national
aspirations which he was called upon to encourage, and
of the oppositions to his foreign and financial policy
with which, from time to time, he was compelled to
cope. The Spanish conquests in America form so vast
a subject in themselves that it would under any circumstances be impossible to include them in these volumes.
Charles had in fact little or no share in the actual
process of conquest, but in the organisation of the
new colonies he took a lively interest, and therefore the
influence of his personality upon the fortunes of his
trans-oceanic territories has been in outline indicated.

In the Netherlands there was no want of stirring

incidents.   There was plenty of fighting on the French
border and against the Duke of Guelders.   Charles in
person chastised Ghent for its opposition to his will,
and wrested Guelders from the Duke of Cleves.   These
were tasks forced upon him ; they were none of his own
seeking.   Of more permanent importance were his active
persecution of heresy, differing widely from his moderate
and deliberate treatment of it in Germany, and the
measures by which he not only extended his Netherland
provinces to their ultimate number of seventeen, but
gave them that feeling of national unity which rendered
possible their struggle with his son.   It is held, indeed,
by some writers, that the separation of the Netherlands
from the Empire, and therefore their promotion to the
rank of an independent nation, should date not from the
Peace of Westphalia of 1648, but from the arrangement
enforced by Charles at Augsburg just a century earlier,
in 1548.

Charles was never in Italy before 1529 nor after
1543.   The year 1541 may, indeed, almost be taken as
the final date, for in 1543 he merely landed at Genoa
and paid a flying visit to Piacenza and Cremona, to
pass thence by the Brenner into Germany.   Only in the
war of 1536 did he take any personal part, and that
of infinitesimal importance, in the great fight with
Francis I. on Italian soil.   Yet from his reign dates the
paramount power of Spain in Italy, and to his individual
will was due the vital result that Milan was to be
Spanish rather than Imperial.   Italy therefore would
seem properly to occupy a large space in these volumes.
The campaigns, inasmuch as they were not personally

conceived nor directed by Charles, have been reduced to
the narrowest scale consistent with intelligibility. I have
preferred to enlarge on the statecraft, the object of which
was to thrust France beyond the Alps, and to adjust
the relations between the remaining independent states
and the provinces which were directly ruled by Spain.

If success in Italy is only in part to be ascribed
to the personal action of Charles, it can scarcely be
doubted that he was immediately responsible for the
failure in Germany, although it may well be questioned
if any other could have succeeded. He was here acting
on the defensive, whatever momentary appearances
there may be to the contrary, against the encroachments of Lutheranism and princely particularism, which
were so closely allied as to seem at times identical.
In this defence he was somewhat worsted. Germany
during his reign was to become less rather than more
united in religion, and she was to lose almost all trace
of her national solidarity. The forces of rebellion,
religious and political, had been accumulating for
generations, and the Catholic Emperor proved powerless to stay the avalanche. Not only was Charles's
attention constantly occupied with German affairs, but
each visit seemed to provoke a crisis in the relations
of one religion to the other, and of Emperor to princes.
Thus it is that success or failure in Germany is, on
the whole, the surest clue in the labyrinth of Charles's
life. Yet it is essential to remember that such success
or failure depended often on conditions wholly foreign
to Germany, such as the temper of Spain, the mineral
wealth of the Indies, the factions of Italy, the activity

of French or Turk, the intrigue or inertia of the Papacy.

Whatever method be adopted for the treatment of the Emperor's biography, the most refractory element to handle is the Pope. It so happens that throughout the reign the personal interests of the successive Popes, if Adrian VI. be excepted, are almost purely Italian and dynastic. If the power of the Papacy, as well as its interests, had been confined to Italy, it could be treated as one of several Italian states, and even its recurring intrigues with France would have readily found their place in the history of the settlement of Italy. But the Roman court formed in one shape or another an integral part of the German problem, and this interaction between German and Italian politics adds infinitely to the complexity of the reign.

To one portion at all events of the Pope's relations to Charles I have thought it possible to give a minimum of space. The General Council which twice met at Trent was of high importance in the optimistic calculations of the Emperor and in the nervous anxieties of the Pope. Each meeting added to the exasperation already existing between the two powers and between the Emperor and his Lutheran subjects. Both sessions, however, were abortive as far as the objects of Charles were concerned. Such results as there were, were for the present of speculative and theological rather than of practical political importance. The Council of Trent is during this reign a mere *torso*; it can only be viewed in its full proportions in the history of a later period.

It may reasonably be asked if the biography would not be made more effective by the omission of some of its minor sections, of the chapters relating to Spain, the Netherlands, the Indies. The book would thus be rendered certainly shorter, and probably more readable, but it would be less useful and less faithful. Such a treatment would conceal the most essential feature in the Emperor's career—the intricacy of his task. The real interest of his life is not dramatic, nor even personal; it consists rather in a peculiar combination of character and circumstance. Gigantic issues, such as the supremacy of Crown, princes or people, of Catholicism or Lutheranism, the future of the New World, of Italy, of the Netherlands, appear to depend on the wisdom or unwisdom of one who was neither by nature nor education a Titan among statesmen. The problems for Charles were too numerous to find mention here. The problem for the student of his life is, How will the slight-built frame emerge with life and credit from the clash of warring elements which it was his recognised duty not to evade but to control?

The character of Charles has seldom inspired enthusiasm, but he was, taking him all in all, so just a man that his biographer feels pledged to do him justice. In this attempt there is danger lest he lapse into doing less than justice to the Emperor's opponents. Their actions and characters cannot be presented in their entirety; in their attitude of hostility the less amiable features are necessarily the more prominent. Were I, for instance, to write a life of Luther, I should give a very different impression of his character from that which may be pieced together from the references to him in these pages. The nobler, the softer, the more intellectual sides of the reformer's nature have but the most indirect bearing on my subject. If the far-famed scene at Worms be excepted, Luther is usually seen at his very worst when brought into contact with the more marked political events of Charles's reign. We see nothing of his cheerful family life, hear nothing of his virile eloquence, read nothing of his loving care for the education of the young. But there are ample opportunities for his violence, his coarse utterance, his obstinacy, his inconsistency. His conduct towards the deluded peasants, his acquiescence in Philip of Hesse's bigamy, his alternate rejection and acceptance of authority or of foreign alliance, his very scolding of Zwingli, or Bucer, or Melanchthon, are unfortunately the episodes on which it may be necessary to touch, if not to dwell. Yet these disagreeables are no more the whole of Luther than are March winds and dust the whole of spring.

To write a just biography it is necessary, so it seems to me, to face in the same direction as that in which its subject faced; to see the contours over which his eyes must range, to look past and beyond the hollows which the formation of the ground must hide. It does not follow from this that the biographer sees with the self-same eyes, nor is the use of modern mechanical appliances forbidden. Objects may have been blurred to the commander in the action, which keener eyesight or Time's improved field-glasses have made clear to the scientific visitor of the field. Such a visitor, even apart from mere difference of sight, will recognise errors of judgment, false deductions, unjustifiable optimism. This is the task of legitimate biographical criticism, and it will be the more faithfully performed if the critic have some general sympathy with the actor's plan. To wander round to points of vantage which, by the nature of the circumstances, the subject of the biography can have never reached, to view the field under every variety of climatic conditions which he was never fortunate or unfortunate enough to experience, may result in an impartial history of a period, but it is not the method suited to biography. But thus it is that the biographer may appear only less unjust than Charles himself to the Emperor's chief enemies, such as Francis I. or Luther. It may be true enough that Luther was a prince of table-talk and the prophet of the true religion; that Francis was an inimitable squire of dames and the apostle of the higher culture. They could not, however, have presented themselves to the Emperor in these aspects. When the opponent is only met when in the act of spitting one's poultry or pillaging one's church, it is impossible to recognise in him the quondam cynosure of the county ball, or the preacher of the Nonconformist chapel. Nor can the biographer with ease or propriety follow the foeman home to the ball-room or the chapel.

I can claim at least for my task that it is not superfluous. No biography of the Emperor has been written in English since the great work of Robertson, now a century and a quarter old, nor is there, within my knowledge, a complete biography of serious value in any foreign language, although the sixth volume of Signor de Leva's excellent history of Charles V. in relation to Italy may probably bring the writer into port.[1] I may assure my readers that if I had thought that they could endure six volumes, I could have written them with greater ease than two.

[1] Signor de Leva died when his work was yet unfinished.

BIBLIOGRAPHICAL INTRODUCTION

THE regulations imposed upon writers in the Series of Foreign Statesmen precluded the use of references and footnotes. When the plan of this volume was altered, I determined, after some hesitation, to convert the prohibition into an act of renunciation. I had few scruples as to abandoning the explanatory or supplementary footnote, which is often the fruit of laziness or literary incompetence, for it is far easier to bury a stubborn fact or episode at the bottom of the page than to make it a living portion of the text. My decision against page references was due to quite another cause. As I had made my preliminary studies on the other plan, to have added references throughout would have entailed an indefinite postponement in the publication of my book.

Closely connected with the subject of references is that of bibliography. For the sake of those who may be tempted to carry their studies further than the mere reading of an English book, I have called attention in each chapter to such works as partake of the character of a monograph, and especially to those of comparatively recent date. Very occasionally also I have similarly treated separate documents which have a quite limited bearing. This system will, I hope, to some slight extent compensate for the lack of page references.

Any attempt at a complete bibliography of a subject

so enormous would be out of place in a book of this character. I only indicate the sources which seem to me of chief practical value. It will suffice merely to mention the names of the more important among the older historians, such as J. G. Sepúlveda, P. Mejia, Peter Martyr of Angleria, L. de Avila, P. de Sandoval, B. L. Argensola, F. Guicciardini, Paolo Giovio, G. Ruscelli (*Lettere di principi*), G. Ribier (*Lettres et mémoires d'État*), J. Sleidan.

On passing to works written or edited in more recent times, it may be convenient to introduce some sort of classification, although it is impossible to avoid a certain measure of cross-division. I propose therefore to divide the authorities into four classes : (1) Documents bearing directly on the reign of Charles V. ; (2) histories of Charles, or of any aspects of his personal career ; (3) general histories which may treat with some detail or the whole or parts of his reign ; (4) biographies of characters closely connected with Charles at one epoch or another. These latter are frequently of value, not only as giving atmosphere to the picture, but as supplying telling details for the foreground and middle distance. The selection must necessarily be arbitrary, for it would be impossible to include the vast literature on Erasmus, Luther and Melanchthon, and the French biographies, such for instance as that of the Constable Montmorenci.

The collections of documents are of the utmost importance, and I have striven to construct from their materials at once the foundations and the adornments of my fabric. Those which seem to me to be of most service are :—

K. Lanz.   *Correspondenz des Kaisers Karl V.*, 3 vols., 1844-46.
K. Lanz.   *Staatspapiere zur Geschichte des Kaisers Karl V.*, 1845.
C. Weiss.   *Papiers d'État du Cardinal Granvelle*, vols. i.-iv., 1841-43.

A. von Druffel. *Briefe und Akten zur Geschichte des sechzehnten Jahrhunderts* (*1546-1555*), vols. i.-iv., 1873-96 (a fifth volume by W. Goetz, 1898, continues the collection).

L. P. Gachard and C. Piot. *Collection de voyages des souverains des Pays-Bas*, 1884.

Calendars of State Papers : (1) *Henry VIII., Foreign and Domestic to 1546* ; (2) *Edward VI. and Mary* ; (3) *Spanish to Jan. 1547* ; (4) *Venetian to 1558*.

E. Albèri. *Le Relazioni degli ambasciatori Veneti al senato durante il secolo decimosesto.* Series I. vols. i.-iii. ; Series II. vol. iii. ; Series III. vol. iii., 1839-55.

J. Fiedler. *Relationen Venetianischer Botschafter über Deutschland und Österreich im XVI. Jahrhundert. Fontes rerum Austriacarum*, xxx., 1870.

G. Turba. *Venetianische Depeschen vom Kaiserhofe*, vols. i., ii., 1889.

G. Canestrini. *Legazioni di G. C. Serristori*, 1853.

Nuntiaturberichte aus Deutschland im Auflage des k. Preuss. hist. Instituts in Rom, ed. by W. Friedensburg, G. Kupke and L. Cardauns :

(1) *Die Nuntiaturen des P. P. Vergerio, 1533-36.* Abt. I. Bd. 1, 1892.

(2) *Die Nuntiatur des Giov. Morone, 1536-38.* Abt. I. Bd. 2, 1892.

(3) *Die Legation Aleander's, 1538-39.* Abt. I. Bde. 3, 4, 1893.

(4) *Die Nuntiaturen Morones und Poggios, die Legationen Farneses und Cervinis, 1539-40.* Abt. I. Bd. 5, 1909.

(5) *Die Gesandschaft Campeggios, die Nuntiaturen Morones und Poggios, 1540-41.* Abt. I. Bd. 6, 1910.

(6) *Die Nuntiatur des Verallo, 1545-46.* Abt. I. Bd. 8, 1898.

(7) *Die Nuntiatur des Verallo, 1546-47.* Abt. I. Bd. 9, 1899.

(8) *Die Legation des Kardinals Sfondrato, 1547-48.* Abt. I. Bd. 10, 1907.

(9) *Die Nuntiaturen des Pietro Bertano und Pietro Camaiani, 1550-52.* Abt. I. Bd. 12, 1901.

[This invaluable series is still in progress. It may be supplemented by the monographs on Aleander's mission at Worms mentioned in Chapter IV., and by F. Dittrich, *Nuntiaturberichte Giovanni Morones, 1539-40 ; Quellen und Forschungen aus dem Gebiete der Geschichte*, i. 1, 1892.—F. Dittrich, *Nuntiaturberichte Giovanni Morones vom Reichstage zu Regensburg, 1541 ; Historisches Jahrbuch*, iv., 1883.—H. Laemmer, *Monumenta Vaticana historiam ecclesiasticam saeculi XVI. illustrantia*, 1861.—L. Pastor, *Correspondenz Contarinis, 1541*, 1880. The nunciature in Spain is the subject of R. de Hinojosa's *Los Despachos de la diplomacia pontificia en España*, 1896.]

Deutsche Reichstagsakten, herausgegeben durch die Münchener historische Kommission; Jüngere Reihe. Vol. i. ed. by A. Kluckholm, 1893 ; vols. ii.-iv. ed. by A. Wrede, 1896-1905. [This collection at present only covers the earlier years of Charles V.'s reign.]

H. Virck and O. Winckelmann. *Politische Correspondenz der Stadt Strassburg im Zeitalter der Reformation.* Vol. i., 1879 ; vol. ii., 1887.

J. J. I. von Döllinger. *Dokumente zur Geschichte Karl's V., u.s.w.* Bd. 1 *die Beiträge zur politisch-kirchlichen und Culturgeschichte der sechs letzten Jahrhunderte,* 1862.

W. Bradford. *Correspondence of the Emperor Charles V.,* 1850.

E. Le Glay. *Négociations diplomatiques entre la France et l'Autriche; Collection de doc. inéd. sur l'histoire de France,* 2 vols., 1845.

A. Champollion-Figeac. *Captivité du roi François Ier. Ibid.* 1 vol., 1847.

G. Molini. *Documenti di storia Italiana,* 2 vols., 1836.

I Diarii di Marino Sanuto, 1879 and following years.

G. van Male. *Lettres sur la vie intérieure de Charles-Quint,* ed. by Baron de Reiffenberg, 1843.

Commentaires de Charles-Quint, ed. by Baron Kervyn de Lettenhove, 1862.

L. P. Gachard. *Correspondance de Charles-Quint et d'Adrien VI,* 1859.

E. Charrière. *Négociations de la France dans le Levant* : in *Collection de doc. inéd. sur l'histoire de France,* 1848-53.

M. Colmeiro. *Cortes de los antiguos reinos de León y de Castilla,* vol. iv., 1882 [the text of the proceedings to 1537 with Introduction], 2 vols., 1883-86. M. Danvila has edited vol. v., 1903.

Colección de documentos ineditos para la historia de España (tracts or documents relating to Charles V. and his reign will be found in vols. i., ii., iii., iv., vi., viii., ix., xiv., xxiii., xxiv., xxv., xxvi., xxxviii., xlii., xlix., l., lxxv., xcvii.).

The events of the reign in the American colonies have been treated in these volumes in the barest outline, but those who wish to make a study at first hand of Charles V.'s colonial legislation may be referred to *Colección de documentos inéditos relativos al descubrimiento, conquista y organización de las antiguas posesiones españolas de Ultramar,* 2nd series, vols. i., iv., vi., ix., x. The early history of the Philippines finds illustration in vol. ii. Many documents of interest are scattered through the volumes of the earlier series.

The military events of the reign in Italy and North Africa find admirable illustration in the memoirs of Martin Garcia Cerezeda, 3 vols., printed by the *Sociedad de Bibliofilos Españoles* in *Relaciones historicas de los siglos XVI y XVII,* 1896.

Of biographers who may be called modern our own Robertson is the *doyen*, for the first edition of his *History of the Emperor Charles V.* falls well within the eighteenth century. It may be worth remarking that the biography which is frequently called by the name of W. H. Prescott is merely an edition of this, though the chapter on the Emperor's retirement is new, embodying, as it does, the researches of Stirling and Mignet on the life at Yuste. Upon Robertson follows the well-known book of F. A. Mignet, *Rivalité de François Ier et de Charles-Quint*, 2 vols., 1875. All lovers of history still regret the death of H. Baumgarten before he finished his admirable *Geschichte Karls V.*, 3 vols., 1885-93, which only extends to 1539. On the other hand, G. de Leva, who brought down to 1552 his *Storia documentata di Carlo V in correlazione all' Italia*, 5 vols., 1862-94, died when in sight of goal. This careful study is, in fact, a general history of the reign, though with special reference to its Italian aspects. Of great value, in spite of its necessary compression, is L. P. Gachard's history of Charles in the *Biographie Nationale*, vol. iii., 1872. A. Henne has written with much fulness his *Histoire de Charles-Quint en Belgique*, 10 vols., 1858-60. This may be supplemented by T. Juste's *Les Pays-Bas sous Charles-Quint*, 1861, which, perhaps, should rather be classed as a Life of Mary of Hungary, and his *Charles-Quint et Marguerite d'Autriche*, a study on the minority, emancipation and accession to the Empire.

On the court of Charles may be consulted the interesting studies of A. de Ridder, *La Cour de Charles - Quint*, 1889, and its *Ordonnances* in *Messager des Sciences historiques de Belgique*, 1893-94.

Important for other aspects of the reign are W. Maurenbrecher's *Karl V. und die deutschen Protestanten 1545-1555*, 1865, which contains documents from Simancas, and his *Studien und Skizzen zur Geschichte der Reformationszeit*, 1874; L. P. Gachard's *Trois années de l'histoire de Charles-Quint, 1543-1546*, in *Bulletin de l'acad. royale des sciences, etc., de Belgique*, Series ii. 19, 1865; L. Pastor's *Die kirchlichen Reunionsbestrebungen während der Regierung Karls V.*, 1879. E. Gossart has lately published two useful pamphlets, *Charles-Quint et Philippe II. Étude sur les origines de la prépondérance politique de l'Espagne en Europe*, 1896, and *Notes pour servir à l'histoire du règne de Charles-Quint*, 1897. M. de Foronda has had the original idea of showing where Charles was on every day of his life: *Estancias y viajes de Carlos V desde el día de su nacimiento hasta el de su muerte*, 1895. A good old-fashioned book on the Emperor's coronation is Gaetano Giordani's *Cronaca della venuta e dimora in Bologna del sommo pontefice Clemente VII per la coronazione di Carlo V Imperatore*, 1848. It is copiously supplied with notes and documents.

At the head of the general histories which are of value for the reign of Charles must stand L. von Ranke's *Deutsche Geschichte im Zeitalter der Reformation*, of a part of which there is a well-known English translation by Lady Austin, recently revised. Reference must be made also to Ranke's *Fürsten und Völker von Süd-Europa im sechzehnten und siebzehnten Jahrhundert*, 1857: an earlier edition of this was translated by W. R. Kelly, 1843. I am particularly indebted to four, more recent, German historians of whose works I have made constant use, viz. F. von Bezold, *Geschichte der deutschen Reformation*, 1890; G. Egelhaaf, *Deutsche Geschichte im sechzehnten Jahrhundert bis zum Augsburger Religionsfrieden*, 2 vols., 1892; G. Wolf, *Deutsche Geschichte im Zeitalter der Gegenreformation*, vol. i., 1899; L. Janssen, *Geschichte des deutschen Volkes seit dem Ausgang des Mittelalters*, vols. i.-iii.; L. Pastor's edition of 1897. This last work is marred by an excessive spirit of partisanship, but it is extremely rich in illustrative matter. Several volumes of Heeren and Ukert's series are very useful for various sides of the Emperor's reign, especially K. Haebler, *Spanien unter den Habsburgern*, vol. i., 1907; A. Huber, *Geschichte Österreichs*, vols. iii. and iv., 1888; C. F. von Stälin, *Wirtembergische Geschichte*, vol. iv., 1873; S. Riezler, *Geschichte Baierns*, vol. iv., 1899; K. T. Wenzelburger, *Geschichte der Niederlande*, vol. i., 1879. With the latter should be read P. J. Blok's *History of the People of the Netherlands*, an English translation from the Dutch by Ruth Putnam. M. Lafuente's *Historia general de España*, 1888, has a fairly full treatment of the Emperor's career in Spain. Other aspects of the reign may be studied in

M. Creighton.   *A History of the Papacy during the Period of the Reformation.*

F. Gregorovius.   *Geschichte der Stadt Rom im Mittelalter.*

J. A. Froude.   *History of England.*

P. Friedmann.   *Anne Boleyn: a Chapter of English History, 1527-36,* 1884

R. B. Merriman.   *Thomas Cromwell: His Life and Letters,* 1902.

M. Philippson.   *La Contre-révolution religieuse au XVIe siècle,* 1884.

F. Picatoste.   *Los Españoles en Italia,* 1887.

M. Danvila's work, *El Poder Civil en España*, 1885, may be placed either in this or in the preceding class. It treats of Spanish civil history as a whole; but that of the reign of Charles, complete in itself, is found in vol. ii., while vol. v. contains numerous important documents.

Among biographies which have a direct bearing on the reign of Charles the foremost is F. B. von Bucholtz, *Geschichte der Regierung Ferdinand des Ersten,* 9 vols., 1831-38, an old book but still full of life, and excellently provided with documents. The story of the Emperor's sister Eleanor has been written by E. Moeller, *Éléonore d'Autriche et de Bourgogne,* 1895. The *Revue des deux mondes* of 1898 contains articles on the Emperor's mother, *Jeanne la Folle,* by C. De Mouy. The following selection of the lives of other characters is given a little at haphazard :—

E. Le Glay.   *Études biographiques sur Mercurino Arborio di Gattinara.*

G. Müller.   *Documenti per la vita di Girolamo Morone,* in *Miscellanea di storia Italiana,* vol. iii.

E. Petit.   *Andrea Doria,* 1887.

E. Strauss.   *Ulrich von Hutten,* 3 vols., 1858-60.

F. Dittrich.   *Gasparo Contarini, 1483-1542,* 1885.

M. de los Heros.   *Pedro Navarro (Documentos ineditos,* vols. xxv. and xxvi.).

A. M. Fabié.   *Vida y escritos de Francisco Lopez de Villalobos* (the Emperor's physician), 1886.

M. Lenz.   *Briefwechsel Landgraf Philipps des Grossmütigen von Hessen mit Bucer,* 1880.

J. Wille.   *Philipp der Grossmüthige von Hessen und die Restitution Ulrichs von Wirtemberg, 1526-1535,* 1882.

G. Voigt.   *Moritz von Sachsen, 1541-1547,* 1876.

E. Brandenburg.   *Moritz von Sachsen,* vol. i., 1898.

G. Voigt.   *Markgraf Albrecht Alcibiades von Brandenburg,* 2 vols., 1852.

My obligations to numerous other works will be found in the notes to the several chapters, but I may be allowed here to pay in advance some part of my debt to such helpful writers as G. Turba, S. Issleib, and M. Lenz.

I hope that all the writers above and hereafter mentioned, who are still alive, will accept once for all the expression of my sincere acknowledgment for the aid which I have derived from them. I have frequently embodied their ideas in my pages, and, perhaps, often, if unwittingly, their very phrases.

My gratitude is due to the Editor of the *Pilot* for allowing me to reprint an article on the Youth of Charles V., which forms part of my first chapter, and also three articles on the Character of Charles V., which, with very trifling additions and alterations, reappear as my concluding chapter.

I have owed very much to help of many kinds rendered to me during the latter stages of my book by Miss D. K. Broster, late of St. Hilda's Hall, Oxford.

EDWARD ARMSTRONG.

THE RED HOUSE, OXFORD,
   September 3, 1901.

Note.—Works published since September 1901 are mentioned in the Introduction to the Second Edition, but I have added the later volumes of Series, such as the *Calendars of State Papers* and the *Nuntiatur-berichte aus Deutschland*, to the lists already given.

September 18, 1910.

BIBLIOGRAPHICAL INTRODUCTION
TO THE SECOND EDITION

In presenting the second edition of my book my first duty is to thank my readers for the encouragement given to a history, which, if it was to be true, must be always difficult and often dull, and my reviewers for the criticisms and suggestions which were even more welcome than their praise. Such additions as I have made are mainly due to my wish to meet these suggestions. Dr. A. Hasenclever, for instance, rightly pointed out that, while I had given an adequate account of the smaller Italian states, I had accorded less liberal treatment to the German states, which in the end more closely affected the Emperor's fortunes. I have therefore given a short account of the several dynasties with which Charles had to reckon at the beginning of his reign. Similarly I have somewhat strengthened the paragraphs on Spanish economic history, though I felt unable to meet the wish of Mr. Stanley Leathes for a more exhaustive statement. In spite of recent researches I doubt if the time is as yet ripe for very definite conclusions, and I feared, moreover, that a subject so highly technical would break the continuity of what is essentially a biography. Other additions are in the main illustrative details drawn from the fresh publications of the last eight years.

The output of books bearing directly or indirectly upon Charles V. during these eight years is indeed considerable. Of these the contributions to Spanish history are the largest. The fifth volume of the *Cortes de Leon y Castilla* was published by Manuel Danvila in 1903, and this is particularly valuable as containing the proceedings of the celebrated session of 1538. A. Rodriguez Villa has printed (1902-5) the correspondence by Martin de Salinas, which must be of the highest importance for any detailed history of the reign. Salinas accompanied Charles to Spain in 1522, as agent for Ferdinand, and was mainly at the Spanish Court till 1539, though he was with Charles in Italy and Germany in 1529-30, and again met him at Naples on his return from Tunis, and took part in his Provençal campaign. The letters of Castiglione, translated by Julia Cartwright (Mrs. Ady), are also helpful for the Emperor's life in Spain down to 1529, when the writer died. Professor Altamira in the third volume of his excellent *Historia de España* treats of all the Habsburg kings, giving especial weight to the social and economic aspect of the dynasty. K. Haebler devotes the whole of his volume in the series of Heeren and Ukert to Charles V. He gives the best account that I have yet read of the rising of the Communes, and in this connection it may be mentioned that M. Danvila has continued his collection of documents relating to the revolution in the *Memorial historico Español*. The economic and constitutional questions of the reign are also admirably handled. These are the subjects of the *Estudios historicos* of F. de Laiglesia, who supplies invaluable data for the income, the expenditure and the debts of the Spanish Crown. Both these works more than confirm the favourable estimate which I had

formed of Charles V.'s economic policy, and are a useful
corrective to commonly received opinion. Dr. Lea lived
just long enough to complete his magnificent work
on the Spanish Inquisition : his memory will live not
only in these stately volumes, but in the career of
many younger students to whom he gave ungrudging
aid.

Next in importance to the recent works on Spain are
those on the relations of Charles V. to the Papacy, and
particularly to Paul III. Dr. Pastor has devoted a
very substantial volume to this Pope ; L. Cardauns has
elaborately treated the documents bearing on the critical
years 1535 to 1538 ; C. Capasso has discussed the
policy of Paul III. with regard to the Imperial domina-
tion in Italy ; while A. Segre, in his *Carlo III di Savoia
dal 1536 al 1547*, has traced the misfortunes of the
Emperor's ill-used connection. The Conciliar policy of
Charles V. from 1538 to 1543 is the subject of a
monograph by A. Korte, while the despatches printed
by W. Friedensburg in vol. x. of the *Nuntiaturberichte* are of first-rate importance for the Papal-
Imperial quarrel in the years 1547 and 1548.

Two new volumes of the *Reichstagsakten*, edited
by A. Wrede, form the most important document-
ary contribution to the German history of the reign.
W. Bauer has written a useful book on the early
relations between Charles and Ferdinand, ending with
the grant of the Austrian Habsburg territories to the
latter. The stream of monographs flows steadily forward, but the fourth centenary of Philip of Hesse's
birth, November 13, 1904, occasioned a strong freshet.
Among the pamphlets and articles on this hero of the
Reformation may be mentioned a simple and pleasant
biography by Egelhaaf. English readers will delight

in the translation of that graphic and highly-flavoured book, the *Memoirs of Bartholomew Sastrow*. The despatches of Bertano and Camaiani, edited by Kupke in vol. xii. of the *Nuntiaturberichte,* lead the reader step by step to the tragedy of the Emperor's life. The services of Charles V. to Germany form the climax of the unpublished papers of the late Onno Klopp, which Dr. L. König has collected in a book entitled *Deutschland und die Habsburger*, 1908. The writer regarded Charles as the champion of German Imperialism against a disruptive oligarchy, which betrayed national to personal interests. He believed that the depreciation of Charles by German Protestants has been due to their adherence to the prejudiced views of Sleidan, who offered his pen first to Philip of Hesse, and later to Maurice of Saxony, rather than to the independent judgment of Melanchthon, for whom Charles was to the end a wise, indulgent and beneficent ruler, who loved and practised justice and mercy.

The later volumes of the *Calendars of State Papers*, both those on *Henry VIII.*, edited by Dr. Gairdner and R. H. Brodie, and the Spanish series by the late Martin A. S. Hume, throw light on many sides of the Emperor's reign. The articles in the *Cambridge Modern History,* vol ii., touch my subject closely, especially those of Stanley Leathes on Habsburg and Valois, and of A. F. Pollard on the German Reformation. The fifth volume of the *Histoire de France*, edited by E. Lavisse (1903), is useful for the French side of the struggle between Charles and Francis. For the relations with Henry VIII. we have H. A. L. Fisher's *History of England from 1485 to 1547*, while A. F. Pollard's volume from 1547 to 1603 has just been published. T. M. Lindsay's *History of the Reformation* in two volumes (1906-7) gives a useful and temperate account of the religious problems of the reign.

This selection of books, all written within the last nine years, will prove that the issues of Charles V.'s fateful reign are still subjects of living interest, and that the character of the Emperor and his chief opponents and supporters have still their charm or their repulsion for students in the fourth century from his birth.

THE RED HOUSE, OXFORD,
September 18, 1910.

AUTHORITIES MENTIONED IN THE BIBLIOGRAPHICAL INTRODUCTION OR IN THE FOOTNOTES

Albèri, E. *Le Relazioni degli Ambasciatori Veneti*, 1839-55. See Introduction, p. xix.

Allgemeine deutsche Biographie.

Altamira y Crevea, R. *Historia de España*, vol. iii., 1906.

Argensola, B. L. *Anales de Aragón*, 1630.

Avila, L. de. *Comentario de la guerra de Alamania hecha por Carlos V. Biblioteca de autores españoles*, xxi., 1858.

Bardi, A. *Carlo V e l' assedio di Firenze (Arch. Stor. It. 1893).*

Barga, H. *Die Verhandlungen zu Linz und zu Passau*, 1897.

Basset, R. *Documents musulmanes sur le siège d'Algers*, 1890.

Bauer, W. *Die Anfänge Ferdinands I.*, 1907.

Baumgarten, H. *Geschichte Karls V.*, 3 vols., 1855-93.

Baumgarten, H. *Zur Geschichte des Schmalkaldischen Krieges (Hist-Zeitschrift*, 1876).

Bax, E. B. *German Society at the Close of the Middle Ages*, 1894.

Bax, E. B. *The Peasants' War in Germany*, 1899.

Bezold, F. von. *Geschichte der deutschen Reformation*, 1890.

Biographie nationale de Belgique.

Blok, P. J. Trans. by R. Putnam. *History of the People of the Netherlands*, vol. ii., 1899.

Boehmer, E.   Bibliotheca Wiffeniana I., 1874.

Bofarull, F.   Predilección de Carlos V. por los Catalanes (Memorias de la R. Acad. de Buenas Letras de Barcelona, v., 1896).

Bonn, M. J.   Spaniens Niedergang während der Preisrevolution der 16. Jahrhunderts, 1896.

Bonwetsch, G.   Geschichte des Passauischen Vertrages von 1552, 1907.

Bourrilly, L.   L'Ambassade de la Forest et de Marillac à Constantinople, 1535-38 (Revue historique, 1901).

Bradford, W.   Correspondence of the Emperor Charles V., 1850.

Brandenburg, E.   Moritz von Sachsen, 1898.

Brandi, K.   Passauer Vertrag und Augsburger Religionsfriede (Hist. Zeitschrift, 1905).

Brieger, T.   Aleander und Luther, 1521 (Quellen und Forschungen zur Geschichte der Reformation, vol. i., 1884).

Brieger, T.   Beiträge zur Geschichte des Augsburger Reichstags, 1530 (Zeitschrift für Kirchengeschichte, 1891).

Brieger, T.   Der Speierer Reichstag von 1526, 1909.

Bucholtz, F. B. von.   Geschichte der Regierung Ferdinand des Ersten, 9 vols., 1831-38.

Burgon, J. W.   The Life and Times of Sir Thomas Gresham, 1839.

Busch, K. E. W.   Drei Jahre englischer Vermittlungspolitik, 1884.

Busch, K. E. W.   Cardinal Wolsey und die kaiserlich-englische Allianz (1522-25), 1886.

Calendar of State Papers.   See Introduction, p. xix.

Cambridge Modern History, vol. ii., 1903.

Canestrini, G.   Legazioni di G. C. Serristori, 1853.

Capasso, C.   La Politica di papa Paolo III e l' Italia, 1901.

Cappa, R.   Estudios criticos acerca la dominacion española en America. Various dates.

Cardauns, L.   Paul III., Karl V. und Franz I., 1535-36 (Quellen und Forschungen aus italienischen Archiven, xi., 1908), followed by Zur Geschichte Karls V. (xii., 1909).

Cardauns, L.   See Nuntiaturberichte, Introduction, p. xix.

Cartwright, Julia (Mrs. Ady).   Baldassare Castiglione, vol. ii., 1908.

Cat, E.   De Caroli quinti in Africa rebus gestis, 1891.

Cave, J.   Relation inédite (Mélanges d'archéologie et d'histoire publiés par l'École française à Rome, xvi., 1896).

Cerezeda, M. G.   Tratado de las Campañas . . . de los ejércitos del Emperador Cárlos V, 1521-45.   See Introduction, p. xx.

Chabert, F. M.   Journal du siège de Metz en 1552, 1856.

Champollion-Figeac, A.   La Captivité de François Ier.   See Introduction, p. xx.

Charrière, E. *Négociations de la France dans le Levant.* See Introduction, p. xx.

Cimber et Danjou. *Archives curieuses*, Series I., iii., 1835.

Claretta, Baron G. *Notizie per servire alla vita del Gran Cancelliere di Carlo V, Mercurino di Gattinara (Memorie della R. Acc. delle Scienze di Torino*, 1897). See also *Société Savoisienne d'Histoire et d'Archéologie*, 1898.

Colección de documentos inéditos para la historia de España. See Introduction, p. xx.

Colección de documentos inéditos relativos al descubrimiento . . . de las posesiones españolas de Ultramar. See Introduction, p. xx.

Colmeiro, M. *Historia de la Economia politica en España*, 1863.

Colmeiro, M. See *Cortes de Leon y Castilla.*

Commentaires de Charles-Quint. See Introduction, p. xx.

Cortes de Leon y Castilla. See Introduction, p. xx.

Creighton, M. *A History of the Papacy*, vol. vi., 1882.

Danvila, M. *El Poder Civil en España*, 1885.

Danvila, M. *La Germania de Valencia*, 1854.

Danvila, M. *Historia critica y documentada de las comunidades de Castilla (Memorial historica español*, xxxv.-xl., 1897 *seq.*).

Desdevises du Dezert, G. *L'Espagne de l'ancien régime*, 1899.

Deutsche Reichstagsakten. See Introduction, p. xx.

Dittrich, F. *Nuntiaturberichte Giovanni Morones.* See Introduction, p. xix.

Dittrich, F. *Gasparo Contarini, 1483-1542*, 1885.

Döllinger, J. J. I. von. *Dokumente zur Geschichte Karl's V.* See Introduction, p. xx.

Dormer, D. J. *Anales de Aragón, 1525-40*, 1697.

Druffel, A. von. *Briefe und Akten.* See Introduction, p. xix.

Druffel, A. von. *Des Viglius von Zwichem Tagebuch des Schmalkaldischen Donaukriegs*, 1879.

Druffel, A. von. *Die Sendung des Kardinals Sfondrato an den Hof Karls, 1547-48 (Abhandl. der hist. Classe der k. bay. Akad. Wiss.* xx., 1893).

Druffel, A. von. *Kaiser Karl und die Römische Kurie, 1544-46 (Vier Abhandl. des Münchener Akad.*, 1877-90).

Druffel, A. von. *Über den Vertrag zwischen Kaiser und Papst von Juni, 1541 (Deutsche Zeitschrift für Geschichte*, iii., 1889).

Egelhaaf, G. *Deutsche Geschichte im sechzehnten Jahrhundert*, 2 vols., 1892.

Egelhaaf, G. *Landgraf Philipp von Hessen (Schriften des Vereins für Reformationsgeschichte*, 1904).

Fabié, A. M. *Francisco Lopez de Villalobos*, 1886.

Ficker, J.   *Die Konfutation des Augsburgischen Bekenntnisses*, 1891.

Fiedler, J.   *Relationen venetianischer Botschafter.*   See Introduction, p. xix.

Fischer, G.   *Die persönliche Stellung und politische Lage König Ferdinands vor und nach den Passauer Verhandlungen*, 1891.

Fisher, H. A. L.   *History of England, 1485-1547*, vol. v. of *Political Hist. of England*, 1906.

Fita, F.   *Los tres procesos de San Ignacio de Loyola (Boletin de la R. Acad. de Historia*, xxxiii., 1898).

Foronda, M. de.   *Estancias y viajes de Carlos V*, 1895.

Frédéricq, P.   *Corpus documentorum inquisitionis haereticae pravitatis Neerlandicae (to December 31, 1528)*, 1889-1903.

Frédéricq, P.   *De Nederlanden onder Keizer Karel.*

Friedensburg, W.   *Nuntiaturberichte.*   See Introduction, p. xix.

Friedensburg, W.   *Am Vorabend des Schmalkaldischen Krieges (Quellen und Forschungen aus ital. Archiven*, 1897).

Friedensburg, W.   *Eine ungedrückte Depesche Aleanders (ibid.*, 1897).

Friedensburg, W.   *Der Reichstag zu Speyer, 1526* (Jastrow's *Historische Untersuchungen*, v., 1887).

Friedensburg, W.   *Zur Geschichte des Wormser Konvents (Zeitschrift für Kirchengeschichte*, 1900-1901).

Friedensburg, W.   *Die Chronik des Arborio Besozzi, 1548-63* : in *Fontes rerum Austriacarum*, Abt. I. Bd. 9 (*Scriptores*), 1904.

Friedrich, J.   *Der Reichstag zu Worms, 1521, nach den Briefen des Nuntius Hieronymus Aleander (K. Bay. Akad. Wiss.* xi.).

Fritsche, B.   *Die päpstliche Politik und die deutsche Kaiserwahl*, 1909.

Gachard, L. P.   *Correspondance de Charles-Quint et d'Adrien VI*, 1859.

Gachard, L. P.   *Biographie nationale*, iii., 1872 (*Life of Charles V.*).

Gachard, L. P.   *Relation des troubles de Gand (Collection de chroniques belges*, 1846).

Gachard, L. P.   *Retraite et mort de Charles-Quint au monastère de Yuste*, 1854-55.

Gachard, L. P., and Piot, C.   *Collection de voyages des souverains des Pays-Bas*, 1884.

Galindo, L.   *Historia . . . de España respecto de sus posesiones en las costas de Africa (Memorias de la R. Acad. de Historia*, xi., 1884).

Gebhardt, B.   *Die Gravamina der deutschen Nation gegen den römischen Hof*, 1895

Giordani, G.   *Cronaca della venuta e dimora in Bologna del sommo pontefice Clemente VII*, 1848.

Giovio, Paolo (Jovius).   *Historiarum sui temporis libri XIX.*, 1550-52.

Goetz, W.   *Die bayerische Politik im ersten Jahrzehnt der Regierung Herzog Albrechts V.*, 1896.

Gossart, E.   *Charles-Quint et Philippe II*, 1896.

Gossart, E.   *Notes pour servir à l'histoire du règne de Charles-Quint*, 1897.

Gossart, E.   *Charles-Quint roi d'Espagne*, 1910.

Gounon Loubens, M. J.   *Essais sur l'administration de la Castille au XVIe siècle*, 1861.

Gregorovius, F.   *Geschichte der Stadt Rom im Mittelalter*, vol. viii., 1880. Translated by A. M. Hamilton.

Grethen, R.   *Die politischen Beziehungen Clemens VII. zu Karl V.*, 1887.

Griessdorf, H. C. J.   *Der Zug Karls V. gegen Metz (Hallische Abhandl. zur neueren Geschichte*, xxvi., 1891).

Guicciardini, F.   *Storia d' Italia*.   Several editions.

Haebler, K.   *Die wirtschaftliche Blüte Spaniens im 16. Jahrhundert und ihr Verfall*, 1888.

Haebler, K.   *Spanien unter den Habsburgern*, vol. i., 1907.

Haebler, K.   *Zur Geschichte der kastilischen Comanidades (Hist. Zeitschrift*, xcv., 1905).

Harleian Miscellany, iv., 1809.

Hasenclever, A.   *Politik Kaiser Karls V. und Landgraf Philipps von Hessen vor Ausbruch des Schmalkaldischen Krieges*, 1903.

Hasenclever, A.   A Review of Recent Books on Charles V. and the Treaty of Passau (*Hist. Zeitschrift*, civ., 1910).

Hausrath, A.   *Aleander und Luther auf dem Reichstage zu Worms*, 1897.

Hecker, O. A.   *Karls V. Plan zur Gründung eines Reichsbundes*, 1906.

Helps, G.   *The Spanish Conquest of America*, 1855-61.

Henne, A.   *Histoire de Charles-Quint en Belgique*, 10 vols., 1858-60.

Heros, M. de los.   *Pedro Navarro*.   See Introduction, p. xxiv.

Herre, P.   *Barbara Blomberg*, 1909.

Hinojosa, A. de.   *Los Despachos de la diplomacia pontificia en España*, 1896.

Höfler, K. von.   *Der Aufstand der castilianischen Städte*, 1876.

Höfler, K. von.   *Don Antonio de Acuña, genannt der Luther Spaniens*, 1882.

Höfler, K. von.   *Zur Kritik und Quellenkunde der ersten Regierungsjahre Karls V. (Denkschrift der Wiener Akad., phil.-hist. Kl.* xxv., xxviii , 1876 and 1878).

Huber, A.   *Geschichte Österreichs*, vols. iii., iv., 1888.

Issleib, S.   *Moritz von Sachsen gegen Karl V. bis zum Kriegszuge 1552 (N. Arch. für Sächs. Geschichte*, vi., vii., 1885 and 1886).

Issleib, S.   *Von Passau bis Sievershausen (ibid.* viii., 1887).

Issleib, S.   *Die Wittenberger Kapitulation, 1547 (ibid.* xii., 1891).

Issleib, S.   *Die Gefangenschaft des Landgrafen Philipp von Hessen (ibid.* xiv., 1893).

Issleib, S.   *Das Interim in Sachsen, 1548-52 (ibid.* xv., 1894).

Issleib, S.   *Philipp von Hessen, Heinrich von Braunschweig und Moritz von Sachsen, 1541-47*, 1904.

Janssen, L.   *Geschichte des deutschen Volkes seit dem Ausgang des Mittelalters.* See Introduction, p. xxiii.   Translated by A. M. Christie.

Juste, T.   *Les Pays-Bas sous Charles-Quint*, 1861.

Kannengiesser, P.   *Der Reichstag zu Worms, 1544-45*, 1891.

Kannengiesser, P.   *Karl V. und Maximilian Egmont, Graf von Buren*, 1895.

Kervyn de Lettenhove, Baron H.   *Commentaires de Charles-Quint*, 1862.

Klopp, O.   *Deutschland und die Habsburger*, edited by L. König, 1908.

Kluckhohn, A.   See *Deutsche Reichstagsakten.*

Köhler, W.   *Die Doppelehe des Landgraf Philipps von Hessen (Hist. Zeitschrift*, lxxxv., 1905).

Kooperberg, L. M. G.   *Margaretha van Oostenrijk*, 1908.

Korte, A.   *Die Koncilspolitik Karls V., 1538-43 (Schriften des Vereins f. Reformationsgeschichte*, lxxxv., 1905).

Kühn, W.   *Geschichte des Passauischen Vertrag von 1552*, 1906.

Laemmer, H.   *Monumenta Vaticana*, 1861.

Lafuente, M.   *Historia general de España*, 1888.

Laiglesia, F. de.   *Estudios históricos, 1515-55*, 1908.

Lumia, I. La.   *La Sicilia sotto Carlo V*, 1862.

Lanz, K.   *Correspondenz des Kaisers Karl V.*, 3 vols., 1844-46.

Lanz, K.   *Staatspapiere zur Geschichte des Kaisers Karl V.*, 1845.

Lavisse, E.   *Histoire de France*, vol. v., 1903.

Lea, H. C.   *Moriscos of Spain*, 1901.

Lea, H. C.   *History of the Inquisition in Spain*, 1906-1907.

Le Glay, E.   *Négociations diplomatiques entre la France et l'Autriche.* See Introduction, p. xx.

Le Glay, E.   *Études biographiques sur Mercurino Arborio di Gattinara.*

Lenz, M.   *Die Schlacht von Mühlberg*, 1879.

Lenz, M.   *Die Kriegführung der Schmalkaldener gegen Kaiser Karl an der Donau (Hist. Zeitschrift*, 1883).

Lenz, M.   *Briefwechsel Landgraf Philipps von Hessen mit Bucer*, 1880.

Leva, G. de.   *Storia documentata di Carlo V in correlazione all' Italia*, 5 vols., 1852-94.

Lindsay, T. M.   *History of the Reformation*, 2 vols., 1906-1907.

Loaysa, G. de.   *Cartas al Emperador Cárlos V, 1530-32*, 1848.

Massignani, R.   *Il primo duca di Parma e Piacenza e la congiura del 1545*, 1907.

Maurenbrecher, W.   *Forschungen zur deutschen Geschichte*, vol. iii.

Maurenbrecher, W.   *Karl V. und die deutschen Protestanten, 1545-65*, 1865.

Maurenbrecher, W.   *Studien und Skizzen zur Geschichte der Reformationzeit*, 1874.

Mayerhofer, J.   *Zwei Briefe aus Rom, 1527 (Hist. Jahrbuch, 1891).*

Mejia, P.   *Historia imperial*, 1655.

Mencke, J. B.   *Scriptores rerum Germanicarum*, vol. iii., 1730.

Mignet, F. A.   *Rivalité de François I*er *et de Charles-Quint*, 2 vols., 1875.

Moeller, C.   *Éléonore d'Autriche*, 1895.

Molini, G.   *Documenti di storia italiana*, 2 vols., 1836.

Mouy, C. de.   *Jeanne la Folle (Revue des deux mondes*, 1898).

Moses, R.   *Die Religionsverhandlungen in Hagenau und Worms*, 1889.

Navenne, F. de.   *Pier Luigi Farnese (Revue hist.*, 1901-1902).

Ney, J.   *Geschichte des Reichstags zu Speyer, 1529*, 1880.

Nitti, F.   *Leone X e la sua politica*, 1892.

Nuntiaturberichte.   See Introduction, p. xix.

Pastor, L.   *Correspondenz Contarinis, 1541*, 1880.

Pastor, L.   *Die Reise des Kardinals Luigi d' Aragona beschrieben von Antonio de Beatis*, 1905.

Pastor, L.   *Geschichte der Päpste seit dem Ausgang der Mittelalter*, vols. iv. and v.   Translated edition by F. I. Antrobus and R. F. Ker, in progress; to 1549, 1906-1909.

Peter Martyr (Vermigli, P. M. de).   *Opus epistolarum*, 1670.

Petit, E.   *Andrea Doria*, 1887.

Philippson, M.   *La Contre-révolution religieuse*, 1884.

Picatoste, F.   *Los Españoles en Italia*, 1887.

Pichot, A.   *Charles-Quint: chronique*, 1854.

Pieper, A.   *Die päpstlichen Legaten und Nuntien in Deutschland, Frankreich und Spanien*, 1897.

Politische Correspondenz der Stadt Strassburg.   See Introduction, p. xx.

Pollard, A. F.   *History of England, 1547-1603*, vol. vi. of *Political Hist. of England*, 1910.

Prescott, W. H.   Edition of *Robertson's History of Charles V.*, 1857

Professione, A.   *Dalla battaglia di Pavia al sacco di Roma*, 1890.

Quarterly Review.   A Grand Tour in the Sixteenth Century, July 1908.

Rachfall, F.   *Die Trennung der Niederlände vom deutschen Reiche (Westdeutsche Zeitschrift*, xix. 2, 1900).

Randi, C.   *La Guerra di sette anni sotto Clemente VII (Arch. della Soc. Rom.* vi. 34).

Ranke, L. von.   *Deutsche Geschichte im Zeitalter der Reformation*, 6 vols., edition of 1882.   An early edition translated in part by Lady Austin; revised by R. A. Johnson, 1905.

Ranke, L. von.   *Fürsten und Völker von Süd-Europa*, xlii.-xliv. of *Sämtliche Werke*, 1874.   An early edition translated by W. R. Kelly, 1843.

Ranke, L. von.   *Die römischen Päpste*, xxxvii.-xxxix. of *Sämtliche Werke*. An early edition translated by Lady Austin, 1847 ; revised by G. R. Dennis, 1908.

Reiffenberg, Baron de.   *Histoire de l'Ordre de la Toison d'Or*, 1830.

Ribier, G.   *Lettres et mémoires d'estat*, 1666.

Ridder, A. de.   *La Cour de Charles-Quint*, 1889.

Ridder, A. de.   *Ordonnances de la cour de Charles-Quint* (*Messager des sciences historiques de Belgique*, 1893-94).

Riezler, S.   *Die bairische Politik im Schmalkaldischen Kriege* (*Hist. Abhandl. der Baier. Akad.*, xxi., 1894).

Riezler, S.   *Geschichte Baierns*, vol. iv., 1899.

Robert, U.   *Philibert de Chalon, Prince d'Orange* (*Boletín de la R. Acad. de la Historia*, 1901-2).

Robertson, W.   *History of the Emperor Charles V.*, 1769.

Rodríguez Villa, A.   *Italia desde la batalla di Pavía hasta el saco de Roma*, 1885.

Rodríguez Villa, A.   *La Reina Doña Juana la Loca*, 1892.

Rodríguez Villa, A.   *Memorias para la historia del asaltó y saco de Roma*, 1885.

Rodríguez Villa, A.   *El Emperador Carlos V y su corte, según las cartas de M. de Salinas*, 1903-5.

Romano, M.   *Cronaca del soggiorno di Carlo V in Italia dal 29 luglio 1529 al 25 aprile 1530.*

Rozet, A., et Lembey, L. F.   *L'Invasion de la France et siège de Saint-Dizier par Charles-Quint en 1544*, 1910.

Ruscelli, G.   *Lettere di principi*, 1526.

Salinas, M. de.   See *Rodríguez Villa, A.*

Salvá, A.   *Burgos en las comunidades de Castilla*, 1895.

Sandoval, P. de.   *Historia de la vida y hechos del Emperador Carlos V*, 2 vols., 1634.

Schirrmacher, F. W.   *Briefe und Akten zu der Geschichte des Religionsgespräches zu Marburg und des Reichstags zu Augsburg*, *1530*, 1876.

Schirrmacher, F. W.   *Johann Albrecht I., Herzog von Mecklenburg.*

Schultz, H.   *Der Sacco di Roma ; Karls V. Truppen in Rom* (*Hallische Abhand. zur neueren Geschichte*, xxxii., 1894).

Schlomka, E.   *Die politische Beziehungen zwischen Kurfurst Moritz und Heinrich II., 1550-52*, 1884.

Segre, A.   *Carlo III di Savoia . . . dal 1536 al 1545*, 1902.

Sepúlveda, J. G.   *Opera*, 4 vols., 1780.

Simonetti, A.   *Il Convegno di Paolo III e Carlo V in Lucca, 1541*, 1901.

Sozzini, A.   (*The Sienese War*) *Arch. Stor. Ital.* ii., 1842.

Springer, J. *Beiträge zur Geschichte des Wormser Reichstages, 1544-45*, 1882.

Staffetti, L. *Carlo V a Spira nel 1544 (Arch. Stor. Ital.,* 1892).

Stirling-Maxwell, Sir W. *Cloister Life of the Emperor Charles V.,* 4 vols. from 1852.

Stirling-Maxwell, Sir W. *The Chief Victories of the Emperor Charles V., designed by Martin Heemskirck in 1553.* Privately printed, 1870.

Tausserat-Radel. *Correspondance politique de Guillaume Pellicier, 1540-1542,* 1899.

Trefftz, J. *Kursachsen und Frankreich, 1552-56,* 1891.

Turba, G. *Venetianische Depeschen vom Kaiserhofe (Dispacci di Germania,* 2 vols., 1889, 1892).

Turba, G. *Beiträge zur Geschichte der Habsburger, 1548-58,* 1901.

Turba, G. *Verhaftung und Gefangenschaft des Landgrafen Philipp von Hessen, 1547-50 (Arch. für österr. Geschichte,* xxxiii., 1896).

Turba, G. *Über den Zug Karls V. gegen Algier (ibid.* xxvi., 1890).

Turba, G. *Geschichte des Thronfolgerechtes in allen habsburgischen Ländern,* 1903.

Tytler, P. F. *England under the Reigns of Edward VI. and Mary,* 2 vols., 1839.

Ulmann, H. *Franz von Sickingen,* 1872.

Ursu, L. *La Politique orientale de François Ier,* 1909.

Vaissiere, P. de. *Charles de Marillac,* 1896.

Van der Straeten, E. *Charles-Quint musicien,* 1894.

Vetter, L. P. *Die Religionsverhandlungen auf dem Reichstage zu Regensburg, 1541,* 1880.

Vigo, P. *Carlo Quinto in Siena nell' aprile del 1536, relazione de un contemporaneo,* 1884.

Villa, A. R. See *Rodríguez Villa, A.*

Virck, H. *Melanchthons politische Stellung auf dem Reichstage zu Augsburg (Zeitschrift für Kirchengeschichte,* 1887).

Voigt, J. *Markgraf Albrecht Alcibiades von Brandenburg-Kulmbach,* 1852.

Voigt, G. *Moritz von Sachsen, 1541-47,* 1876.

Wilkins, C. A. *Geschichte des spanischen Protestantismus im 16. Jahrhundert,* 1888. Translated by R. Challice, 1897.

Wille, J. *Philipp von Hessen und die Restitution Ulrichs von Wirtemberg, 1526-35,* 1882.

Winckelmann, O. *Der Schmalkaldische Bund und der Nürnberger Religionsfriede,* 1892.

Witter, J.　*Die Beziehung und der Verkehr des Kurf. Moritz mit dem römischen König Ferdinand, 1547-52*, 1886.

Zeller, J.　*Quae primae fuerint legationes a Francesco I. in Orientem missae, 1524-38*, 1881.

Zeller, J.　*La Diplomatie française vers le milieu du XVIe siècle, d'après la correspondance de G. Pellicier ambassadeur à Venise, 1539-42*, 1880.

CONTENTS

CHAPTER I

PAGE

Birth of Charles—His mother's loss of reason and his father's death—He inherits the Netherlands and Franche Comté—Sketch of recent Netherland history—Prospective difficulties—Childhood of Charles —His amusements, appearance, and education—His early betrothal to Mary Tudor—He is declared of age—His subservience to his minister, the Lord of Chièvres—Love affair of his sister Eleanor . 1

CHAPTER II

Death of Ferdinand of Aragon—Charles's Spanish inheritance and its difficulties—His voyage to Spain and journey through Asturias— His visit to Juana—Death of Jiménez—Charles enters Valladolid— The Cortes of Castile—Unpopularity of the Flemings—Charles holds the Cortes of Aragon at Saragossa—His visit to Catalonia —His election to the Empire—Discontent in Castile—Riot at Valladolid—The Cortes at Santiago and Corunna—Charles sails for England, leaving Adrian of Utrecht as regent—Outbreak of revolt in Toledo, and social war in Valencia—Inauspicious opening of the reign 16

CHAPTER III

Rivalry of Charles and Francis for the Empire—Condition of Germany —Growth of territorialism—The Habsburg territories—The Suabian League—Acquisition of Württemberg by Charles—Importance of the Empire to Charles—Certainty of a French war—The hostility of Spain and France—Attempt at friendship between Charles and Francis—The treaty of Noyon—The alliance proves impossible— The value of English friendship—Henry VIII.'s leaning towards Charles—Visit of Charles to England—His coronation at Aix— Aleander's estimate of his character—His welcome in Germany . 45

CHAPTER IV

PAGE

The Diet of Worms as a forecast of the reign—The problem of Luther—
The attitude of the Pope, the princes, and prelates—Public feeling
in Germany—Luther at Worms—Charles's declaration against him
—Publication of the ban—Development of the personality of
Charles—Apparent success of his policy—Constitutional reforms in
Germany—Cession of the Austrian provinces to Ferdinand—De-
parture of Charles for the Netherlands, England, and Spain   .   70

CHAPTER V

Revolt of the Castilian Communes—Its social and geographical distribution—The Santa Junta and its petition—Reaction of the nobles
in favour of the Crown—Dissension among the Communes—Battle
of Villalar—Capitulation of Toledo—French invasion of Navarre—
Social war in Valencia—Arrival of Charles and his artillery—
Punishment of the rebellion in Castile and Valencia—The Inquisition and the Moorish peasantry—A Moorish war—Revolt in
Sicily against the viceroy—Victory of the nobles and the Crown—
Comparison of the three movements   87

CHAPTER VI

Importance of a mutual understanding to Pope and Emperor—Leo X.'s
attitude during the Imperial election and afterwards—He finally
decides for alliance with Charles—His desire for war in Italy—
The resources and alliances of Charles and Francis—The condition
of Italy—The Medici and Venice—The smaller dynasties—The
smaller republics—The Orsini and Colonna, the Guelphs and Ghibellines—Italian sentiment and Italian soldiery—The weakness of
Charles in Naples and Sicily—The separation of France from
Milan by Piedmont, Montferrat, and Saluzzo   .   .   .   119

CHAPTER VII

Opening of hostilities with France—Imperialist successes and reverses—
Wolsey's anxiety for peace—The treaty with England—The capture
of Milan and Tournai—Death of Leo X.—Election of Adrian VI.—
Papal neutrality—Papal Imperialist victory of Bicocca—Treaty of
Windsor—Death of Adrian VI.—Revolt of Bourbon—Abortive

PAGE

proposals for peace—Invasion of Provence—Advance of Francis I.
on Milan—Siege and battle of Pavia—Reception of the news by
Charles—Alternative policies of Lannoy and Gattinara—Decision of
Charles—Removal of Francis to Spain—His interview with Charles
—Course of the negotiations—The question of Burgundy—Treaty
of Madrid—Release of Francis—Marriage of Charles with Isabella
of Portugal 136

CHAPTER VIII

Panic in Italy after the French defeat—Danger of Clement VII.—
Dreams of Italian independence—The Morone conspiracy—Milan
capitulates to the Imperialists—Moncada and Colonna surprise
Rome—Overtures for peace between Pope and Emperor—The
march of Bourbon upon Rome—Storm and sack of the Holy City
—The responsibility of Charles for the tragedy—Indignation in
Spain—Ideas of the secularisation of the Papacy—Indecision of
Charles—The treaty with Clement VII.—European combination
against Charles—French successes in Italy—Siege of Naples—
Helplessness of Charles—Weakness of Papal policy—Failure of
the French at Naples—Imperialist victory of Landriano—Treaties
of Barcelona and Cambrai—Visit of Charles to Italy—His coronation at Bologna—Departure for Germany . . . 167

CHAPTER IX

Germany since 1522—The Council of Regency and its financial proposals
—The Knights' war—Defeat and death of Sickingen—Collapse
of the Council of Regency—The Edict of Worms a dead letter—
Proposals for a General Council—Difficulties and imprudence of
Ferdinand—The Peasant revolt—Responsibility of Luther—
Varying character of the revolt—Attitude of the towns towards it
—Its suppression—Comparison of the German and Spanish risings
—Effects of the revolt on Lutheranism—Charles loses his oppor-
tunity—Lutheranism finds support with the Princes—The diet of
Speyer of 1526—Death of Louis of Hungary at Mohacs—Election
of Ferdinand in Bohemia—His contest with Zapolya in Hungary
—Effects of his new position upon his policy—Luther finds refuge
in territorialism—Organisation of Lutheranism—Diet of Speyer of
1529 and the Protest—The Zwinglian movement—Philip of Hesse's
connection with it—Luther and non-resistance . . . 202

CHAPTER X

PAGE

Charles in Germany—His favourable reception—Death of Gattinara—
Diet of Augsburg—The Lutheran Confession and Catholic Confuta-
tion—The legate Campeggi—Moderation of Charles—Recess of
Augsburg—Ferdinand's election as King of the Romans—Charles's
ministers, Cobos and Granvelle—Mary of Hungary appointed regent
of the Netherlands—The League of Schmalkalde—Policy of Bavaria—
Comparison between Charles and Ferdinand—The Turkish danger—
The convention of Nuremberg—Advice of the Confessor Loaysa—
Reasons for the Emperor's truce with Lutheranism—Charles marches
to meet Solyman—Charles's failure in Germany   .   .   .   241

CHAPTER XI

Charles forms a defensive Italian League—Francesco Sforza at Milan—
The restoration of the Medici—The Italian republics—Elements of
opposition to Charles in Italy—Attitude of Clement VII.—Marriage
of Catherine de' Medici—Death of Clement VII.—Accession of
Cardinal Farnese as Paul III.—Condition of the Spanish possessions
in North Africa in the reign of Ferdinand—Defeat of Ugo Moncada
at Algiers—Settlement of the Knights of St. John at Malta and
Tripoli—The power of Barbarossa—Expedition of Charles against
Goletta and Tunis—His visit to Sicily—Death of Francesco Sforza
—Francis I. reopens the question of the Milanese succession—His
refusal of the Emperor's proposals—French invasion of Savoy—
Charles challenges the French King before Pope and Cardinals   .   268

CHAPTER XII

Charles at Rome and Siena—His journey to North Italy—The French
war of 1536—The Emperor's invasion of Provence—Reasons for his
retreat—Indecisive results of the campaigns of 1537—The truce of
Nice—Effects of the war upon Charles's position in Italy—Cosimo
becomes Duke of Florence—Hostility of the Strozzi to Cosimo and
Charles—Marriage of Ottavio Farnese with the Emperor's natural
daughter Margaret—Meeting between Charles and Francis at Aigues
Mortes, and their subsequent alliance—Death of the Empress—
Schemes for permanent friendship with France—The Emperor's
journey through France—The revolt of Ghent—Punishment of the
city by Charles—Rupture of the negotiations with France—The
question of the Emperor's insincerity   292

CHAPTER XIII

PAGE

German history since 1532—The loss of Württemberg—Anabaptism at Münster—The revolution at Lübeck and the Danish war—Decline of Catholicism—Hostility of German Catholics to the Papacy—New religious policy of Charles—The truce of Frankfurt—Death of George of Saxony—Advance of Protestantism—Bigamy of Philip of Hesse—Religious conference of Regensburg—Causes of its failure —Intrigues of France—Moderation of Charles—His ill-humour against Bavaria—His reconciliation with Philip of Hesse . . 316

CHAPTER I

Birth of Charles—His mother's loss of reason and his father's death—He inherits the Netherlands and Franche Comté—Sketch of recent Netherland history—Prospective difficulties—Childhood of Charles —His amusements, appearance, and education—His early betrothal to Mary Tudor—He is declared of age—His subservience to his minister, the Lord of Chièvres—Love affair of his sister Eleanor.

THE fortunes of the Habsburgs have proverbially been made by marriage ; yet death rather than wedlock was the direct cause to which Charles of Ghent owed his greatness. When in 1496 the third child of Ferdinand and Isabella married the heir to the German possessions of the Habsburgs and the territories of the house of Burgundy, none could have foreseen that her elder brother and elder sister would be swept away in their young married life, and that neither heir nor heiress would survive to inherit the crowns of Spain. Still less probable might it seem that Charles, during thirty-eight years, should supplant his own living mother in the government of her inheritance. Such unexpected fortune was no matter for congratulation, for a dominion so vast and so conglomerate was not an enviable heritage. It is a hard lot to be born to the impossible, and harder still if the heir to the impossible has the conscience or ambition which compels him to attempt his task, while lacking the indolence or intelligence which would prompt him to abandon it.

Charles was born at Ghent on February 24, 1500.
The world received him with pomp and gaiety. His
great-grandmother, Margaret of York, carried him to
church; his aunt, Margaret of Austria, was his sponsor.
The dragon on the Belfry ejected Greek fire from mouth
and tail in honour of the heir of Austria and Burgundy.
From the tower of St. Nicholas to the Belfry torches
and paper lanterns swung merrily on a gallery of rope.[1]
At least the child had a bright entry into life. This
life was early to be clouded, for he scarcely knew his
parents. In November 1501 Philip the Handsome and
his wife Juana left the Netherlands for Spain. When
the latter returned at the close of 1504 her intellect was
already troubled; her mother in her will contemplated
the possibility that she might be unable or unwilling to
reign. Upon Isabella's death her daughter and son-in-
law journeyed to Spain to take possession of their
kingdom of Castile (April 1506), and until 1517 Charles
never again saw his mother.

On Juana's arrival in Spain it was recognised that
she was unfit to rule; whether her father or her husband
should exercise authority in her name was not so
obvious. Public opinion decided in favour of Philip as
being the less known and the less competent, and
Ferdinand sailed for Naples to secure that newly-won
kingdom against Castilian intrigues. The chief measure
of Philip's short regency was the close confinement of
his wife; the publicity which he gave to her malady
shocked Castilian sentiment, but it virtually decided the
question of succession for the future. In September
1506 he died; Ferdinand, returning, assumed the
regency of Castile for his afflicted daughter, until his

---

[1] A very full account of the first days of Charles's life may be found in
A. R. Villa's *La reina Juana la Loca*.

grandson Charles should be of age. The other grand-parent, the Emperor Maximilian, aware that impossible claims sometimes brought pecuniary consolation, also urged his title to the guardianship. It is, however, important to remember that there was as yet no certainty that Charles would succeed to the Spanish crowns, for his mother was by right Queen of Castile and heiress of Aragon, and she might outlive him.

Meanwhile, on his father's death, Charles had inherited the Netherlands and Franche Comté. The Netherlands alone were a sufficiently wealthy and laborious inheritance for one ruler, although they did not yet include the provinces of Guelders and Utrecht, nor the Frisian territories. Hitherto the period of Austrian rule had been little more than an interruption at once to commercial progress, and to the development of governmental centralisation. It would be unfair to ascribe this to the Habsburg marriage, for it was the lawless violence of the Flemings, after the death of Charles the Bold, which forced his daughter Mary to bring to an issue the lagging negotiations for her marriage with Maximilian. There was no other alternative but French conquest or the dissolution of the complex state into its primary elements, for the only bond as yet was personal. The Flemings had destroyed the monarchical institutions which had given some measure of unity to the Low Countries; they had judicially murdered the ministers who represented the Burgundian traditions; they had striven to cast loose the French-speaking provinces, the union with which seemed to threaten their national law and language.

On Mary's early death Maximilian had to fight hard for the regency during his son's minority. For four months he was the prisoner of the citizens of Bruges, and

in no slight peril of death. Under a weak government
the old factions of Hoeks and Kabeljaws revived in
Holland and Zealand, intermingling with the troubles
in Flanders, with civil war in the German diocese of
Utrecht, with the struggle of Charles of Guelders against
the Burgundian government. These factions, like those
of Guelf and Ghibelline, had almost lost such significance
as they had once possessed ; they were traditional feuds,
not so much of class against class, but of family against
family, and town against town. The ravages of civil
war and oppressive taxation exasperated the peasantry,
and the so-called Bread and Cheese War of North
Holland was in reality a social revolt. Maximilian's
capable general, Albert of Saxony, beat down Flemings,
Hoeks, and peasants, but at a fearful cost. Disaster
had even infected the high seas, for the whole herring
fleet was one year captured by the French.

The few years of Philip's direct government were
relatively peaceful, and the commercial treaty with
England, named the *Magnus Intercursus*, gave some
relief (1496); but on his death troubles broke out anew,
if not in so acute a form, under the second regency of
Maximilian, while the Baltic fleet in 1511 fell into the
hands of the Hanseatic squadron. The bane of the
Netherlands was now, however, Charles of Egmont, Duke
of Guelders and Count of Zutphen, who for thirty-eight
years was to prove a constant factor in the difficulties
of Charles's life. The duke was the son of Adolf of
Guelders, whose quarrel with his father Arnold had been
utilised by Charles the Bold to annex their territories.
After the Duke of Burgundy's defeat and death Adolf
had been released from his Burgundian prison, and re-
assumed his sovereignty; he died fighting against the
French in the cause of Flemish nationality; the

Flemings had indeed wished him to marry Mary of Burgundy, and so form a truly national Low Country dynasty. His son Charles was then at Maximilian's court, and was soon after taken prisoner by the French. On Maximilian's capture at Bruges the French king released Charles of Egmont, and henceforth used him as a tool against his Habsburg enemies. His subjects, from hatred to the Burgundian, were devoted to their duke in spite of his financial oppression. He was clever, unscrupulous, and faithless—a general of no ordinary ability, disconcerting his enemies by a rapidity of movement which seemed to make him ubiquitous. Aided, now openly, now secretly, by the French, he was at constant war with Maximilian, with Philip, and again with Maximilian; at one moment raiding Brabant, at another driving the Bishop of Utrecht from his territories of Drenthe and Overyssel.

The Burgundian rulers were, as counts of Holland, titular lords of Friesland, but they had never established an effective sovereignty, although Charles the Bold was on the point of so doing. Maximilian, much to the disgust of Philip's government, had mortgaged the territory to Duke Albert of Saxony (1498). The province, to all appearance, passed entirely out of the sphere of Burgundian influence. It had long been laid waste by the chronic feuds of two factions, the Schieringers and Vetkoopers, and by the attempts of the chief city Groningen to establish its authority over the smaller towns and rural districts. To these sources of disorder was now added the struggle for the independence of Friesland, or at least of Groningen, from the Saxons; while the counts of East Friesland, who had established an independent lordship beyond the Ems, threw themselves, now on one side, now on the other, into the conflict between Groningen and the Saxons. It was certain that Charles of Guelders would not long stand out of so promising a fight.

The ruler of the Netherlands had other difficulties of a character more permanent, depending less on popular violence or unpopular government. It is difficult to draw a hard-and-fast line between Dutch and Flemings. Yet the Dutch provinces were, as a whole, distinct in character and interests from the Flemish; and much more deeply were the commercial and manufacturing Flemish provinces divided from the French-speaking states of Artois, Hainault, West Flanders, Luxemburg, and Franche Comté, where noble influences predominated in spite of the thriving towns of Artois, Hainault, and Walloon Flanders. It was an additional inconvenience that political and ethnological distinctions did not correspond. The French-speaking provinces of Franche Comté, Luxemburg, and Hainault were held under the Empire, but Artois and Flanders were French fiefs, and Charles was, as Count of Flanders, a peer of France. Nor was geography kindly to the Habsburg-Burgundian territories. Without Guelders and Utrecht, Holland and Zealand had an inadequate pastoral and agricultural *hinterland.* The great diocese of Liège, French in language and sympathy, yet politically connected with the Empire, separated, but for the narrow strip of the Burgundian lordship of Namur, Limburg and Luxemburg from the Flemish group. Lorraine interposed its substantial form between Franche Comté and the Netherlands. Even the bishoprics of Cambrai and Tournai were obstacles to complete geographical and political consolidation. Franche Comté, indeed, had a far closer connection with the Swiss than with the Netherlands, while the fortunes of Limburg and Luxemburg were destined to be quite distinct from those of the Dutch and Flemish provinces.

Such then was the first problem paper which was set to Charles in his early youth. It was his task to revive the monarchical institutions, which had scarcely as yet recovered from the shock of Charles the Bold's tragedy ; to make those institutions popular, and so create a national unity among alien races and jarring interests, hitherto connected by a bare personal union. For this purpose he must prove the necessity of the monarchy to commerce and manufacture; he must protect his frontier against French aggression, the Channel against piracy, his fisheries and factories against English competition. It would be his ambition to fill in and round off by annexation his straggling Netherland possessions ; to eliminate, or at least emasculate, the Imperial and French suzerainty, which must sometimes be a danger and always an annoyance. He must, in fact, weld a number of independent and antiquated atoms into a modern state, bind it together by obedience, and give it the principle of life in the sentiment of loyalty which would inevitably harden into patriotism. To effect all this the ruler's means were at the moment scanty. He had succeeded to a wasted heritage; the cloth factories and breweries, which were the peculiar industries of the Netherlands, had dwindled; the live stock, which was the fortune of the country districts, had diminished ; in some ports of the Zuyder Zee a few sail represented the fishing fleet of the age of Charles the Bold.

It is time to turn to the child whose first task has been described. If Charles never knew a mother's care, he had an admirable substitute in the guidance of his father's sister, Margaret. Juana's malady had been intensified by the loss of her faithless, worthless husband. Margaret retained all her senses, although she had been contumeliously rejected by her betrothed, Charles VIII. of France, and had lost by death two young husbands full of promise. On her brother Philip's death, Maximilian, as guardian of his grandson, had made Margaret his viceregent in the Netherlands. Here she had no light task—on the one hand holding her own against the nobles of the French party, on the other endeavouring to instil into her father Maximilian's irretentive brain the rudiments of economy and common-sense. Charles could scarcely have entered into political life under better tutelage, although his aunt's masterful nature may have checked the development of his own individuality.[1]

During the first fifteen years of Charles's life it is only possible to get occasional glimpses of a retiring, inarticulate boy.[2] He is seen dancing with his sisters round a bonfire on St. John's Day; Maximilian gave him a wooden horse—emblem of his future prowess, and the boy also had a sledge in the form of a ship with masts, ropes, and flags. In games, like most children, the prince liked to be on the winning side. Mimic combats were fought between Turks and Christians. Charles was always a Christian, and the page who commanded the paynim host complained that the Christians were always made to win. In after life the balance was not infrequently redressed. If teasing is a token of affection, the boy was fond of animals, for he loved to poke his stick between the bars at the bears and lions in the royal cages. He shot skilfully with the bow, and at ten took a real pleasure in the chase—

[1] For the opening years of Margaret's administration see *Margaretha van Oostenrijk*, by L. M. G. Kooperberg, 1908.

[2] Of much interest for the early life of Charles is C. Moeller, *Eléonore d'Autriche*, 1895.

a feature which delighted the old Emperor, for otherwise, he wrote, the boy could not be his legitimate grandson. On one occasion the bag, unfortunately, comprised a man; but the victim was "only an artisan, a drunkard and ill-conditioned."

Charles as a boy is described as graceful and well-built, but his face was colourless, and he looked delicate. Habsburg blood betrayed itself in the projecting lower jaw, which Charles faithfully transmitted to generations of Spanish kings. Even in youth the misunderstanding between the jaws not only embarrassed mastication, but caused hesitation in the speech. The pleasing features were a clear, steady eye, and a calm, intelligent forehead; these, late in life, still gave at once a pleasant and a dignified expression to the face.

Malines was the home of the prince's childhood. The life of most young people of royal birth is apt to be monotonous, and that of Charles was the more cramped by the peculiarly strict etiquette of the Burgundian court. Not only every functionary, but every object of the table and the wardrobe had its own ceremonious usages, from the prince's shirt to his table napkin and his toothpick. Had the two largest knives upon the table not lain in the form of a Burgundian cross they would have been suspected of *lèse-majesté.* Harmony is the best antidote for monotony; thus music was an early taste which lasted Charles through life. With his sister Eleanor he was taught the clavichord and other instruments by the organist of the chapel.[1] But music not infrequently is the source of discord. A little later, at the court of Brussels, its merits and demerits were much debated. Lannoy, afterwards viceroy of Naples, held that some forms

[1] See E. van der Straeten, *Charles Quint musicien,* 1894.

thereof made men effeminate, whereon the votaries of music and their opponents nearly came to blows. Charles in person intervened, proposing a tournament as a bloodless means of ascertaining the manhood of musicians, who proved by their victory that sounds were not incompatible with arms.

The opening of the sixteenth century was a golden age for education, and Charles was carefully educated— at least, in intention. He was taught to read and write by Juan de Vera, who, in 1505, gave up his charge to another Spaniard, the humanist, Luis Vaca, who, after six years, was succeeded by Adrian of Utrecht, Dean of Louvain. The boy was not, however, a willing pupil; he complained, it is said, of being educated as if he were intended for a school-master. The future ruler of a polyglot empire was a singularly bad linguist. Roman Emperor as he became, he knew very little Latin. German was never one of his few accomplishments; as late as 1548 German towns, wishing to make a favourable impression, pre-sented their addresses in Spanish. Two years after he became king of Castile and Aragon he only knew a few words of the national language; his knowledge of Italian was barely elementary. Flemish was the tongue of his birthplace, but he did not begin to learn it until he was thirteen. French was his natural language, but he neither spoke nor wrote it with any elegance, though Maximilian begged him in 1513 to write some pretty letters *en walon* to his relations in Spain. The time spared from modern languages Charles did not lavish on more educational if less utilitarian studies. Of theology the champion of Catholicism knew little or nothing; he could scarcely read the Vulgate, and in his later years his comprehension thereof must needs be aided by very simple commentary. Mathematics he learnt when over thirty, in the belief that they were essential to the career of a great captain. His gorge rose at the humiliation of becoming the pupil of a mathematical professor, and so Francisco Borja took the lessons and transmitted them by rote to the imperial student. It is small wonder that the mediator, a Borgia though he was, developed into sainthood.

If Charles learnt little from his actual tutors, he owed much to Henry, Count of Nassau, who superintended them. This genial nobleman might not be thought a wholly desirable guide for youth. He gave great banquets, and liked to see his friends well primed ; so he thought-fully provided a monster-bed with sheets and counterpane and bolsters at head and foot, and hereon, when they could no longer stand, his guests were laid. Nassau did not teach Charles to drink, but inspired him with the love of history, stirred the somewhat sluggish blood, kindled the imagination with stories of the Burgundian house, of Philip the Good and Charles the Bold. He was until his death in 1538 one of Charles's most intimate counsellors and companions, fighting, negotiating, and administrating in his master's cause.

When only seven Charles made his first public speech, for his aunt Margaret cleverly brought the child to support her demand for a subsidy before the Estates at Louvain. Its purport was understood rather from his gestures than from the sounding quality of the boyish voice ; but at all events, adds the chronicler, the people could not fail to be well pleased. At eight, so far as is known, the prince wrote, or rather signed, his first love-letter.[1] This was also his personal entry into inter-

---

[1] This letter has been ascribed to the year 1513, but Dr. Gairdner shows strong reasons for connecting it with the espousal ceremonies of 1508. See *Camden Miscellany*, vol. ix., 1895.

national political life, for the letter was addressed to
Mary Tudor, to whom he presented a jewel bearing the
monogram K, and the posy *Maria optimam partem
elegit, quae non auferetur ab ea.* Charles was, indeed,
wedded by proxy to the English princess, who, "with
moost sadde and pryncely countenaunce . . . spake
parfittely and distinctely in the frensche tonge by a
longe circumstaunce the wordes of matrimonye for hir
partie . . . without any basshing of countenaunce,
stoppe or interrupcion therein . . . whiche thyng
caused dyverse and many . . . not only to mervayle
but also in suche wyse to rejoyse that for extreme
contente and gladnes the terys passed out of theyr ies."

This seemed, indeed, a notable moment in Tudor-
Habsburg history; it was the last of Henry VII.'s
many diplomatic triumphs. The king's poetical secretary, Petrus Carmelianus, might well rejoice that the
flourishing red roses of the Tudors were so planted and
spread abroad in the highest Imperial gardens and
houses of power and honour, that their branches bound
together the twin Imperial eagles. This was no
nominal, momentary union; it was confirmed in 1513,
and the boy-bridegroom visited his brother-in-law,
Henry VIII., in his newly-won city of Tournai, his first
royal visit. Next year, it is true, the future king of
Spain and queen of France were parted in the shuffling
of the cards. But, although Mary Tudor married the
old French king, statesmen on both sides still yearned
for the more natural alliance. Before six years had
passed Charles was pledged to his betrothed's younger
namesake, and thirty-four years later he showed all a
young lover's eagerness in courting this second Mary
Tudor for his son Philip.

In 1515 Charles was, at the instance of the Estates,

suddenly declared of age in his Netherland provinces. This act was directed against the influence, not only of Maximilian, but of Margaret, without whose knowledge or consent it was proposed. It would be natural to suppose that the youth of fifteen played some part in this palace revolution ; it was, at all events, a moment when any latent force of character might well have unveiled itself. Yet Charles's passivity suffered him to fall under the spell of the leader of the nobility, Guillaume de Croy, Lord of Chièvres, who since 1509 had been his governor and grand chamberlain. In this capacity at the Burgundian court Chièvres enjoyed peculiar opportunities of exercising influence upon his master, from whom, except during the hour of dinner, he was never separated by day or night. The all-powerful minister belonged to the French branch of the house of Croy, but he possessed large estates within the Burgundian frontier. As long as the Walloon noble lived, the career of Charles as a ruler scarcely opened. The experienced English diplomatist Pace described the young king as an idiot surrounded by a corrupt council. The Papal legate Campeggi, who, later, had much reason to reject any claim to vicarious infallibility, rashly pronounced him more fit to be governed than to govern.

Flattery, whose function it is to place an exaggerated emphasis on truth, early laid stress upon the modesty of Charles, and upon his attention to public business. Even as his first little speech had aided his aunt to extract a subsidy, so his punctual attendance at Council was doubtless to the benefit of Chièvres. The enforced interest in public affairs must have been irksome to one whose natural tastes were hunting and shooting, but it was educational. Self-sacrifice was the preparation for

self-reliance. Modest Charles certainly was. So dependent was he upon his ministers that his name is scarcely
mentioned in despatches, save as a minnow to be spun
in the preserved waters of royal matrimony. Engaged
or half-engaged some ten times before he married, he
seems scarcely to have expressed an opinion on the
choice of a wife. Once, indeed, when the name of
Renée of France was mentioned, his face brightened, and
he said with emphasis that she would be the best,
because she would bring him Brittany. A little later
his motives were more personal; at least in 1518 he was
credited for some fantasy for the Hungarian princess,
his future sister-in-law, as being " of high stature and fair
complexion for to bring fair generation."

It was in a love affair, after all, though not his
own, that Charles first showed his strength of purpose.
Marriage was a subject of much interest at the court of
Brussels, which has been called a sort of matrimonial
agency. Before Charles succeeded to his Spanish kingdoms, his sister Mary had already left for her short, if
comparatively happy, marriage with the ill-fated Louis
of Hungary, while Isabella had begun her miserable life
with the brutal and lustful Christian II. of Denmark.
Ferdinand and the youngest sister Catherine were being
brought up in Spain. Only Eleanor, eldest and dearest
of Charles's sisters, was still at Brussels, the cynosure of
European princes' eyes. Upon her the brilliant Count
Palatine Frederick fixed his fancy. He was the most
finished nobleman of the court, and, though seventeen
years his senior, Charles's earliest personal friend. The
affection was returned, and reciprocity led to clandestine
correspondence. But Eleanor was being reserved to
replace her deceased aunt upon the throne of Portugal.
Chièvres set Charles on the track of one of the Palatine's

love-letters.   Under pretext of wishing good-morning to
his sister, he snatched it, before she had time to read it,
from her bosom, and, after a brief hand-to-hand conflict,
secured the prize.   He was white and trembling with
wrath at his friend's presumption or deceit.   "Upon
this his constancy into a like affair," wrote Spinelli to
Henry VIII., "many do conject in him good stomak
and couraggy, and how that he shall not lightly forget
the offences, and how he will be fast in his determyna-
cions, and much extime the honnor of the worlde."
This singularly sound forecast of the character of
the hitherto problematic boy of seventeen gives,
perhaps, the first glimpse into the secret chambers of
Charles's personality.   Court gossip attributed other
virtues to the young ruler, such as a loathing for
drunkenness, a dislike for flattery, and strong, outspoken
indignation at backbiting.   These characteristics, although only guaranteed by rumour, may be credited to
Charles's youth, for they certainly find their place in his
riper years.   A little incident points to the possibility
of young ambition.   The court physician, Marliani, in-
vented for Charles the device of the Pillars of Hercules,
with the words *Plus oultre*.   The prince was one day
found scratching the legend upon a pane of glass with
his dagger's point.   Nevertheless, ambition was the last
vice or virtue which critics or flatterers attributed to the
future sovereign of innumerable lordships.   If ambition
had really taken root it proved unusually slow of
growth.   At his first tournament in Spain the young
king's shield bore, not the adventurous *Plus oultre*, but
the more modest *Nondum*.   The life of Charles henceforth was to seek alternate guidance from these same
two legends, *Yet further* and *Not yet*.

CHAPTER II

Death of Ferdinand of Aragon—Charles's Spanish inheritance and its difficulties—His voyage to Spain and journey through Asturias— His visit to Juana—Death of Jiménez—Charles enters Valladolid— The Cortes of Castile—Unpopularity of the Flemings—Charles holds the Cortes of Aragon at Saragossa—His visit to Catalonia— His election to the Empire—Discontent in Castile—Riot at Valladolid—The Cortes at Santiago and Corunna—Charles sails for England, leaving Adrian of Utrecht as regent—Outbreak of revolt in Toledo, and social war in Valencia—Inauspicious opening of the reign.

On January 23, 1516, died Ferdinand of Aragon. His relations with his son-in-law Philip and his grandson Charles had been unfriendly; gossip reported that he wished the latter dead, and that he bribed Margaret to keep him out of Spain. He has been credited with designs for leaving Aragon, or at least Naples, to his favourite grandchild Ferdinand, who was born, educated, and beloved in Spain. Adrian of Utrecht had, however, visited him in Charles's interest in 1515, and dissuaded him from dividing the Spanish kingdoms or their revenues, if ever he had cherished such intentions. The will of Isabella had left Castile to Juana, and after her to Charles, and Ferdinand's will made a similar provision for Aragon. Both grandparents had recognised that, owing to their daughter's malady, her son's reign must begin at once. Until his arrival the regency of Castile was entrusted to Cardinal Jiménez, and that of

Aragon to Ferdinand's natural son, the Archbishop of Saragossa.

Charles was first proclaimed king at Brussels, where Ferdinand's funeral obsequies were celebrated in the cathedral of St. Gudule. Twice the king-at-arms of the Golden Fleece called aloud " Don Ferdinand," thrice the answer came, " He is dead," and on this, the great standard clattered to the ground. Then cried the herald, " Long live donna Jehanne and don Charles, by the grace of God Catholic Kings," whereon Charles, doffing his mourning, received and brandished the sword of justice. In Spain this assumption of the royal title was regarded as a breach of custom, and caused comment and discontent. Nevertheless Jiménez had his young master proclaimed in Castile, while courteously pushing into the background Adrian, to whom the Flemish government had given full powers as governor of Spain, in the event of Ferdinand's death.

As the Netherland provinces, which Charles had inherited from his Burgundian ancestors, were a group of duchies, counties, and lordships, with little internal unity, so his Iberian inheritance was a conglomerate of kingdoms and counties, with no common constitution. Castile and Aragon were separated by long traditions of hostility, which their personal union under Ferdinand and Isabella had by no means obliterated. Their parliamentary institutions were distinct in form and character; the privileges and position of their nobility were different; their frontiers were divided by a hostile tariff. Several of the smaller kingdoms had long been incorporated with Castile, although the monarch's official style preserved the record of original independence. Even the recent conquest, the kingdom of Granada, was connected by a real union, for the town of Granada sent its proctors to the Castilian Cortes. Navarre, however, although formally annexed under Ferdinand to the Castilian crown, retained its Cortes, its local *fueros* or charters, its frontier duties. It was still sentimentally attached to its ousted French dynasty, and to the eighteenth century was by economic interests tied to France rather than to Spain.

With the crown of Aragon were connected the kingdom of Valencia and the county of Barcelona, and with the latter the counties of Cerdagne and Roussillon, which stretched far into Southern France. But Aragon, Valencia, and Catalonia had separate Cortes, differing from each other in their form, and each maintained the right of recognition of their king or count. Beyond the peninsula lay the kingdom of Majorca, the kingdom of Sardinia, the kingdom of Sicily, and the kingdom of Naples, each absolutely distinct from the other, each with its national traditions of government, its ethnological peculiarities. Yet further afield lay the Spanish possessions in North Africa, and the colonies in the islands and on the mainland of America.

It is fortunate that the purely Spanish history of these complex possessions usually reduces itself to that of Castile. The importance of Navarre in Charles V.'s reign was mainly diplomatic and military; Valencia was shattered by a social war; Roussillon was the scene of a French invasion; otherwise there is little to tell. The minor kingdoms supplied soldiers and politicians, but little money. They were virtually disorderly oligarchical republics, of which the king acted as occasional president with great discomfort and little profit. In the reign of Charles V. Spain meant Castile; he would have wished that it were not so.

Ferdinand and Isabella had reduced Castile to admirable order, which had not wholly disappeared after the queen's death. The nobility had been sedulously kept in due subordination. Their power over their vassals was slight, and in great contrast to that of the nobles of Aragon, whose authority was uncontrolled; but they were still very rich, very proud, and very factious. The towns were entirely different from the great commercial centres of France, Italy, and Germany. They preserved much of their original character of military colonies, with large territories around them, and, although manufactures had already thriven in several cities, the gentry were usually a predominating element. As a counterpoise to the great nobles Isabella had shown favour to the towns, and under Ferdinand's weaker regency their pretensions had increased.

The Crown, under normal circumstances, could exercise much control over the towns through their *regidores* and *corregidor.* The former composed the governing body, and had been originally elective. This system had gradually been supplanted by one of Crown nomination and purchase, so that the *regidores* had become presumably the creatures of the king. Even more closely connected with the monarchy was the *corregidor,* who was from the first a royal functionary. His powers were formerly concurrent with those of the *regidores,* but he had become, before the reign of Charles, virtual governor of his town. The office was highly unpopular, but, in spite of remonstrance it had, from being an exception, now been universally imposed on all the principal Castilian cities. A body termed *jurats* still represented non-official interests, having a voice, if not a vote, in the municipal government, and watching, with a right of protest, the pro-

ceedings of the *regidores*.   The condition of the towns
necessarily affected the parliamentary institutions of
Castile, upon which supply depended, for, although
nobles and ecclesiastics were occasionally summoned,
the Cortes really consisted of thirty-six representatives
of eighteen towns.

The Spanish clergy were, owing to the royal rights
of nomination, completely under the Crown's control,
and this was no doubt increased by the introduction
of the Inquisition, which was practically, if not tech-
nically, a purely royal institution worked, not through
the bishops, but through the friars.   At the head
of the administrative stood the powerful Council of
Castile or Royal Council, mainly consisting of lawyers,
and chiefly concerned with the supervision and execution of the law, although its competence extended
to all matters affecting the welfare of the States.   From
this the Council of State, or Privy Council, was not
as yet fully differentiated, nor from this again the
Council of War.

Such in its general outlines was Charles's Iberian
inheritance, and if to the rule of the Spanish kingdoms
be added the government of the young North African
and American dependencies, and the protection of
Naples and Sicily against French and Turks, it seemed
likely to supply material for a strong man's long life,
and Charles was weakly and longevity improbable.

The immediate presence of Charles in Spain seemed
essential.   Strong as Jiménez was, the regent could
with difficulty rule a people that would scarcely brook
a king.   Noble factions, kept under by the catholic
kings, blazed out afresh; towns resisted the levy of
a standing national force; it seemed not improbable
that the nobility would proclaim Charles's younger

brother king, and Ferdinand, genial, ambitious, and hot-headed, with none of the affection inspired by early companionship, was not unlikely to accept, if he did not invite, their overtures. Fate seemed to be against Charles's first visit to his kingdom. His Netherland councillors were already at variance with Ferdinand the Catholic's Castilian enemies, who had long found a refuge at the court of Brussels. Since Ferdinand's death the Spanish element had perceptibly increased. All enemies of Jiménez, all place-hunters, flocked to Brussels. So numerous were the knights of Santiago that it was found possible to hold a chapter. If the Grand Chancellor stirred from home, he was followed by from fifty to a hundred mules, each mounted by an applicant for office. English, French, Spanish, and Imperial factions jostled with each other. All parties but the French strove to overthrow Chièvres, and, with this end, to lure Charles from the Netherlands. Letters professedly from Spain painted its condition in the most sombre colours, but then these letters were found to bear a Brussels watermark. Meanwhile Chièvres was in possession, and must have been fully conscious that his influence would be imperilled by the atmosphere of Spain.

It was really impossible to leave the Netherlands until the friendship of France was assured, and therefore the negotiations for the indeterminate treaty of Noyon[1] delayed Charles for some six months; it was impossible to sail until the passage money had been raised and a guarantee for the security of the voyage obtained from the English king. It was no easy or

---

[1] This treaty is described at greater length hereafter in connection with the international relations of Charles. It provided for his marriage with the infant daughter of Francis I., and the clauses bearing on the disputed ownership of Naples and Navarre were wholly in favour of France.

inexpensive matter to find shipping for a household of
five hundred and for a miscellaneous following of three
hundred more. When all was settled, westerly winds
kept the royal fleet in port.[1] For weeks Charles was
forced to find amusement in Walcheren, now making
parties to the big ships, now wandering through the
lanes, vocal with birds, to Westhoven, with its rabbit
warren, its rich meadows and gardens, and its firm,
sunny beach. At Middelburg Charles was seen by a
keen observer, one Antonio de Beatis, chaplain of the
Cardinal of Aragon, who brought a Cardinal's hat for
a nephew of Chièvres, the boy-bishop of Cambrai, of
whom more will be heard hereafter.[2] Antonio's
judgment was unusually favourable for those early days.
The face was long and thin, and, unless he thought
about it, the lower jaw dropped and the mouth fell
open. Yet the expression was attractive and extremely
dignified; and these are the precise characteristics on
which Charles's visitors expatiated in later years. His
figure was beautiful, and the lank, straight legs the
shapeliest that could be seen. A month later Antonio
saw Francis I. at Rouen, and his master's verdict was
that the French king's legs were too slight for so large
a body. These respective royal legs may be thought to
provide a key to character; the weaker knee throughout was that of Francis.

After this visit the wind suddenly changed to E.N.E.,
and the pilots said that the king must sail at once.

[1] The following account of the voyage of Charles and his journey through
Spain is mainly derived from the *Relation du Premier Voyage de Charles Quint
en Espagne*, written by his attendant, Laurent Vital, and printed in the
Collection des Voyages des Souverains des Pays-Bas, by MM. Gachard et Piot,
vol. iii. 1881. It is supplemented from the letters of the English envoy, Sir
Thomas Spinelli, in Cal. State Papers, Henry VIII., vol. ii. part ii.

[2] *Die Reise des Kardinals Luigi d'Aragona, beschrieben von Antonio de
Beatis*, ed. by L. Pastor, 1905. See also *Quarterly Review*, July 1908.

The ships were well found in salt meat and dried fish, butter and good beer, but great was the confusion in getting the baggage aboard. The king could not sleep for the noise of the luggage lowered to the hold, and the chanties of the sailors hauling at the cable. The keeper of the wardrobe failed to get a cart, and was left on shore with the royal clothes; he had to row six miles by night with a drunken and extortionate boatman; "but God," he piously exclaims, "helps drunkards." An officer of the stables in similar plight had his boat run down by a hoy, was dragged on board the admiral's ship, and, fortunately for himself as it proved, was unable to join his horses.

On September 8 the fleet set sail from Flushing. Difficulties still dogged the king. The lighter, faster ships scouted in advance, and kept the Channel clear; but a pirate, professing to be a friendly Southampton merchantman, sailed round and round the slow-going vessel of the provost-marshal, with intent to delay it and cut it off. The Duke of Alba's son ran aground off the banks of Zealand, and must needs be forwarded to Spain by land. At night the ship with the royal stud was burned, with all its crew and passengers and freight, "a piteous ensample to warn the company": henceforth the regulations as to lights were stringent, although the king and his sister were allowed lanterns, for fear that they should slip in the dark and hurt themselves.

Every detail of the stormy voyage is known. The royal ship was a thing of beauty. Her foresail bore the Crucifixion and the device of Charles, the pillars of Hercules with the legend *plus oultre* between them. On the mainsail was painted the Holy Trinity, on the mizen St. Nicholas; St. Christopher graced the sprit-

sail, and on that of the forecastle St. James slew
infidels above the figure of the Virgin, who stood
upon the moon, crowned with seven planets. The
king's outfit was worthy of his sails, and was as
prudent as it was highly coloured. The crimson satin
tunic had a high collar lined with scarlet; over this
was a sleeveless cape lined with marten, fastened by
a brooch, and reaching just below the waist. His
scarlet stockings were protected by high leggings. On
his head he wore a double cap of scarlet, fastening
under the chin. To give warmth to body and neck
and arms he would enfold himself in a mantle of fine
velvet lined with lamb's wool. "Thus," wrote the
sympathetic Master of the Wardrobe, "he was protected from the impetuous sea winds."

At dawn the royal trumpets sounded on the poop,
while three times a day the German fifes and drums
made such melody as might be. Charles breakfasted
after early prayers. He would then talk or listen to
his fool Jan Bobin, or watch the two long columns of
ships astern. After early dinner the passengers read
or played chess and cards till supper. The boatswain
then called the crew together, and by the various
notes of his whistle gave his orders. If these were
not obeyed, the rope's end made the sailors run like
rats to the appointed work. The crew were content
with short evening prayers, but certain young sailors
sang elaborate sacred music until the bell rang for
bed.

The weather was at times extremely rough, and
the misguided efforts of the servants to reach the table
with their dishes were a constant source of laughter.
The ladies suffered sadly from sea-sickness, but Charles
was ill but once, and was much the better for it.

During a dead calm boats would ply from ship to
ship. The admiral visited the king in the hope of
replenishing his cellar. "Sire," he craftily began, "I
have still a tin pot full of fresh butter which I will
give you; I would also send some red wine if I had
any." Charles laughed and said, "Gentle admiral, I
quite understand that one who gave you wine would
do you pleasure; now, as you are a good comrade, and
have given me some butter, I make you a present of
the best wine I have." So the wine was sent, and the
butter arrived, and the king and his sister ate thereof
as of a most exquisite dainty.

The ordinary incidents of a voyage were not lacking.
We are told of the catching and eating of the porpoise,
the wager of a passenger to swim from ship to ship
with a bottle of wine round his neck, the Andalusian
smack bound for the Channel which made the king
a welcome gift of figs and oranges, raisins and pome-
granates, the promise of wine to the first sailor who
sighted land, and the consequent cry of "There it is!"
seven good hours before the fact.

The land sighted proved not to be Biscay, for which
the fleet was making, but the Asturian coast. Charles
determined to land with his more immediate following,
and, shunning the dirty little port of Tazones, he was
rowed up the estuary at dead of night to the humble
village of Villa Viciosa. Most of his suite put back to
Santander, for there were no carts nor mules for transport. The first night was a veritable picnic; the great
lords and ladies tried their prentice hands at cooking,
and eggs and bacon proved a good foundation for an
omelette, if only there had been butter. On the morrow
hunger and thirst were relieved by a municipal gift of
sheep and oxen, and skins of wine.

The first few weeks in Spain formed the most romantic episode in Charles's life. Nothing can have been in greater contrast to the solid uneventful comfort of Netherland existence. The king learned to know a portion of his realm which he was never likely to see again. When the fleet first appeared, the inhabitants, believing it to be French or Turkish, hurried their women and stock into the mountains and beset the passes. On recognition of the Castilian flag, the reception was hearty but very rude. The peasants were all hidalgos, boasting descent from the conquerors of the Moors; but their jackets were of coarse gray wool, their legs and feet were bare, their chins were razorless; they were, write our two informants, for all the world like Irishmen. The women were less uncouth; black knitted ribands with paternosters of jet, coral, or amber set off the whiteness of their necks, but their coarse red stockings, when they wore them, were innocent of garters, and the creases distressed the fastidious Netherland observer.

For six weeks Charles wandered through the wild hill country without even entering an important town. There were only forty horses for two hundred gentlemen and ladies. Charles himself rode a hobby lent him by the English envoy Spinelli; the ladies were packed in ox-carts; for lack of bedding the great Lord Chièvres slept on straw; the king, when taken ill, had to lie in an extemporised arbour, owing to the vermin in the houses. The country, however, compensated for any hardships, with its wooded hills and smiling valleys teeming with fertility to the Netherlander's experienced eye, but only sufficiently cultivated to keep alive the scattered villages, for the Asturians plumed themselves on their gentility. There was no want of amusement. Each village gave its bull-fight in the king's honour. The men held mock reviews, pelting each other with fallen oranges, or they danced with snapping of fingers and knocking of shoes. The dancing and singing of the girls was much more elaborate ; some shook tambourines and had jingling anklets, belts, and armlets, in Moorish fashion. The huge linen headgear of the women, differing from village to village, caused unfailing merriment. It was explained as a penalty, inflicted because they killed their children, rather than see them converted to Christianity as were their fathers. They petitioned Charles for the removal of the burden, but he cautiously replied that he would make no novelties without consulting the Council of Castile. Another survival of the Moorish period was the turban, worn still by some of the peasantry, and by the aged Marquis of Villena, who rode to visit Charles with ample folds of linen around his head, just as though he were one of the Three Kings in Scripture.

On the last day of October the Constable of Castile met Charles, and henceforth he was among his nobles, who had been told that he could not meet them in the barren mountains. Before the king would show himself to his people, he visited his mother at Tordesillas, where she lived with extreme simplicity and in virtual confinement with her daughter Catherine. Juana was in a reasonable and cheerful mood, but she was surprised to find Charles and Eleanor grown up, and asked if they could really be her children. A little later Charles tried to remove his child-sister from her gloomy surroundings, but her secret abstraction caused his mother such paroxysms of grief that she had to be restored. Experts might now term Juana's malady hysteria rather than insanity, but there is no question that she was unfit to rule her country ; she could not even command herself. Lucid intervals alternated with wild storms of passion, with deep melancholy, and dislike for religious duties.   In Castile there was natural reluctance to believe Isabella's daughter mad, and much sympathy for her close confinement.   In the coming Cortes Charles was urged to give her a household befitting the queen, and when the ensuing troubles came he was accused of neglecting the measures which might have produced a cure.   Yet it cannot be doubted that Juana's case was one which death alone could heal, and it was not until 1554 that the healer visited the queen.

The gloom of Tordesillas is relieved by a lively boyish letter[1] written by Charles "with his own fair hand" to Henry of Nassau.   "Pretty ladies," he writes, "are not to be found here; I pretend, indeed, to have found one who pleases me, but she is nothing very grand, for she has quite an inch of paint on her face : you can imagine what that must be."   After bewailing the poor fare of Spain, so different from that which Henry must be enjoying, especially on fish days, he concludes, "Every one talks of what he loves, and so I answer your letter sooner than all the others, and indeed I think that if we did not sometimes have a quiet chat, I should become as wise as Solomon ever was.   And truly I should have need to be, for there are sharp practitioners here, and one has a deal to do to give the right reply to everything.   Anyhow, after all this nonsense I shall never forget my Henry.   Would to God he were here, or I, sometime or other, there.   And now I must stop, praying God that it may please Him

---

[1] This letter, originally published by N. C. Kist in *Kerkhistorisch Archiv*, has been reprinted from the MS. at Brussels by E. Gossart in *Charles Quint*, 1910. To illustrate Charles's dislike to paint and powder, he quotes from R. Villa s *Juana la loca*, p. 285, an order given on August 24, 1518, that his sister Catherine is to have her face washed with fresh river water only, and that no paint or other cosmetic is to be applied.

to make me much more clever, and to give you plenty of good wine, which I do not believe you lack."

While Charles was at Tordesillas the news reached him that his grandmother's great minister was dead. Jiménez, knowing that his end was near, had craved for the sight of his master. The king's delay was ascribed to want of will, to the influence of the Flemings, who did not wish Charles to meet his subjects, and least of all his minister. Charles's letters hitherto had been full of affectionate regard, but his last, which suggested retirement on the score of age and infirmity, is thought to have been the immediate cause of the veteran's death : the letter was, however, written in consequence of a violent recurrence of the Cardinal's malady, as an act of consideration rather than of cruelty. It was clear that Chièvres would now be all-powerful in Spain as in the Netherlands. For the see of Toledo, the primacy, was selected his nephew, the boy-Cardinal de Croy : he was mulcted, it is true, of some two-thirds of its revenues for the benefit of Spanish magnates.

At length, on November 18, Charles made his entry into Valladolid, the capital of Old Castile. The magnificent procession was headed by thirty falconers with birds on fist, some wearing the king's livery of white, yellow, and red, others, the red and green of Ferdinand. Then followed the new royal guard of two hundred halberds, the fifty light Spanish lancers, the drum and fife bands of the nobles, the king's twenty chargers with grooms at head. Behind the royal stud rode three hundred Spanish and Flemish nobles; after them again marched two hundred halberds more, with the foreign ambassadors, and the heralds in their midst ; and then at length appeared the king.

Charles looked his best in a surcoat of his colours, crimson silk with silver and gold brocade over the steel

armour. On his head he wore, not a helmet, but a
black velvet cap with a long ostrich feather attached,
with a ruby and a pendent pear-shaped pearl. From
childhood he had a good seat, and he proved it now,
for his horse pranced, neighing and foaming, "with the
majority of its legs always in the air," as though it
found the streets of Valladolid too narrow for its enterprise. Yet in spite of its pawings and caracolings,
writes the eye-witness Vital, "the king no more stirred
nor swayed than if he had been glued thereon." The
nobility from all Spain gathered to see their king, and
the inevitable round of tournaments succeeded. Castile
was a land of contrasts; if the nobles wore a fortune upon
their backs, the streets of the capital were knee-deep in
mud; it was difficult to provide a banquet; the clergy
rudely refused quarters to the royal suite; thieves plied
their trade without fear of serious punishment.

After the preamble of pleasure the business of the
reign began. The Castilians were not in the best of
humours. The nobles found difficulty in obtaining
audience; the Flemings, or at best the Spaniards, who
had long haunted the Burgundian court, stood between
them and the light and warmth of Crown favour.
The Count of Benevente, kept waiting by the Grand-
Chancellor of Burgundy, Jean le Sauvage, gave vent to
his offended dignity by beating the culprit's servants.
As a concession to the pride and indolence of the nobles
the chain across the royal gateway was removed, that
they might ride in without dismounting. It soon trans-
pired that the king's reluctance to give audience was
due to his almost total ignorance of Spanish, and this
after nearly two years of reigning.

The Cortes opened on February 2, 1518. The town
deputies from the first showed fight against the foreigner;

they would not suffer the presidency of the Chancellor
at their first meeting; they objected to Charles's old
advisers, the Bishop of Badajoz and Garcia de Padilla.
In the first royal session Charles was required to swear
observance to the customs and privileges of the kingdom, and to confine office and benefices to its natives.
When he took the oath in general terms he was pressed
to be explicit on the latter question.   He testily replied
that he had already sworn, and with his obstinate
attitude and ambiguous answer the deputies had to
profess contentment.   The oath of allegiance was at
length taken to Charles and his mother conjointly, and
a liberal subsidy was granted for three years.

The eighty-eight petitions of the Cortes did not differ
substantially from those of previous or succeeding
sessions.[1] Much emphasis was indeed laid on the
exclusion of foreign influence, and on the prohibition of
the export of articles of primary importance, but neither
feature was a novelty.   Several petitions were, however,
of personal interest to Charles.   He was requested to
marry at once, and not to allow Ferdinand to leave
Spain until he himself had children.   To these suggestions he gave an evasive answer, but to the petition
that he would learn Spanish he replied that he had
already begun the study.   The Cortes noted with
satisfaction the statement in the royal speech that
Charles intended to hold Navarre, incorporated by his
grandfather with the crown of Castile; they offered
their persons and their property for its defence.   This
was no obscure hint that Spain intended resistance to
the growing pretensions of Francis I., to which Spaniards

---

[1] The proceedings of this and subsequent sessions of the Cortes to 1558 are
to be found in *Cortes de los antiguos reinos de León y de Castilla*, vol. iv., 1882,
edited by M. Colmeiro, and vol. v., 1903, by M. Danvila.

believed Chièvres to be unduly complaisant. The
demand for the king's immediate marriage pointed in
the same direction, for this involved a breach of the
recent treaty of Noyon, the matrimonial arrangements
of which would have delayed it for many years.

Generous as was the subsidy granted by the
deputies, their outspoken criticism had given evidence
of bitter hostility to the Flemish ministers. The large
fortune which Jiménez had left to local charities was
swept into the royal coffers. He had destroyed the
fortresses of Navarre in order that they might not
harbour French invaders or native malcontents, and
this formed the pretext for the confiscation. All who
were disappointed at the election to the see of Toledo
bore a grudge against the ministers; among these was
the Duke of Alba, whose son was interested, and he
refused to accompany Charles to Aragon. The Chancellor was accused of selling justice. The letters of
Peter Martyr, although not by birth a Spaniard, breathe
hatred against the greedy, drunken foreigners who were
longing for home, and yet would not go until they had
filled their pockets with all the coins that Spain contained. Castilians, he writes, complained that Charles
was not king, but the subject of Chièvres; that he was
led like a muzzled calf, unable to turn his head unless
the Flemings willed; that Castilians, the conquerors
of Spain, were treated as if born in a sewer, by men
whose only gods were Bacchus and Cytheræa. The
Constable, the Admiral, even Adrian of Utrecht, warned
Charles of the consequences of his subservience. He
was only beginning to speak Spanish, and, indeed,
spoke little of any tongue. "He says little, is not of
much ability, and is entirely ruled by his Flemish
governors," was the verdict of an Italian envoy. The

Marquis of Pescara, who was to become his greatest
general, reported that he had no talent, and that in
three audiences he had not said three words.

It was suspected that Charles did not intend to
keep his alleged promise as to Ferdinand. On the
walls of the churches of Valladolid appeared placards—
" Woe unto thee, Castile, if thou sufferest the Infant
Ferdinand to be removed." It was, perhaps, known
that Charles, when holding his last Netherland Estates,
had engaged to send Ferdinand to his Burgundian
provinces. No sooner had Charles left Valladolid for
Aragon than he despatched his brother to the Netherlands. This act was not merely due to jealousy. The
government had information that the prince's half-
uncle, the Archbishop of Saragossa, was plotting with
Castilian magnates to place the younger brother on the
throne. Nevertheless the necessity, if necessity it were,
was most unfortunate, for Spaniards doted on the
active, genial, quick-witted prince, who had been
brought up among them, and who outshone his silent,
foreign brother. While the heir-presumptive was thus
unceremoniously exiled, the king, whom the nation
implored to marry the Portuguese Infanta, was pledged
by a disadvantageous treaty to French babes-in-arms,
sister after sister. Already at Rome it was reported
that Charles counted for nothing, and that the opposition of the Spanish magnates would soon lead to
some great confusion.

In Aragon Charles found resistance more obstinate
than in Castile. The existence of a standing committee
of the Cortes created an additional difficulty. He could
not constitutionally issue the writs for the Cortes until
he was declared king, and to be king he must take the
oath to this committee. Its members stated that if

they swore allegiance, Charles must formally recognise
Ferdinand as heir-presumptive ; if he refused, they
would only grant him the title of administrator for
his mother. The Castilian Count of Benevente took
up the cudgels on his king's behalf, remembering, doubtless, the exclamation of Isabella, that she wished to
conquer Aragon to make it a kingdom in deed and not
in name. He offered his person and his property to
subdue the kingdom, that Charles might grant the
laws that he, and not the Aragonese, might list. The
natural consequence was a sanguinary street fight, with
a list of twenty-seven casualties, and only Charles in
person could reconcile the Castilian nobleman with the
Aragonese champion, the Count of Aranda. The combat probably cleared the air, for Charles was recognised
as co-regnant with his mother ; but then began the
interminable wrangle over subsidies—a foretaste of the
parliamentary difficulties with which it was the fate
of Charles to wrestle throughout his life and in each
of his scattered inheritances.

The much-vaunted constitution of Aragon was a
very nightmare of self-misgovernment. The three lower
Estates had some vague volitions in favour of the
justice and order which Charles and his counsellors
were honestly resolved to introduce. But to the nobles
justice was anathema. They had a vested interest in
the robbery of strangers and the irresponsible oppression of their subjects. Their castles, said Peter Martyr,
were robbers' caves, malefactors' sanctuaries. "Every
hour," wrote the Bishop of Armagh to Wolsey, "was
murder and robbery without punishment . . . many
of the lords being possessed of all their lands by robbery ; so that there is likely to be no end of these
Cortes, unless justice be set apart." And Armagh added,

with true Irish grace, that when he told the Council
of the Cardinal's administration of justice in England
to the fear of all evil-doers, high and low, they rejoined
that they lacked his Grace's presence and wisdom among
themselves.

Philanthropy and political economy were scouted
in the parliamentary system of Aragon. Charles was
forced to withdraw his edicts for the food supply of
the people, because the Aragonese "preferred to live
by their own laws, however noxious, than do anything
suggested by the king." The municipality of Saragossa
purposely prolonged the session, because it enjoyed the
monopoly of provisions; it starved the poor in order
that it might rob the Court—"a pennyworth of everything for tenpence" was the English envoy's curt
comment. This was not wholly to the king's disadvantage, for ultimately the people rose against its
government in his favour. The subsidy was granted;
but even if it had not been docked under pretext of
old royal debts it would not have liquidated the costs
of Charles's first visit to his kingdom of Aragon.

Yet fortune, though unkind, had not been wholly
curst. An epidemic had carried off many of the king's
Flemish suite, and among them the hated Chancellor.
Charles replaced the latter by Mercurino Gattinara,
a Piedmontese who had passed from Savoyard into
Burgundian service. He was a foreigner, it is true,
yet not provincial but cosmopolitan—a fit minister
for a heterogeneous empire. Gattinara was, moreover,
honest, agreeable, enthusiastic, and he knew Spain
well. Charles never had a more devoted or more
popular minister.

On his way to Barcelona Charles heard of the
Emperor's death; the tension with France was neces-

sarily tightened ; European interests were overshadow-
ing the local pretensions of sections of the peninsula ;
time was becoming day by day a more important
factor of success. The complexity of the situation
was enjoyed by the Catalonian Cortes, equally arrogant
with those of Aragon and surpassing them in sarcastic
impudence. But here too, ultimately, the deputies
proved to be, as those of Aragon and Castile, men of
flesh and blood, which is probably Sandoval's method
of hinting that they were equally corrupt. Charles
was acknowledged king, and a subsidy granted. He
had still to face the prospect of meeting the quarrelsome nobility and municipalities of the kingdom of
Valencia, but at this moment, while still at Barcelona,
the news arrived of his election to the Empire.

As Spanish complications had driven Charles from
the Netherlands, so now European claims called him
away from Spain. He was nothing loth to leave. He
deputed Adrian of Utrecht to hold the Cortes of
Valencia, little recking that the Cortes were certain
to contest the legality of the deputation. From Barcelona he hurried to his port of departure on the
Galician coast. He was, however, not so quick as to
avoid the disturbances of the political atmosphere
which were likely to retard his voyage. In Castile
the resolute stand made by the " pigmy states " of
Aragon and Catalonia had occasioned humiliation and
accentuated discontent. To the old grievances of
foreign influence and the drainage of Spanish money
were added those of the king's approaching departure,
his premature demand for a fresh subsidy, his failure
to make a progress through Castile. Above all and
everything, popular indignation was quickened by the
wild rumour that Charles meant to abduct his mother

from her kingdom. Well received at Burgos, he found
trouble at Valladolid. The writs had already been
issued for Cortes to be held at Santiago in Galicia.
This was the crowning insult. Charles had spent
nearly two years in his minor kingdoms, and but five
months in Castile ; yet now he summoned the Cortes
to an out-of-the-way corner of the realm, in a province
which was not even represented by one of its own
towns, but only by the neighbouring city of Zamora.

Toledo, the capital of New Castile, had been the
city most deeply injured by the royal government.
For long she had been striving for common measures
of defence against the Crown. She now set aside the
deputies elected, as was customary, by lot, because
they were too favourable to the Court, and despatched
a deputation which had more effect upon the passions
of the populace at Valladolid than upon the ears of
the Flemish minister. Hither, too, came the great
Andalusian noble, Pedro de Giron, and told Charles
to his face that he had not kept his word to him.
Personal interests of the nobles were already intermingling with the blind patriotism of the masses. In
vain the king, by purging the magistracy of Valladolid,
obtained a promise of support at the coming Cortes.
The people set its own rulers at naught ; the great
bell clanged to arms ; Charles owed it only to a violent
storm that his escort was able to brush aside the people
thronging to the gate, and that he escaped detention
by a furious mob.

On March 30, 1520, the Cortes were opened at
Santiago. The writs had directed the *corregidores* to
see that good men only, acceptable to the Crown and
desirous of the public welfare, should be elected, and
that they should, according to custom, receive from

their constituencies full powers, a form for which accompanied the writ. In these forms it is expressly
stated that the new subsidy which was demanded
should be levied only after the expiry of the term of
the current grant. Thus the accusation frequently
brought against Charles—that he wished to impose a
new tax concurrent with that already granted—is unjust: he merely asked that it should be voted in
advance, because his absence would prevent a session
of the Cortes when the term of the present subsidy
had expired. The growing opposition, indeed, was
not caused by the demand for a subsidy, but by the
king's intended departure. The necessity for this was
not, on the face of it, the outcome of Castilian interests,
but a corollary of his election to the Empire. The
Castilians,—proud beyond every other people, regarding
all other nations as their inferiors,—saw their kingdom,
in Peter Martyr's words, reduced to a province ruled
from the icy ocean of the North. They were, moreover,
conscious of their need for governance : Castile, cried
nobles and towns alike, could not exist without a king.

The royal speech was delivered by the Bishop of
Badajoz, President of the Cortes. Its tone was conciliatory and almost apologetic. The deputies were reminded that Charles had accepted the Empire with the
written consent of all the prelates, the grandees, the
knights, and the members of his Council, and the cause
of his acceptance was the defence of Christendom against
the infidel. Had not Galba, elected like himself in Spain,
journeyed to Rome for his coronation ? Had not the
Emperor Alfonso left Castile ? The Netherlands had
acquiesced in their ruler's departure, although that had
apparently been for ever : Castile therefore should suffer
its king's absence patiently, that he might become the

greatest power in all the world. After a space of three years at most Castile should be the garden of his pleasures, the fortress of his defence, the strength of his attack, his sword, his horse, the seat of his repose and rest. He would leave justice well secured, the coasts and Navarre well defended, his troops and household salaried for three years. He promised to prohibit the export of horses and precious metals and other forbidden objects. The Cortes were warmly thanked for the current subsidy, the most generous that had ever been accorded to the Crown ; they were warmly entreated to grant a further aid of three annual instalments, when the term of those already conceded had expired.

When the long royal speech reached its end Charles, in person, addressed his faithful Commons. His short apprenticeship in Spanish rendered his address curt and unadorned. " All that the Bishop of Badajoz has said to you has been said by my command, and there are three points only which I desire to repeat : firstly, that I am grieved at my departure, as you have heard, but I cannot act otherwise with due regard to my honour and the welfare of my kingdoms ; secondly, that I promise you on my royal word of honour to return and take possession of these kingdoms at the close of three years from the day of my departure, or earlier, if earlier be possible ; thirdly, that for your contentment I am content, on my royal word of honour, not to bestow office in these kingdoms on such as are not natives thereof, and this I swear and promise."

The deputies were not mollified by their king's appeal. Only those of Burgos, Seville, and Granada voted for the subsidy; while the majority were in favour of redress before supply, begging that the petitions should be answered before an aid was granted. Gattinara, the

Chancellor, replied in the king's name that Charles could not consent to an innovation so unconstitutional, but that he would consider the petitions before sailing. The question of a subsidy was again put, and the votes were equal. That the deputies were no mere delegates is proved by the fact that in the case of Granada and Jaen the two members voted on opposite sides, although, on a further declaration that the king could not depart from the custom, the second member for Granada joined his colleague, thus giving the Crown a majority of one vote. Once more, on April 4, the deputies were asked for a definite Yea or Nay. As the replies were indeterminate, the session was prorogued until the 22nd, when the Cortes met at Corunna, the port of embarkation. Here Charles, to create a favourable impression, issued an ordinance against the export of horses and precious metals, and against the bestowal of office upon foreigners. Then once again the subsidy was put to the vote. Eight towns and one member for Jaen now voted for the aid ; his colleague, with seven towns, rejoined, not with a negative, but in ambiguous terms. Shortly afterwards the members for Valladolid joined the majority on the promise that the petitions granted at the Cortes of Valladolid should be put in force.

The Bishop of Badajoz now assured the deputies that Charles gratefully accepted the subsidy—that he bore no grudge against the towns whose members had refused, although he had reason to be displeased with their deputies, and would report their conduct to their constituencies. It was then announced that Adrian of Utrecht would be left as Viceroy, while a Spaniard should, in the king's absence, command the troops. The sixty-one petitions were then presented and answered, and the Cortes were dissolved without further incident.

Such is a summary of the official reports of this session—the first great parliamentary struggle of Charles's reign, and, as far as they go, they are of indisputable authority. But the official history is only a half of the whole. Two most important towns were not represented, for Toledo had sent no constitutionally appointed deputies, while those of Salamanca appear in no division list. This abstention has never been quite explained. The members for Salamanca arrived late and unprovided with regular powers, but these were afterwards brought by the *corregidor*. Sepulveda states that the members were excluded by the Crown; it is possible that they refused to accept their powers from the hands of a Crown official. Whatever the action of the members for Salamanca may have been, there is no question as to that of the informal delegates of Toledo. Headed by a leader of the coming revolution, Pedro Laso de la Vega, they stimulated resistance alike to the king's demands and to his departure. So dangerous were they thought that they were ordered to leave Galicia, while Charles cashiered the members of the opposition in the municipality of Toledo, and ordered its champion, Juan de Padilla, to repair to court. The ministers moreover, it is alleged, though perhaps on insufficient evidence, browbeat and bribed the deputies of the Cortes into acquiescence. Yet it must be admitted that their resistance was creditable to their courage. The Castilians had ever a legal mind, and if they receded from pretensions which were proved to be unconstitutional this was no proof of corrupt subservience. It has been naturally assumed that the growing practice of nomination of aldermen by the Crown weakened the independence of the Cortes, many of whose members were, by local custom, aldermen. An analysis of the division lists of the Cortes of Santiago shows little evidence of this tendency. On the occasion when the votes were equal, ten aldermen or other officials and six popular members voted for the Crown, while for the opposition were either ten or nine aldermen and seven or six non-official members. These figures are of interest, although it would be wrong to lay excessive stress upon them, since the practice of election of deputies varied almost from town to town.

The subsidy once granted, Charles could sail as soon as the north wind permitted. He had won a tactical victory, but on the wider field of strategy had conspicuously failed. Toledo was already in full revolt, while far away in Valencia a social war was actually raging—due in no slight measure to the carelessness and the interested motives of the Crown. The king's last act—his appointment of Adrian as sole regent—was the crowning insult. A greater contrast to the last Cardinal-regent, Jiménez, could scarcely be conceived. Adrian had little experience and less competence ; he had neither birth nor courage. Above all, he was one of the hated foreigners, although even Spaniards acquitted him of the charges of theft and avarice which he had honestly criticised in his compatriots. The very terms of his commission seemed intended to wound Castilian pride, for he was dispensed from all laws, usages, and privileges which might hamper his absolute power, and from all the customary ceremonies of installation. Charles had spontaneously promised to confer no office upon a foreigner, and yet such was his own representative ! Some of the towns protested against the appointment ; others, while bending to the royal will, prayed that it might not form a precedent.

Seldom has a ruler begun his reign so badly. It may

be admitted that the policy of the Crown was inspired by Chièvres, but Charles was now twenty and old enough to gauge the temper of his people. In one respect only had he won esteem. In the national game of cane-throwing, his graceful horsemanship had delighted the spectators, and was a presage of the later compliment that Charles, by gaining the Empire, had cost the Spanish army its best light-horseman. There may even have been some presentiment that the silent youth would not always be "spell-bound under the ferule of Chièvres."

Charles was not alone to blame for the coming troubles, nor even were his Flemish ministers wholly culpable. Since Ferdinand's death Jiménez had been unable to control the insubordination of both towns and nobles; Ferdinand himself had only tided over the dangerous hour. Long before the young king landed, confusion—a mere euphemism for revolution—had been foretold. It was only uncertain what form this would first take. Would the Crown be the primary object of attack, and, if it were, would the burgher or the grandee be its assailant? Would towns and nobles, after years of ineffectual sparring, close for a decisive round, or would rival magnates drag Crown and people into their personal or hereditary squabbles, and so convert an in-significant dog-fight into an all-consuming civil war? Antecedently it seemed probable that revolt would originate with the nobles, for each one of the Catholic Kings' more important measures, whether the *Hermandad* or the Inquisition, or the creation of the judicial bureaucracy, had directly or indirectly the aim of reducing the turbulent nobility. Meanwhile, however, the towns had outgrown their leading-strings; the favour of Isabella, and, after her death, the neglect of Ferdinand, had encouraged pretensions which could not be tolerated by a monarch who meant to reign.

Prediction was unusually difficult, for there was, in fact, a strain of madness, not only in the queen, but in the nation. The feverish excitement, the strenuous action, the rigorous discipline, of the reign of the Catholic Kings had given place to the inevitable reaction of morbid irritation or natural opposition. In the line, *quicquid delirant reges plectuntur Achivi*, the substantives, save for scansion, might not infrequently be transposed. Nevertheless, if Charles suffered for his people's madness, and if, whatever his conduct, he must have suffered, the fact remains that in his first attempt to govern Spain he unquestionably sinned.

CHAPTER III

Rivalry of Charles and Francis for the Empire—Condition of Germany
—Growth of territorialism—The Habsburg territories—The Suabian
League—Acquisition of Württemberg by Charles—Importance of
the Empire to Charles—Certainty of a French war—The hostility
of Spain and France—Attempt at friendship between Charles and
Francis—The treaty of Noyon—The alliance proves impossible—
The value of English friendship—Henry VIII.'s leaning towards
Charles—Visit of Charles to England—His coronation at Aix
—Aleander's estimate of his character—His welcome in Germany.

CHARLES had excused his hurried departure from Spain
on the plea of the Electors' importunities, and the
obligations of the coronation ceremony imposed upon
him by the Golden Bull. To his own election he had
contributed little or nothing, and it is therefore unnecessary here to follow closely the fluctuations of that
disgraceful market. He, or more probably his Flemish
counsellors, had grumbled at the ruinous cost of bribery,
and had been taken to task severely by his grandfather
and aunt for such ill-timed parsimony. Maximilian had
already secured a majority for his grandson, but his
death threw the votes once more into the melting-pot,
and the whole process of corruption had to be restarted,
but on the same lines and by the same agents.

At one moment only did Charles take a personal
part in his candidature. Margaret, despairing of his
success against Francis I., suggested that he should
transfer his interest to his brother Ferdinand, as being

45

less formidable in the eyes of the German princes, and less objectionable to the Pope.   Her nephew indignantly rejected the proposal, which he stigmatised as a trick of the French king, who would marry his daughter to Ferdinand, and so divide the power and interests of the Habsburgs, that he might bring their house in ruin to the ground.   He himself was the eldest; for him, Maximilian had appealed to the Electors; to him they had promised their votes; should these votes be diverted to his brother, it would mean for himself not only the loss of Empire, but of honour, of all the wealth that had been lavished on the election, of all the possessions that remained to him.   If he were Emperor, Charles continued, he could perform many a great exploit: he could not only maintain the dominions that God had granted to him, but could mightily enlarge them, and so give peace to the whole of Christendom and exalt the holy Catholic faith, which was its chief foundation.   The idea of Ferdinand's candidature was forthwith dropped. Results, as often afterwards, justified the obstinacy of Charles in facing an apparently hopeless situation. When he had once made up his mind, he was already, as an English envoy had expressed it, as immovable as an image.

Charles owed his first success, as his final failure, on German soil to a flood-tide of German feeling.   Of this sentiment the Electors themselves had little.   The Archbishop of Trèves was an avowed partisan of France, while his neighbour of Cologne kept wavering.   Albert of Mainz and his brother, Joachim of Brandenburg, in spite of their debt to Maximilian's favour, were bought by Francis.   Louis, Elector Palatine, had an old score to pay off against the Habsburgs, for Maximilian in the Landshut Succession War of 1504 had declared against the Palatinate line, and had annexed slices of its territory. So also Frederick of Saxony had once and again suffered at Maximilian's hands for his loyalty to constitutional principles; yet he alone closed his ears to the French charmers, and kept an open mind. But, if French corruption was first in the field, the Imperial financiers had the greater staying power, and this, combined with bodily fear, decided the day for Charles. In the great trading centres, Augsburg, Ulm, and Nuremberg French bills of exchange were refused; the house of Fugger declined Francis I.'s custom and threw all the weight of capital into Charles's scale.

In the Rhineland public sympathy was emphatically in favour of Maximilian's grandson. The Renaissance had not denationalised the German humanists, who were anti-French and anti-Latin. Charles wisely dwelt on his German blood and ancestry, on his resolve rather to increase than lessen ecclesiastical and civil freedom. Francis was less prudent in boasting of his power to defend Germany against the Turk, and to preserve her from anarchy within. The Germans could seldom be persuaded to take the Turkish danger seriously : the Sultan seemed so far away. Of the six Electorates four lay on the Rhine, and Brandenburg on the rivers of the Baltic. The Habsburg lands were, as Charles urged, the natural bulwark against the Moslem. To the military classes the ideal of strong government held up by Francis was a scarecrow rather than a lure. He had promised to make the roads in Germany as safe as they were in France, and this was "very ill liked," wrote Pace, who was in Germany watching Henry VIII.'s slender chances of election. The very Swiss, tied as they were to Francis by golden chains, caught the Teutonic contagion, and declared against him ; with a French king as both Emperor and Duke of Milan the cantons would be between the upper and the nether grindstone. Their mercenaries were ordered to withdraw from the service of Ulrich of Württemberg, a French *protégé*. A large army of the Suabian League, which had then expelled Ulrich from his duchy, moved within reach of Frankfort under Sickingen and Frundsberg to overawe the Electors. The Papal legate, who was believed to support Francis, was threatened with violence, and Pace thought that, if Charles were not elected, the Electors would be torn in pieces.

Francis, when his own chance was lost, strove to divert the votes to Joachim of Brandenburg, while the Pope recommended Frederick of Saxony. But Joachim's own brother, Albert, declared that he was a fool, and Frederick, so-called the Wise, was persuaded that, if he had the wisdom, he had not the resources to rule the unwieldy Empire. Thus, then, on June 28, 1519, Charles was unanimously elected to the joy of all true Germans, who fondly thought that he, too, was one of them.

It may be wondered that Charles should have been anxious to add the government of the Empire to his other tasks. If the rule of Spain and the Netherlands were difficult, that of Germany was infinitely harder. In this endeavour no Emperor had as yet succeeded. Germany was ethnologically and sentimentally, but not politically, a nation. Apart from the feeble attempts at constitution-making during the last two reigns, she had none of the elements of common political life. The diet was a congress rather than a parliament ; the princes frequently did not attend in person ; the rights of the Imperial cities were quite uncertain ; the assembly could not enforce the decisions at which, with infinite difficulty, it arrived, and still less could the Emperor enforce them.   In spite of numerous experiments there was no permanent national system of taxation, no national judicature, police, or army.   The necessary result of this was, in parts of Germany, a mediæval anarchy which had long ceased to survive in other European states.   This, however, was not for the monarchy its most formidable obstacle, since many interests were involved in the restoration of order, and anarchy as a permanent condition is impossible.

German history is that of the development of the Second Estate, the nobility.   The greater feudal units, Brandenburg, Electoral and Ducal Saxony, Bavaria, the Palatinate, Hesse, Württemberg, Juliers-Cleves, and others, had blossomed into states, virtually sovereign, and connected by the loosest federal tie.   Each had its estates, its court without appeal, its territorial army, its own system of finance, a large measure of control over its clergy, its own foreign policy.   If these states were inclusive, they were also exclusive; no Imperial official, military or judicial, administrative or financial, had any authority within their borders.   This was natural enough, for the great princes had been in their origin the highest Imperial officials; owing their power mainly to Imperial commission, they had but kicked down the ladder by which they had mounted.   It is true that these states were seldom geographically complete; they were streaked by fiefs belonging to rival princes, by the possessions of nobles and knights who held directly of the Empire, by Imperial towns and ecclesiastical principalities; they were hampered sometimes by the powers of the great archbishops, themselves rival princes.   But the tendency was towards the extension of their influence within a certain geographical area, even over those who were not con-

stitutionally subject, and towards a practical fusion of
the very different rights and titles under which they had
acquired the several atoms which composed the territory.
This is what is meant by the growth of territorialism.

Among territorial families the greatest beyond comparison were the houses of Wittelsbach, Wettin, and
Hohenzollern. Each of these possessed an Electorate,
but, on the other hand, each was divided into two main
lines. The three Bavarian branches of Wittelsbach, those
of Ingolstadt, Landshut, and Munich, had, indeed, lately
merged in the latter, and together formed a powerful
state. The Palatinate, Bavarian in name, was in effect
a Rhenish territory wholly distinct from Bavaria, except
that it held the so-called Upper Palatinate, contiguous
to Northern Bavaria and lying with its back to the
Bohemian mountains. The solidarity of the territory
was weakened by the appanages of cadet lines, Neuburg,
Veldenz, Sulzbach, and Zweibruck. The Ducal branch
always coveted the Electorate, which was settled by the
Golden Bull on the Palatinate, and the recent Landshut
Succession War had aggravated ill-feeling. In neither
line was there a ruler of any eminent ability. Louis,
Elector Palatine, was a normal hunting, drinking
princeling. The brothers, William and Louis, ruled
Ducal Bavaria nominally in common, but while military
affairs were the special department of the latter, William
virtually controlled policy. He in turn had the good
sense to be guided by his Chancellor, Leonard von Eck,
who was among the most competent, if least scrupulous,
statesmen of this age. It is possible that the reputation
of the Chancellor has somewhat unduly overshadowed
that of the Duke. They died in the same year (1550),
and, therefore, the Method of Differences cannot be
applied to determine their respective merits.

The Electoral Ernestine and the Ducal Albertine lines of Saxony bore no good feeling towards each other, and the clumsiness of the partition of the Wettin territories made in 1485 multiplied opportunities for friction.   The Elector Frederick was the most statesmanlike among the greater princes; he had championed the cause of a representative constitution against Maximilian, and showed sympathy with the new religious movement, though without committing himself.   His death in 1525 perhaps prevented a more moderate solution of the religious problem.   George, Duke of Saxony, a careful, conscientious ruler, was hitherto distinguished by consistent efforts to reform his clergy, regular and secular, by establishing state control over the monasteries, and by enlarging the powers of civil jurisdiction.   He strove also to limit the abuses of indulgences by applying the proceeds, as far as possible, to local religious purposes. His zeal for moral reform was shortly, however, to give place to his desire to protect his subjects from all taint of doctrinal heresy.[1]

The Hohenzollern were divided between the Brandenburg and Franconian lines.   In their case there was no hostility, but geographical separation prevented effective co-operation, and their ambitions were distinct.   The Electoral Brandenburg line coveted control over Pomerania, once a fief, which cut it off from the Baltic, and also over the sees of Magdeburg and Halberstadt.   It likewise had interests in Bohemia and the Bohemian Crownland, Silesia.   The Franconian line, which from time to time separated into the Ansbach and Bayreuth branches, would look for elbow-room at the expense of the Franconian Imperial cities, above all the traditional

---

[1] See *Akten und Briefe zur Kirchenpolitik Herzog Georgs von Sachsen*, vol. i., by F. Gess, 1905.

enemy Nuremberg, and the rich neighbouring bishoprics.
The natural rival of the Brandenburg line was the house
of Wettin, whose interests came into collision on the
Bohemian borders, in Magdeburg and Halberstadt, and
in the eventual succession to Cleves-Juliers. The
Brandenburg Elector's brother, Albert, had replaced a
Wettin in the Archbishopric of Mainz, while a Franconian
cousin succeeded another Saxon prince in the Grand-
mastership of the Teutonic Order. The Franconian
Hohenzollern, on the other hand, had a long-standing
feud with the Bavarians, whose designs on the Imperial
cities and bishoprics were very similar. The Elector
Joachim I. had no especial merits, either moral or political;
his main object was to regain the Emperor's favour, in
spite of the obvious snubs which Charles administered
until the interests of their common Catholicism produced
a friendlier feeling. The Franconian brothers, George
and Casimir, early adopted Lutheran principles, though
with varying degrees of warmth : they were, however,
closely connected with the Court of Vienna, and Casimir
died at Ofen in the campaign of 1527, leaving as his
heir the notorious Albert Alcibiades. The two little
states were administered conjointly until their division
between George and Albert in 1541. A brother of
George and Casimir was the Grandmaster Albert, while
John entered Spanish service and married Ferdinand the
Catholic's fat, ugly, and lame, though well-dowered,
widow, Germaine de Foix.

Among the secondary states Hesse, Württemberg,
Mecklenburg, and Pomerania, had all increased in
importance during the fifteenth century. The two latter
were too far from the centre of gravity to have much
direct influence upon Charles's fortunes, unless trouble
arose with his disreputable brother-in-law, Christian II.

of Denmark. Württemberg was at present princeless,
but the case of Guelders had proved that a prince
dispossessed might be more dangerous than a prince in
possession. None could have foreseen the part that
Hesse was to play owing to the personality of its boy
ruler, Philip.

The ecclesiastical principalities were territories like
the rest; but the absence of the hereditary system
denied them the same opportunities of expansion.
Moreover, they had great urban centres, and their
capitals had with greater or less success asserted their
position as Imperial cities. The chapter, too, was a less
amenable partner than the council nominated by a
secular prince. Yet the relation of Charles to the
Church in Germany would be very different from that
which existed in Spain. He could not have the same
power over the great ecclesiastical princes, three of
whom were Electors. A papal permit to tax the clergy
might have effect upon sees in Habsburg territory,
but little upon Estates of the Empire ; it would be a
mere chance if, on a vacancy, Charles could influence
an election.

In Spain, a revival of the nobility would entail
general anarchy, each noble fighting against each town,
or against each other, but the monarch would have had
the sympathy of all the elements of order. In Germany
there was, indeed, plenty of anarchy, but the Emperor's
probable enemies were the forces of order,—the princes
who, with or without right, had withdrawn large
stretches of the nation from the area of perpetual
anarchy, and were little inclined to sacrifice the fruits
of independent enterprise to a higher unity. It was
certain that any Emperor who meant to rule would have
to reckon with armed opposition from these princes.

Had Luther died in infancy, and the Reformation of the sixteenth century been still-born, conflict was still inevitable for Charles. The Reformation may have altered the time, the manner, the composition of the parties; Bavaria, for instance, would with tolerable certainty have taken the place of Saxony; the towns would perhaps have been with the Emperor rather than against him; but an economic grievance or a personal grudge would have provoked a conflict almost as easily as religious dualism. Napoleon was wrong in his belief that Charles, by embracing Lutheranism, could have conquered Europe at the head of a united Germany. Had Charles declared for Luther, some at least of his ultimate Protestant opponents would have been found in the ranks of uncompromising Catholicism. This is not to minimise the importance of the religious question, for if this did not wholly decide the wherefore, it determined the how and the when.

Not only were the great princes secular and ecclesiastic, independent powers with areas tolerably well defined, and with mutual relations, hostile or friendly, tolerably permanent; but princes and towns were two armies camped up and down within the same country, the princes studying opportunities of attack, the towns the most modern methods of defence. Outside both camps lay the knights, hostile at once to princes, merchants, and ecclesiastics. Lower in the scale was the surging mass of peasants and artisans, uttering inarticulate cries which might express anguish at intensified oppression, or ambitions engendered by a rising standard of comfort and expense. These divisions would not be without their use to an Emperor whose chief object was the restoration of Imperial authority within Germany, but they were fatal to the revival of Imperial power in Italy and in Europe, to united national resistance against the aggressive powers,—the French and the Turks.

The Emperor was threatened not only by the particularism of the princes, but by their combination. The idea of German unity was in the air, and the schemes for its realisation had resulted in an oligarchical constitution, which reduced the Emperor to a cypher. Fortunately, the two tendencies were contradictory one to the other, and a skilful Emperor might utilise each in turn. Maximilian had been singularly successful in two directions : he had broken up an elaborate constitution, by playing upon separatist interests, and he had humbled the most powerful of the rival houses, the Bavarian Wittelsbachs, by the agency of its family jealousy. On the other hand, he had failed in permanently uniting Germany for purposes of expansion. Maximilian had advantages which Charles lacked : he lived in Germany, he was steeped in all that was newest and brightest in German life, and in spite of all defects he exercised a strong personal fascination. Charles, in language and feeling, was not German but Walloon ; he was devoid at once of German virtues and vices ; the nature of events must prevent continuous residence. Could he then possibly succeed where his grandfather had failed ?

Charles owed to Maximilian not only the Empire, and the territorial power of the Habsburgs, which Maximilian had doubled by his Burgundian marriage, but a very useful instrument for their maintenance. The Suabian League was a union of princes, knights, and towns, professedly for the preservation of order in that most disorderly corner of Germany, but it had really been formed in Habsburg interests, to counteract the preponderating influence of Bavaria in the south-west. The Suabian League, with its regular diets, its representative system, its fixed scale of contributions and contingents, its identity of interests, formed a workmanlike power for dealing with emergencies which the central government might well envy. The hereditary dominions of the Habsburgs were, even apart from the Netherlands, so large that, had they been more compact and homogeneous, they would have formed the most powerful of the territorial states. This was not, however, an unmixed advantage, for the territories dissipated or diverted the attentions which should have been concentrated upon the Imperial office. The Habsburgs had, therefore, the same particularist interests as other great princes, and their ideal of Empire would be a power which would give them superiority over territorial rivals, but would not cripple their own territorial independence.

The Suabian League was, in 1519 and 1520, instrumental in adding largely to the Habsburg power. Duke Ulrich of Württemberg had been put to the ban of the Empire for various unamiable practices. He murdered the husband of the lady upon whom he had temporarily fixed his roving fancy, and bestrode his own wife with his spurred boots. During the interregnum of the Empire the League, in execution of the ban, expelled him from his duchy. The sequestrated territory was unable to bear the heavy expenses of the operations, and Zevenbergen, Charles's principal minister in Tyrol, proposed that he should buy the duchy from the League. Charles was then at Barcelona; he had just been elected to the Empire, and had little ready money for further speculation. There were, moreover, other grave objections to the scheme. Ulrich would unquestionably enjoy French support in any attempt at restoration; while this important

accession of territory near their own borders would
inevitably alienate the Swiss, whose favour Charles
was earnestly endeavouring to win. Ulrich deserved
his fate, but his guilt did not prejudice the claim of
his son Christopher, whose mother was sister of the
two powerful Bavarian dukes. Annexation, therefore,
seemed to court an alliance of Bavarians, Swiss, and
French against the common traditional enemy. To
this it may be added that it was contrary to constitutional usage that an Emperor should bestow a
fief upon himself.

Against these objections Zevenbergen urged the
vital importance of this compact and fertile duchy as
a centre for the weak and scattered Habsburg possessions in Western Germany. Its acquisition would far
more than outweigh the losses of the last century to
the Swiss; it would be a bulwark alike against Swiss
and French : rulers of Württemberg, the archdukes
could be kings of the Romans and Emperors when
they pleased, and other princes must ride to court
and serve them. Otherwise, argued the minister,
Ulrich would return, and with French or Swiss support become another Duke of Guelders, a focus of
disaffection in Upper Germany. Already other princes
were scheming a confederacy against the Suabian
League, and if Charles did not show the Suabian
towns that he was strong enough to support them,
they would turn to the Swiss, and the cantonal system
would spread from Suabia to Cologne.

The Suabian League itself added weight to these
arguments, and forced the hand of Charles by pretend-
ing its intention of selling to the Swiss. Charles accepted Zevenbergen's advice, and arbitrarily added
Württemberg to his dominions under the guarantee

of the Suabian League. It is strange that this act
attracted so little comment from the princes. But
it was a slap in the face to the Bavarian dukes, which
they were not likely to forget, although for the present
they assented from their inability to protect Christopher
against his father and from their desire to propitiate
the young Emperor. The proceeding ominously re-
sembled that by which Charles of Burgundy had
wrested Guelders, not only from the duke deservedly
dispossessed, but from his innocent infant son. The
future would depend on the continuance of the Suabian
League, and upon the hold which the Habsburgs could
maintain on Württemberg by garrisons or affection.
For the moment their territorial power was appreciably
increased, and was likely to strengthen Charles's Imperial authority ; while this in turn could traditionally be wielded for the aggrandisement of the family
possessions.

Apart from the dignity of the position, and its
practical utility to his hereditary territories, there
were other powerful reasons which made his election
to the Empire desirable to Charles. If he were not
himself elected it was certain that Francis I. would
win the crown. A powerful French king as Emperor
would render the occupation of the Austrian and Burgundian territories by the Habsburgs uncomfortable,
if not precarious. More especially the possession of
the Empire would affect the balance of power in Italy,
and therefore loosen the Spanish hold on Naples.
Francis I., master of Lombardy by the victory of
Marignano, supported by the very Swiss whom he
had vanquished, and allied with Venice, already excluded the Habsburgs from North Italy. The claims
of the Empire, long dormant, had been stirred from

their slumbers by the restless Maximilian : should they be shaken into life by the rougher hand of France, they would soon evict from the Imperial garden every other non-Italian power.

Historians have, over and over again, ascribed the origin of Spain's decline to the wars of Charles V. with France—wars, it is added, in which she had no interest nor concern. The victory of St. Quentin and the treaty of Cateau-Cambrésis, which closed these wars show, indeed, little trace of Spain's decadence; but, however this may be, it is certain that the French wars were also Spanish wars, fought on Spain's behalf, and leaving to Spain their Italian spoils.

The rivalry of Charles and Francis for the Empire undoubtedly embittered their personal relations ; it per-haps hastened the outbreak of the unending hostilities which followed the election. Nevertheless, these had their origin, not in a German, but in a Spanish quarrel ; they were the continuation of the conflict between the Catholic Kings and a succession of French rulers. Throughout the long reign of Ferdinand and Isabella and the regency of Ferdinand in Castile, friendship between France and Spain had only been intermittent. France, by favouring a rival claimant to the crown of Castile, had wished to prevent its union with Aragon. She had forestalled the scheme of Isabella for a further union with Navarre. Spain in retaliation had done her utmost to prevent the absorption of Brittany by the French Crown, while Catalan corsairs endangered its annexation of Provence. Ferdinand's hand had welded the first great European combination against France ; the nascent navies of the rival powers had passed their prenticeship in conflict from the mouth of the Thames to the Straits of Gibraltar, from Tunis to Marseilles.

From 1495 the Catholic Kings subjected France to a long series of humiliations. On condition that he should have a free hand against Naples Charles VIII. had surrendered to Aragon the provinces of Roussillon and Cerdagne, which Ferdinand's father had been forced to cede. No sooner did his success seem assured than the Catholic Kings manufactured the League of Venice, which entailed withdrawal from his newly-won kingdom. Louis XII. had no better fortune. Ferdinand, having divided Naples with him, in the quarrel which ensued, ejected him from his moiety. Joining in the League of Cambrai against Venice, the Aragonese soon turned his back on his French ally, and, notwithstanding the defeat of Ravenna, contributed to the expulsion of Louis from his duchy of Milan. Spain had indeed become an influential Italian power. Not only did she possess Naples, but she exercised pressure upon Rome. She had restored the Medici to Florence, and so bound the dynasty to herself; she had at least claimed a voice in the settlement of Milan after the French defeat. Nor was this all : having with the occupation of Roussillon opened a way into Languedoc, Ferdinand took advantage of French weakness to seize from the French house of Albret the Spanish portion of Navarre, and had invited the English to revive their old claims on Gascony. It is true that, in his determination to retain the government of Castile against Maximilian and their common grandson, he had patched up a momentary peace with France and married the French princess Germaine de Foix; but this was only an expedient; he was equally ready to marry his late wife's niece, the recognition of whose legitimacy would have been tantamount to the denial of Isabella's title to her crown.

Francis I. had opened his reign with the recovery of Milan. In this campaign Spanish troops had opposed the Venetians, his allies ; had they not been timidly led, they might have stood shoulder to shoulder with the Swiss on the memorable field of Marignano. It was even said that the French victory caused Ferdinand to alter his intentions and to leave the Spanish kingdoms undivided to his elder grandson, that he might be the more competent to maintain the quarrel against France. This, if not a true, was an ingenious hypothesis. At all events, Ferdinand's last act was a new combination with England, the Emperor, and some of the Swiss cantons against France ; and it was this which, after his death, held Francis I. back from an immediate attack on Naples.

Charles, on the other hand, until he became king of Castile and Aragon, had no quarrel with France ; friendship with France had been the polestar of the diplomacy of his father Philip and his minister Chièvres ; the elevation of the latter and the emancipation of Charles was a reaction against the hostile attitude of Maximilian and Margaret towards the French king. When Charles became king of Spain, his ministers naturally strove to continue their previous policy of peace, and to close the long conflict between France and Spain. Thus the treaty of Noyon (1516) was the high-water-mark of Franco-Flemish friendship. Charles, that is, far from dragging Spain into war with France, made it his first object to restore peace between these nations, and he followed this up by reconciling his grandfather Maximilian with France, and by thus breaking up the anti-French combination which his Spanish grandfather Ferdinand had ceaselessly laboured to create.

The treaty of Noyon was an attempt to settle the

vexed questions of Naples and Navarre. Charles was pledged to marriage with the infant French princess; or in the event of her death to a younger sister yet unborn, or failing such a birth to Louis XII.'s daughter Renée. This princess would bring Naples as a dower, but Charles was bound to pay a pension thereon until a son were born, and, if there were no marriage, France would reassert her claims. Charles promised to give reasonable satisfaction to the king of Navarre whenever he should bring his wrongs before him. Spaniards rightly regarded this treaty as a surrender of their interests. Spanish counsellors in the Netherlands loudly inveighed against the negotiations conducted behind their backs; the Council of Castile refused to publish the provisions,—it was, in Wolsey's words, the most slanderous treaty that was ever made.

Spaniards and Englishmen were assured by the Flemish government that the treaty of Noyon would not be permanent—that it was merely the means of enabling Charles to travel to Spain in safety, but it was in reality the climax of a Gallophil policy of long standing. Nevertheless, the alliance with France was doomed to be abortive, because it was impossible that Flemish should override Spanish interests. If his first visit to Spain taught Charles little else, it convinced him that Spanish and not Netherland feeling must guide his foreign policy. He confessed in Spain that he had not understood his rights, and must reconsider the position. The death of his intended baby-bride made this the easier. Chièvres, indeed, was willing to accept her newly-born sister as a substitute, but Spaniards could never suffer that their king, who was now eighteen, should wait for the baby's maturity, while the Portuguese Infanta added to riper charms the promise of a dazzling dowry. Throughout the stay of Charles in Spain the storm was brewing, and after the Imperial election even Chièvres became convinced that war had become inevitable.

Thus the election of Charles to the Empire was not the cause but the result of, or an incident in, the long Franco-Spanish feud. In this the French wars of Charles therefore had their origin; they were a liability, an encumbrance upon Charles's heritage. Unless this be fully realised, neither the cause of the hostilities, nor the purport of their conclusion, nor even the responsibility and character of Charles, can be fully understood. War could only be avoided if the young king continued to make Spain subordinate to the Netherlands, and, indeed, to the French-speaking provinces thereof. His election was a diplomatic victory, because it strengthened his weak position in Italy; but France would not have made this a *casus belli*, for the nation, whose aims were not so aggressive as its master's, was not ill-pleased at the king's failure, and even Francis could find consolation in the next day's hunt or the next evening's love-making.

At Burgos, on his way to Corunna, Charles received from Francis an ultimatum requiring him to execute the terms of Noyon, and to determine in favour of France all the questions relating to Navarre and Naples, Milan, Burgundy, and Flanders, which were to form the inharmonious refrain of the discordant duet of Charles and Francis. The reply was a polite adjournment until after the coronation of the Emperor. This coronation was the pretext of Charles's hurried withdrawal from Spain. He had alienated the Spaniards by his long delay in visiting his kingdom; it was natural that he should hasten to avoid a similar offence to Germany. More important, however, than the coronation ceremony was the interview with the English king, which should sterilise the results of his approaching meeting with Francis I. Henry's visit to France had been postponed in order to allow Charles to reach England first. But the sand was fast running down, and a further adjournment was impossible without offence to the French king. This then was the real cause of Charles's extreme haste to leave Corunna as soon as winds should serve.

If fighting was certain, neither side was anxious to begin. The coyness was partly the result of the recent treaty of London (October 1518), which pledged England to take side against the aggressor. Henry VIII.'s great wealth and his successful campaign against Louis XII. made him appear a more desirable ally than he ultimately proved to be. His subsidies would probably determine the attitude of the Swiss; his fleet was already sufficiently powerful to interrupt communications between Spain and Flanders, or to drive French commerce from the Channel; from Calais it was equally easy to invade Picardy or Artois. The balance between the rival powers seemed to depend on Henry's favour, but it was by no means certain into which of the two scales the weight of England would be thrown.

Past history pointed to the probability of an alliance between the successor of Henry VII. and the heir of both Ferdinand and Maximilian, but this was not a matter of course. England had taken active part in the combination against Louis XII., but the rupture of Mary Tudor's marriage with Charles and her wedding with the old French king was the seal of a sudden reconciliation, due to Henry VIII.'s dissatisfaction with his allies. Francis I.'s victory of Marignano had, however thoroughly alarmed the English government, and its diplomatists used their schoolboy knowledge of Alexander or of the Roman Empire to illustrate the danger of a French universal monarchy. England had striven to buy Swiss support for Maximilian, and had joined Ferdinand in the combination which was intended to check Francis I.'s progress southwards.

After Ferdinand's death the movements of Maximilian against the French in Milan proved abortive, but Henry VIII. still urged him to a fresh attack. This danger converted the French king's desire for the conquest of Naples at the expense of Charles into overtures for his friendship, which resulted in the treaty of Noyon. This was concluded in spite of Henry's offer to guarantee Charles's entire possessions, including Navarre and the Two Sicilies, and to make a combined attack on France. He was conscious that his new defensive treaty with Maximilian (October 1516) was a feeble parry to the clever stroke of the French government, which had isolated England. Accordingly, by the treaty of Windsor, he swung back to a French alliance, promised his daughter Mary to Francis, restored Tournai, and arranged for the future interview at the Field of the Cloth of Gold. Charles's ministers fought hard against the cession of Tournai, which was regarded as the key of the Netherlands, but had to be content with Henry's action in widening the Anglo-French treaty into a general European peace, which included Charles, Maximilian, and the Pope (1518). The ostensible purpose of this was a common crusade, as to which the European powers seemed momentarily in earnest, if earnestness may be tested by weighing protocols or counting clauses.

On Maximilian's death Henry VIII. had not been

F

without his ambitions for the Imperial crown, and had
even taken some halting measures to secure it.   His
sympathies might, therefore, naturally be with the other
defeated candidate rather than with his successful rival.
The real offence of Charles, however, had not been his
candidature for the Empire, but the treaty of Noyon;
for Wolsey's whole policy was directed to controlling
the balance and preventing an alliance of France and
Spain behind England's back.   If friendly personal
relations with Charles could ˙be secured previous to
Henry's interview with Francis, the English king would
meet the French on vantage ground.   The ink of the
obnoxious treaty of Noyon was fast fading, and Charles
could therefore anticipate a hospitable welcome on
English shores.   Queen Catherine had abandoned her
usual reserve to press the Emperor's visit; in the
Imperial envoy's presence she praised God for the grace
which she hoped He would do her, that she might
behold her nephew, her greatest desire in the world.
Even Wolsey, whom the envoys had described as unwilling to do anything merely for the sake of Imperialist
beaux yeux, had seemingly been won.   "Come," he
exclaimed, "and you shall be welcome; ask and you
shall have; speak openly and freely, and we shall say
Amen to whatever you say."

Thus it came to pass that Charles landed at Dover
on May 26, 1520, and here he was greeted by Wolsey
with a Latin speech which he could not well understand.
Next day he rode to Canterbury with his royal host, and
received warm welcome from his aunt.   The English
people wondered at the simplicity of his dress and
following, but "it was great joy to see the Emperor,
and more to see the benign manner and meekness of so
high a prince."   When Charles sailed from Sandwich,

Henry VIII. crossed the Channel to meet Francis I., at
the Field of the Cloth of Gold, but immediately afterwards he journeyed to Gravelines, whence Charles
escorted him back to Calais.   In these rides beside his
uncle Charles was beyond the ear of his political school-
master, Chièvres ; he was at length speaking as king to
king.   There was little of the display, and none of the
practical jokes which have made the meeting of Henry
and Francis so celebrated and so tiresome, but there was
the more opportunity for sober conversation, of which
the upshot will appear hereafter.[1]

Charles had been elected Emperor on June 28, 1519,
but in spite of his hurried departure from Spain it was
not until October 23, 1520, that he was crowned at
Aix.   Here, at the high altar, he swore to uphold the
Catholic faith, to defend the Church and her ministers,
to administer true justice, to maintain the rights of the
Empire and recover its lost possessions, to render due
obedience to Jesus Christ, the Roman Pope, and the
Roman Church.   Then the Archbishop of Cologne,
turning to the dense crowd, asked the German nation if
it would be subject to its prince, uphold his government,
and obey his commands, according to the apostolic order,
"Let every man be subject to authority."   The people
gave loud assent.   Charles was then anointed, clothed
in the tunic of Charlemagne,[2] girt with the great
Emperor's sword, crowned with his golden crown, and
then with ring on finger, and ball and sceptre in hand,
he was led to the stone seat of Empire.   On the
following day it was proclaimed that he had assumed

---

[1] For the relations of Charles V. and Henry VIII., in these years, see the
two monographs by K. E. W. Busch ; *Drei Jahre englischer Vermittlungspolitik*,
1884, and *Cardinal Wolsey und die Kaiserlich-englische Allianz* (1522-25), 1886.

[2] This is usually described as the deacon's robe or dalmatic, but F. E.
Brightman suggests that it was not an ecclesiastical vestment but a part of the
Byzantine Imperial costume.

the title of Roman Emperor Elect.   On November 1, he
summoned the Estates to Worms, and thither, in
January 1521, he travelled, to be brought face to face
with Germany and with Luther.

The Lutheran movement was still an unknown
quantity, but it was now recognised as a quantity of
some magnitude ; the stage of insignificance and
indifference was past.   Whatever difficulties it presented must be seriously faced, for they were day by
day yet further complicating the problems which, even
apart from religious dissidence, must tax the ingenuity
of the ruler of Germany.

If the character of Charles had been read aright by
the majority of those with whom he had been brought
in contact, neither the Empire, nor his Habsburg inheritance, nor the Suabian League, would avail him much
in the task of reconciling Germany to the old Catholic
faith, and to a new political order.   It was, however, at
this critical moment that an estimate of his personality
was formed, and that by no mean judge, entirely at
variance with current opinion.   Aleander, whom Leo X.
sent to induce the Emperor to condemn Luther, was no
obscurantist theologian of the old school.   He was a
man of the world and a scholar, essentially modern in
his attitude towards politics and religion, wide awake to
the faults of the Church and the folly of the Papacy, yet
eager to extirpate what he, earlier than most scholars
of his type, believed to be the seeds of social and
ecclesiastical anarchy.   His dispatches have for some
time been among the most important sources for the
history of the diet of Worms, but that in which he
describes his introduction to Charles in 1520 has only
recently been printed.

Aleander on being granted audience, made a little

speech in French to which Charles personally replied,
dwelling on his readiness to risk his life in defence of the
Church and the dignity of His Holiness and the Apostolic
See.   This much might be regarded as a form of speech ;
but Charles had more to say, and all so extremely
to the point, that Aleander could but silently devote to
the powers below the lying and cruel tongues which had
uttered the unjust and wrongful tales now going the
round of Italy.   "Say what they will," the nuncio
wrote, "this prince seemed to me well endowed with
sense, and with prudence, far beyond his years ; to have
much more, however, at the back of his head than he
carries on his face."   Aleander, worldling as he was, was
always susceptible to the impression of the moment, and
the ink of his letter to the pope may well have been
coloured by his hopes.   Yet here was at last a definite
opinion from a competent authority, that the champion
of the Empire and the Church was not such a cypher or
a simpleton as he had allowed himself to appear.

Whatever the character of Charles might be, the
Germans, unlike the Spaniards, were prepared to take
a favourable view.   The election had called forth much
national enthusiasm, which had not yet evaporated.
There were vague ideas that a new Emperor might lay
the brewing religious storm.   Reformers and conserva-
tives might both hope to find in him a champion.   The
princes, and especially those who had intrigued against
his election, had their reasons for advertising their
perfect loyalty.   The towns were honestly hearty in
their welcome, for they believed that he would restore
order, and repress brigandage on the thoroughfares of
trade—a duty which had earnestly been pressed upon
him.   At Worms, therefore, Charles might expect a
sympathetic public and an accommodating diet.

CHAPTER IV

The diet of Worms as a forecast of the reign—The problem of Luther—
The attitude of the Pope, the princes, and prelates—Public feeling
in Germany—Luther at Worms—Charles's declaration against him
—Publication of the ban—Development of the personality of
Charles—Apparent success of his policy—Constitutional reforms in
Germany—Cession of the Austrian provinces to Ferdinand —De-
parture of Charles for the Netherlands, England, and Spain.

At the diet of Worms was cast the horoscope of Charles,
or rather, perhaps, the first five months of 1521 traced
upon the youthful palm the lines of future life. Here
best can be appreciated the unity in diversity of the
Emperor's tasks. The two irreconcilable foes of the
future now met face to face, and for the only time ;
orthodox Emperor and heretic monk, each definitely took
position in the decisive struggle of the reign. Luther's
rescue after his dismissal was the first step in the path
of disobedience which was to lead to the overthrow of
the Ernestine line of Saxony. This diet essayed the
constitutional problem of order and liberty, monarchy
and oligarchy, which the diet of Augsburg, at the close
of Charles's reign, still left unsolved. Outside Worms
gathered the knights, already threatening revolution,
economic and religious ; within could be read the writing on the wall, the Peasant Shoe, which, within four
years, was the symbol of agrarian revolt. Here Charles
made the division of the hereditary territories which
was permanently to separate the Austrian from the

Spanish Habsburgs, and this was the consequence of
the renunciation, in his brother's favour, of the heiress
who was to unite Bohemia and Hungary with Austria.
Here Charles pledged his hand to Mary Tudor: his
son's redemption of the pledge was the last triumph of
the Emperor's reign.

During this memorable diet French aggression led to
the conflict between Habsburg and Valois, which was to
outlive the principals.   Here began the interminable
negotiations with the Papacy, now threatening immediate rupture, now promising eternal friendship.
Already the German people clamoured to be led to Italy
to revive its Imperial rights: in pursuance of this aim
German troops were to conquer at Pavia, storm Rome,
and beleaguer Florence, only to be at the last moment
baulked by the transference of the Italian conquests to
the Spanish Habsburg.

At Worms Charles received the manifesto of the
Castilian Communes; hence he dispatched his commission to the Constable and Admiral; while he was still
here was won the victory of Villalar, the crowning
mercy of Castilian monarchy.   During the last month
of this diet Cortes opened his final siege of Mexico.
Already Solyman's troops were on the march for Belgrad,
already his arsenals and dockyards were giving forecast
of the conquest of Rhodes; already the Danube and the
Mediterranean were marked out as the lines of Mussul-
man attack upon the Christian champion.   Scarcely one
of these interests was to remain in isolation from the
others.   Threads French and English, Lutheran and
Papal, German and Hungarian, Spanish and Italian,
Turkish, African, and American, twine in and out to
form the tapestried story of the reign.

Of all the problems which Charles had to solve at

Worms, that of Luther was the hardest. The graphic letters of the nuncio Aleander[1] represent, perhaps most nearly, the aspect in which it presented itself to Charles. Allowance must, of course, be made for the excitement of a Papal envoy, carefully selected to combat Lutheranism, and for the scorn of an Italian humanist and man of the world for the impudent innovations of a German monk. But Charles also had been brought up outside the area of the national agitation, and in an atmosphere of orthodox Catholicism; he too had as much reason as the Pope to dread an irreconcilable enemy of authority.

The Pope did his best to complicate the situation by urging that Luther should be condemned unheard. Aleander, eager as he was to stimulate Charles to decisive action, did not conceal from the Curia the dangers and difficulties of such a step, although he was strongly in its favour. Leo X. had probably now resolved to throw in his lot with Charles against France, but this was far from obvious to the Imperial government, and Juan Manuel, ambassador at Rome, advised the Emperor to pay some court to Luther. De Chièvres, who was orthodox but not theological, would subordinate ecclesiastical to political interests—the Lutheran question to the French; he would temporise with the Pope in order to win influential Germans. Gattinara, a confessed Erasmian, boldly advocated a General Council,—a policy to which he afterwards returned. Even Glapion, the

---

[1] See T. Brieger, *Aleander und Luther, 1521*, in *Quellen und Forschungen zur Geschichte der Reformation*, vol. i. 1884 ; W. Friedensburg, *Eine ungedrückte Depesche Aleanders von seiner ersten Nuntiatur bei Karl V.*, in *Quellen und Forschungen aus italianischen Archiven*, vol. i. 1897 ; J. Friedrich, *Der Reichstag in Worms, 1521, nach den Briefen des päpstlichen Nuntius Hieronymus Aleander* (*K. Bay. Akad. Wiss.* vol. xi.) ; A. Hausrath, *Aleander und Luther auf dem Reichstage zu Worms*, 1897 ; B. Gebhardt, *Die Gravamina der deutschen Nation gegen den romischen Hof*, 2nd edition,1895.

Emperor's zealous French confessor, strove for a meeting with Luther and Frederick of Saxony, and actually visited Hutten and Bucer at Ebernburg. The evidence does not warrant the belief that he aimed at an understanding with Luther for a disciplinary but not doctrinal reformation, but his action was suspected by the Curia, and illustrates the conciliatory attitude of the Imperial Court. The German councillors inherited from Maximilian had had many a passage of arms with the Papacy. To the end of his days Charles never had, apart from his confessors, a confidential councillor who attained his own standard of religious feeling.

If Lutheranism intensified the national hostility to the Italian Papacy, it was likely also to identify itself with oligarchical opposition to the monarchy. No influential prince was as yet a professed Lutheran, but Aleander represents Frederick of Saxony and the Elector Palatine as working strenuously in Luther's cause. The latter, he wrote, who was stupidity itself, and did not usually say ten words in a year, roared like ten bulls on behalf of Luther. Frederick of Saxony had been Maximilian's ablest constitutional opponent; he had voted for Charles with hesitation; his high character and undoubted talents made him the natural rallying-point for national discontent. This Saxon basilisk,—this serpent rearing his head amid a brood of hissing Lutherans, this marmot with dog-like eyes, who glanced sidelong at his questioner—was the peculiar object of Aleander's fears. Frederick was proud of Luther as an ornament of his cherished university; he resented interference, Papal or Imperial, with his subject. His nephew, John Frederick, Aleander already describes as an actual Lutheran, and so also Philip of Hesse—a mere boy, but full of enterprise and talent. George,

Duke of Saxony, later the bulwark of Catholicism, was now loud in his abuse of the clergy, while the two Bavarian dukes were long to sit upon the fence before planting their feet firmly on the Catholic side.

The great prelates were pledged by their position to the old faith, but they had little power and no courage ; " they let themselves be eaten up like rabbits." Their councillors, as those of other princes, were lawyers and humanists, devoted to the national cause. When the Elector of Mainz wished to burn Luther's books, he was kept up half the night by the gentry of his diocese dissuading him. The immediate danger, however, was the neighbourhood of Sickingen to Worms. This *con-dottiere* had contributed largely to Charles's election ; his aid was indispensable in the event of war with France ; he could add indefinitely to the force already under arms by enrolling the Suabian and Franconian knights. In his camp were the learned controversialist Bucer, and the literary gladiator Hutten, the one knightly representative of the newly-bred swarm of German scholar-satirists. From Ebernburg Hutten poured upon Germany a flood of letters, pamphlets, and satires, now instinct with exalted patriotism and righteous indignation, now poisoned with the venom of disappointed ambition and diseased physique.

Behind Sickingen was ranged the military knighthood of Germany, behind Hutten " the tribe of grammar-mongers and poetasters" with whom Germany was teeming, who believed that learning in Italy was dead, and that the Tiber had flowed into the Rhine. To profess the doctrines of Luther, said Aleander, was with these pedants a sign of learning, and especially of Greek learning : all the lawyers and canonists too were for him, and the majority of monks, friars, and lesser

clergy, save only the parochial rectors : nine-tenths of
Germany cried "Long live Luther," and the other tenth
shouted "Death to the Church." The military and
intellectual classes, for their several reasons, wished for
nothing better than an onslaught on the higher clergy
and their wealth. The populace in town and country
were excited by the social as by the religious bearings of
Luther's teaching. The town of Worms itself was of old
a foe to the clergy and to Roman envoys, and would
gladly have seen them hacked down by Sickingen's
desperadoes. Aleander himself was threatened with
death by Hutten ; landlords refused to take him in. The
delicate Italian, used to a fire from September to May,
sat shivering in a stoveless attic. If he complained of
threats against his person, the ministers shrugged their
shoulders, for Charles had neither men, nor time, nor
means. While every German press was pouring out
Lutheran works, no German, he wrote, dared print an
answer, or if he did, a syndicate of Jews and Lutherans
bought up and burnt the copies.

In this state of public feeling it was impossible that
Charles should consent to Leo X.'s demand for Luther's
immediate condemnation. He had burnt the heretic's
books in his hereditary dominions, but he would not
issue the Imperial ban without the diet's constitutional
consent. He had indirectly owed his election to national
sentiment which was in sympathy with Luther. It
would be madness to flout the official representatives of
Germany, on whose good-will depended support against
France and supplies for his coronation at Rome. Charles
therefore laid the responsibility upon the diet, and this
decided that Luther should be heard. Thus it was that
the heretic was summoned to Worms under Imperial
safe-conduct. Charles must have grudged the opening

words of his letter, *nobilis devote nobis dilecte*, but Aleander was assured that if Luther were roughly addressed, he would not come to be condemned.

When Luther, after his triumphal procession from Wittenberg, reached Worms, he was the greatest power in Germany. On April 16 the two foes of the future met. Luther entered the great hall smiling impudently, as Aleander thought, but a smile is the tell-tale more often of nervousness than of impudence. Brought before Charles, he moved his head up and down and from side to side. He admitted the authorship of his books, but when asked if he would withdraw the doctrines therein contained he replied that the question was difficult, and begged for time. Luther's behaviour had disappointed his supporters. Charles, during the interview, did not speak publicly, but he is said to have remarked, " This man will never make me a Lutheran." He could not believe that Luther had himself written the books which had stirred Germany throughout its length and breadth.

The following day was decisive in the history of Charles and Luther. The monk had recovered his nerve ; not one jot of his doctrines could he find it in his conscience to withdraw. He spoke boldly, impressively, at times fiercely. Neither Pope nor General Councils received quarter. Twice Charles personally intervened. When Luther enlarged upon the Pope's iniquities, the Emperor told him to change his theme, and on his persisting in his denial of the authority of Councils, Charles cut him short. The interview was over. Luther, as he left the hall, raised his hand ; it was the gesture, wrote Aleander, of the *landsknecht* who had dealt a telling stroke. Luther had struck at the mediæval Church and her sworn champion, the mediæval Empire. Charles and his challenger never met again.

The princes visited Charles next morning, and he asked them what should now be done. They begged delay for consultation. "Very well," he replied, "but I should like first to give you my opinion." He then produced a paper composed in French, and written in his own hand; of this a German translation was read aloud to the princes, some of whom turned pale as death. Its terms were these :—"My predecessors, the most Christian Emperors of German race, the Austrian archdukes, and dukes of Burgundy, were until death the truest sons of the Catholic Church, defending and extending their belief to the glory of God, the propagation of the faith, the salvation of their souls. They have left behind them the holy Catholic rites that I should live and die therein, and so until now with God's aid I have lived, as becomes a Christian Emperor. What my forefathers established at Constance and other Councils, it is my privilege to uphold. A single monk, led astray by private judgment, has set himself against the faith held by all Christians for a thousand years and more, and impudently concludes that all Christians up till now have erred. I have therefore resolved to stake upon this cause all my dominions, my friends, my body and my blood, my life and soul. For myself and you, sprung from the holy German nation, appointed by peculiar privilege defenders of the faith, it would be a grievous disgrace, an eternal stain upon ourselves and our posterity, if in this our day, not only heresy, but its very suspicion, were due to our neglect. After Luther's stiff-necked reply in my presence yesterday, I now repent that I have so long delayed proceedings against him and his false doctrines. I have now resolved never again, under any circumstances,

to hear him. Under protection of his safe-conduct he
shall be escorted home, but forbidden to preach and
to seduce men with his evil doctrines and incite them to
rebellion. I warn you to give witness to your opinion
as good Christians and in accordance with your vows."

Such was the Emperor's memorable declaration. It
seems certain that it was his unassisted work. He did
not speak merely as the representative of authority.
The personality of Luther had been repugnant to his
innermost nature; he was the incarnation of the
revolutionary spirit, destructive of the unity of the
Church and the continuity of her rites, which for
Charles were a real religion, and in which to his dying
day he found in all his troubles true consolation.
Reserved as Charles was, the shock struck out the most
outspoken confession of his faith that he ever uttered.
Nowhere else is it possible to approach so closely to the
workings of his spiritual nature, save in the confidential
letters to his brother in the last troubled hours of rule,
when he repeated that it was not in his conscience to
rend the seamless mantle of the Church.

In the subsequent earnest efforts of the princes to
induce Luther to recant Charles took no part. On
April 25 he ordered Luther to leave Worms, and on
the morrow the heretic, after toasting slices of bread
for the day's consumption and fortifying himself with
several glasses of Malmsey wine, set out with two carts
and twenty horsemen on his eventful homeward journey.
A fortnight later arrived the news of his mysterious
disappearance.

The ban was still delayed, for Charles had not yet
received his subsidy, and Germans believed that the
Pope was concerned in the French attacks upon the
Netherlands and Navarre. At length, on May 26,

Aleander cried *Io Pæan,* for his prey had fallen into his net. Frederick of Saxony and the Elector Palatine had left Worms, and the diet on its last day unanimously approved the Edict of Worms. Charles signed it with joyous face, asking Aleander if he were now content. The nuncio had good reason to be content; he frankly confessed that Charles's policy, which he had deplored, was right ; that the ban issued, after hearing of the heretic, with the diet's sanction, had pledged the official German nation to the extirpation of heresy. From the first Aleander had built his hopes on Charles alone : he had seen "nothing good but Cæsar": Charles had the best disposition of any ruler for a thousand years, and if only he could follow his own sound conscience and good sense in despite of interested councillors, all would be well. When success was at length secured, Charles was for Aleander the best person in the world ; his prudence was as consummate as his goodness, his judgment more than human, his impromptu opinions weightier than the mature conclusions of veteran statesmen.

Aleander's praise was no empty panegyric. Luther's brave bearing at Worms has rightly been recognised as his most heroic moment. But this was also, perhaps, the greatest—certainly the first great moment of his antagonist. In after years Lutheranism, as a definite body of doctrines, as an organised political party, was far stronger. But Luther's self was never such a power in Germany as in 1521 ; he was never again so truly the voice from the heart of the people. The cumulative annoyances and aspirations of Germany, ecclesiastical, political, and financial, found in him their mouthpiece. For six months Charles had been warned not to gag Luther, for all policy, internal and external, depended upon humouring his supporters. Luther was a monk, and Charles Emperor and King of Spain. But Luther could command the sole organised force in Germany immediately outside the walls of Worms, and the whole anti-clerical populace within, while Charles had not "four ragamuffin policemen" at his back.

Charles was now twenty-one. He had never been allowed independent action, he was an alien to Germany, his language was not German, he was credited with no force of character. While every word that Luther uttered—and they were numerous—was for Germany an oracle, the Emperor's occasional expressions passed into thin air. The half-educated, inexpressive youth, in spite of his brocaded throne, must have been to the full as nervous as the Augustinian, trained to dialectics, practised in polemics, hardened by defiance. There are moments when it needs more courage to be conservative than radical, and the old faith, whatever its failings, could show the manhood that there was in Charles. The Emperor, had, in fact, at length found a living interest, and this too at the moment when Chièvres was removed by death. The Lutheran question made a man of the boy-ruler. The house of Habsburg was said to mature late. News now reached Spain that Charles had grown a beard, that he was a man in mind, and no longer the boy who sat spellbound under the ferule of Chièvres. Charles never had another schoolmaster; nor was he still *ce bon enfant l'Empereur*, as Leo X. scornfully but wrongly dubbed him. Gattinara, who might claim the succession to Chièvres, told Contarini that Wolsey had expected to find a boy under tutelage as of yore, but was forced to recognise a very different character. "One fault in the world he has," said Glapion to Aleander: "he will not easily forgive an injury." "This I can well believe," wrote the nuncio on the last day of the diet, " for he is a man very serious and determined."

The Emperor's action was justified by its immediate results. His bold personal intervention had stifled further public discussion. In the streets of Worms, indeed, placards were posted at night with the words, "Miserable is the land whose ruler is a child." But it is the privilege of youth to know its mind, and certainty at such a crisis was a power. In spite of Aleander's statistics there must have been many waverers, and these were grateful for a decisive step. Every one had prophesied revolution if Luther were condemned. Charles perhaps more rightly judged that revolution would be the result of his acquittal, for Luther only learned moderation from necessity. The denunciation of General Councils had made a bad impression ; Frederick of Saxony had said that the rascally monk had spoiled all with his fantastical opinions. In vain was the *Bundschuh*, "sign of revolt and riot," placarded on the town-hall walls ; in vain was the nuncio figured hanging head downwards from a gallows. When princes expressed alarm at the reported conspiracy of 400 knights, Charles laughingly reminded them of Mutius Scævola's band of 300, of which he was the only member. Hutten from his watch-tower barked louder than ever, but his barks were apologies for not biting. The restless knights were Lutheran from *ennui* rather than from conviction, and Charles was providing them with pay and employment. Luther had been spirited away, no one knew whither, and not many seemed to care.

Charles had been pledged by the conditions of his election to the formation of a representative central government, and indeed the certainty of his frequent absence from Germany made this the more necessary.

The form which it should assume became a trial of
strength, as in Maximilian's reign, between the monarchical and oligarchical principles.   The princes saw their
opportunity in the accession of a youth, colourless in
character, and hampered rather than helped by the
nature of his hereditary dominions.   Charles, on the
other hand, was aided both by Maximilian's German
advisers, who had for a quarter of a century successfully
combated the consolidation of oligarchy, and by his
Netherland councillors, who had inherited the centralis-
ing traditions of the royal French house of Burgundy.
Germany's chief need was a central court of justice to
administer the law, and a central council to enforce
respect for the court, to execute the decrees of the diet,
and to conduct the administration of the Empire.   Both
court and council had been framed in the previous reign,
but Maximilian's clever opposition had assured their
failure.

At Worms the conflict centred in the Council.
Each party pitched its demands unduly high.   The
princes proposed a permanent Council, irrespective of
the Emperor's, presence or absence, which should decide
all Imperial questions whether foreign or domestic.
In this the several Estates, even the towns, should be
represented, but the Emperor only in so far that the
Estates of his hereditary dominions should elect members.   Under such a constitution the Emperor would
have been powerless; he could not even rely on the
support of his own territories.   The result would have
been a federal oligarchy.

Charles replied with a proposal that the Council should
sit only during his absence from Germany, and under
a regent appointed by himself; out of twenty members
he claimed six nominees, who should be permanent,

while their colleagues were changed quarterly. The direction of foreign affairs was reserved as the Emperor's peculiar function, and his assent should be required for all important decisions. Far from being represented only through the Estates of his territories, Charles demanded that these territories, even the newly-won state of Württemberg, should be excluded from the Council's competence; once more the territorial interests of the Habsburgs took precedence of their Imperial position. Such a scheme would have given to the monarchy a power which it had never yet wielded; it was totally at discord with the capitulations, and was probably but a *ballon d'essai* to test the setting of the wind.

Had either party possessed fixed constitutional principles a deadlock would have resulted. But the Emperor needed the financial support of the Estates, while to individual princes the Emperor's favour was convenient, if fiefs were to be acquired, desirable marriages contracted, or cross-remainder arrangements conducted between neighbouring families. Thus a compromise was found. To the Emperor was conceded the appointment of the president and four members out of twenty-two; the Council should exercise authority only in his absence, but on his return should assist him as a deliberative Council until he convoked a diet. To the Council Charles granted powers to conduct all ordinary business in his absence, reserving the decision on the more important cases; he engaged not to form leagues or alliances affecting the Empire, save with its consent, and withdrew the demand for the independence of his hereditary states. Charles was on the whole the gainer: he had not added to the positive power of the monarchy, but he had foiled the attempt to control

such authority as it possessed. The Court of Justice
was remodelled with less difficulty. Provision was
made for its permanent session under the superintend-
ence of the Council or the Emperor. Of eighteen
members the Emperor nominated four, while in concert
with the Estates he appointed the president and the
two members from the counts and knights. Diets
usually only gave birth to diets, but that of Worms
had brought forth a constitution. Few, however, are
the constitutions that survive their infancy.

The death of Chièvres probably contributed not a
little to produce a friendlier feeling between Charles
and Ferdinand. The latter must have ascribed mainly
to the minister his summary dismissal from Spain, his
native country. There is little doubt that Chièvres
really thought the ambitious young prince a danger.
Gasparo Contarini reports that Chièvres once said to
Charles, "Do not fear the king of France or any other
prince except your brother." The Emperor while still
at Worms, wisely determined to give Ferdinand a
distinct sphere of action, and therefore conferred upon
him the five Austrian provinces remote at once from
the Netherlands and Spain. He had promised a partition of his heritage after his coronation, but character-
istically insisted that it was of grace and not of right.
When Ferdinand became engaged to Anna, the sister
and heiress of the king of Hungary, he could not
decently remain a landless prince. Early in 1522
Charles ceded the Italian-Slavonian appendages of the
Austrian group, and also Tyrol, with the Vorarlberg
and divers Suabian territories. To these he afterwards
added his lands in Alsace and on the Upper Rhine, and
lastly Württemberg. The treaty relating to the more
recent cessions was to remain secret for six years, while

the Alsatian group was only granted for Ferdinand's life. Thus Ferdinand in Tyrol and westwards ruled only as his brother's representative. Owing to the Tyrolese troubles of 1525 the settlement was made public, while in 1540 Charles abandoned the reversion to Alsace. Here, then, in 1521 began the permanent division between the Austrian and Spanish Habsburgs.[1] Ferdinand's share seemed likely to occupy all his energies. In the Austrian provinces the Estates defied or ignored the government, administering the territories under republican forms. The Tyrolese peasants rose on a vague belief that Maximilian in his will had annulled the stringent game laws. The western group was endangered by the restless Duke Ulrich and his French and Swiss allies. It was feared even that Swiss principles might affect Tyrol, where the social and geographical features were very similar to those of the confederacy.

The future of the Austrian territories was not of immediate interest to Charles. He could leave Germany with the consciousness of success. When his first diet closed he might even have repeated Luther's cry on leaving the hall of audience, "I am through, I am through." He had stayed the rout of Catholicism, he had checked the advance of oligarchy, he had enlisted German aid against the onslaught of the foreigner. But the triumph was the less secure because it was so personal. How would it stand the test of the Emperor's nine years' absence?

From Worms Charles travelled northwards down the Rhine to the Netherlands; his next journey to Germany was to be over her southern mountain border.

---

[1] G. Turba, *Geschichte des Thronfolgerechtes in allen Habsburgischen Ländern*, 1903, and W. Bauer, *Die Anfänge Ferdinands I.*, 1907.

On his way to Brussels the Emperor received the
tidings of the victory of Villalar and of the alliance
with the Pope. For nearly a year he remained in the
country of his birth. During this period the long war
in Italy began, and the English friendship ripened
into alliance. On May 26, 1522, Charles left Calais
for England. His thoughts were, however, now mainly
fixed on Spain, and the six weeks of English hospital-
ity seemed, as he wrote to his aunt Margaret, a thousand years.[1] On July 6 he set sail on his third ocean
voyage, bound once more for the port of Santander.
Thither it will be well to follow him, or rather to
precede him, and then retrace the phases of the civil
war, before he arrived to complete the victory which
he had not won, and punish the rebels whom he had
not fought. It is convenient to postpone any account
of the English and Papal alliances, and of the outbreak
of the war, which was to form one of the two abiding
features of the reign, until the ground is cleared of the
opening episode of Spanish rebellion.

[1] For Charles V.'s reception in London, see *The Somers Tracts*, 2nd edition,
vol. i.

CHAPTER V

Revolt of the Castilian Communes—Its social and geographical distribution—The Santa Junta and its petition—Reaction of the nobles
in favour of the Crown—Dissension among the Cummunes—Battle
of Villalar—Capitulation of Toledo—French invasion of Navarre—
Social war in Valencia—Arrival of Charles and his artillery—
Punishment of the rebellion in Castile and Valencia—The Inquisition and the Moorish peasantry—A Moorish war—Revolt in
Sicily against the viceroy—Victory of the nobles and the Crown—
Comparison of the three movements.

THE revolt of the Communes of Castile was only one
of five movements which Charles's government had
to face—or turn its face from—in the early years of
his reign. Of these two were in Spain, two in Germany,
and the earliest in the Aragonese kingdom of Sicily.
All differed in their character and motives, and it is in
character and motive rather than in events that their
interest consists. The elements of discontent were
national and religious, political, social, and economic,
but these were in each case mixed in very different
proportions, some one or other being wholly absent or
subordinate. Every rising proved a pitiable failure,
yet in none was the suppression mainly due to the
direct action of the central government. The principle
of authority asserted itself triumphantly, although its
actual fighting power proved lamentably inefficient.
In the background of the lesser whirlwinds the heavy
black storm of foreign war was either muttering or

raging, but the local disturbances, in spite of their
momentarily drawing towards each other, ran their
own individual course in the foreground, and were
never merged in the more continuous European tem-
pest.

Charles, on sailing from Corunna, had shown his
back, not only to discontent, but to actual rebellion.
Civil war was already raging in Valencia, where the
government, indeed, was not the objective of the
rising. In Castile, on the other hand, it was the
direct outcome of the constitutional opposition offered
to the Crown at Santiago. While Charles was coquet-
ting with Henry VIII. on either side of the Channel,
the revolt ran its course unchecked. Rebels usually
begin to fight under a false flag. Notwithstanding
professions of loyalty, the rising of the Communes
was from the first a revolt against the Crown.[1] The
earliest victims were the deputies who had consented to
its demands, the agents of the monarchy, and foreigners
who had bought from it privileges of trade. If they
could not be caught themselves, their houses, their
furniture, their very poultry, were burnt. Thus at
Segovia the mob murdered two functionaries who de-
precated rebellion, and then dragged from sanctuary
the deputy who had voted the subsidy. In vain the

---

[1] M. Danvila has collected numerous documents relating to the revolt of the
Communes, in *Historia critica y documentada de las comunidades de Castilla*,
xxxv. - xli., 1897 - 1902. See also K. Häbler, *Geschichte Spaniens unter den
Habsburgern*, vol. i., 1907, and *Historische Zeitschrift*, No. 95, 1905 ; K. von
Höfler, *Der Aufstand der Castilianischen Städte gegen Kaiser Karl V.*, 1876, and
Gachard, *Correspondance de Charles-Quint et d'Adrien VI*, 1859. Many
interesting details on the rising are given in A. R. Villa's *La Reina D. Juana la
Loca*, 1892. See also K. von Höfler, " Zur Kritik und Quellenkunde der ersten
Regierungsjahre Karls V.," in *Denkschrifte der Wiener Akademie Phil.-hist. Kl.*
xxv. und xxviii., 1876 and 1878 ; A. Salvá, *Burgos en las comunidades des Castilla*,
1895 ; "Las Comunidades en Cordoba," in *Coleccion de doc. ined. para la hist. de
España*, cxii., 1895.

clergy, Host in hand, strove to protect him; he was hanged head downwards and unshriven. The royal authorities were deposed, the government usurped by the populace. At Burgos the people, after burning the houses of the royal officials and their own deputies, destroyed the splendid palace of the French merchant Jofré; dragged him from the protection of the police, and hanged him under legal forms, for the *corregidor* was forced to sit upon the scaffold and sign his sentence.

Violent as were the revolutionary measures, they were not entirely democratic. In the first manifesto the Crown was accused of violating noble privileges. Among the earliest leaders was Pedro de Giron, a great Andalusian noble, claimant for the duchy of Medina Sidonia, graduated in sedition and a past-master in faction fight. His grievances were, indeed, personal, as were partly those of the fierce and lawless Count of Salvatierra, who headed the rising in Navarre, and boasted direct descent, step by step, from the Gothic kings. But Juan de Padilla and Pedro Laso, the heads of the popular movement in Toledo, the earliest and most obstinate centre of revolt, were gentlemen of high standing. There was not in Castile the contrast between towns and nobles which existed in Germany. The towns had not lost their military, aristocratic character; the nobles in Spain have never had great country seats; their palaces were in the towns; they were, in spite of their huge possessions, an urban nobility; there were towns where the representation was confined to certain noble families. The regent informed Charles that the magnates were instigating the revolution, though it seems more probable that they were watching events and pre-serving towards it at first a not unfriendly neutrality.

The clergy in many instances favoured the revolt; they were intensely national in feeling, resenting the intrusion of foreigners; they had recently, in 1517, resisted an attempt of the Pope to tax them for a Crusade. The strangest figure of the revolt was Antonio de Acuña, Bishop of Zamora, who had in Ferdinand's reign imposed himself on his see in defiance of royal authority. He was perhaps alone overtly republican in his theories—full of wild talk of the liberties of Italian city-states. By him the friars and lower clergy were enrolled in regiments; churches and monasteries were pillaged to support the holy cause; torchlight processions with chant and crucifix, drum and harquebus, stimulated the war fever in his diocese.[1]

The area where revolt was most persistent consisted of the very heart of Spain—of the great river valleys, the Douro and the Tagus, with the intervening country, comprising the bulk of Old and New Castile and Leon. Northwards it spread temporarily to Burgos, and was somewhat violent in Navarre, where it connected itself with the dynastic question and with local factions of long standing. The North - Western provinces and Estremadura seem to have been less seriously affected. In the South Murcia and Jaen were centres of disturbance; their deputies had opposed the Crown in the recent Cortes. But revolt in the South was only transitory, and was rather the revival of old quarrels than a definite movement against the government. Indeed, as in the plague of Athens, all older and lesser maladies determined in the new and gigantic epidemic. Andalusia and Granada were generally loyal, although the deputies of Cordoba had stoutly resisted the subsidy

---

[1] See K. von Höfler, *Don Antonio de Acuña genannt der Luther Spaniens,* 1882.

at Santiago. This town and Seville refused to join
any unlawful association in the king's absence, and
ultimately formed the loyal union of La Rambla, which
offered to raise 6000 horse and 20,000 foot for Charles,
if only he would return to Spain unaccompanied
by foreign troops. These Andalusian municipalities
realised the sources of danger. They begged the
neighbouring nobles to keep outside the walls, and
rigorously forbade armed gatherings round the palaces
of local magnates. Democratic agitators were more
roughly handled; at Cordoba a price was put on the
heads of a cobbler and a friar who had tried to seduce
the lower classes. Moreover in some disaffected districts
small towns here and there held stoutly for the Crown.
Simancas—insignificant save for its strong position on
the Pisuerga—defied Valladolid and endangered the
communications of this great city with its rebel colleagues. Truxillo proved coy to the blandishments of
its powerful neighbour, Salamanca. Vitoria saved the
character of Biscay. Logroño isolated the rebellion of
Navarre from that of Old Castile.

The parliamentary traditions of Spain facilitated a
formal union of the rebel cities, separated by difficult
country or by local interests. At the close of August
1520 they organised a central government, the Santa
Junta. They sent their representatives—men of all
classes—to Avila, which, as the southernmost town of
Old Castile, made a natural geographical centre. The
Junta declared Adrian and the Council to be deposed,
and itself to be the supreme authority. Toledo was
still leading the rebellion, for Pedro Laso was elected
President of the Junta, and Padilla Captain of its
forces.

Adrian was left with no money and few troops. His

feeble efforts to quench the flames made them burn the brighter. Ronquillo, who as magistrate had tyrannised over Segovia, was beaten off from its walls; his attack only served to enlist the moderates of all classes in the popular movement. Even more pregnant with evil consequences were the instructions to Fonseca to march to Ronquillo's aid, after seizing the park of royal artillery at Medina del Campo. The people of this town, which had not previously rebelled, resisted desperately; in the struggle the royalists set fire to some houses, and this central mart, the very Novogorod of Spain, was rapidly destroyed. The fate of Medina in fighting for the common cause gave a unity of sentiment which hitherto was lacking. Segovia cut her pine woods to rebuild the smoking town. At Valladolid the great bell of San Miguel rang the people to rapine. They destroyed the houses of the aldermen and of Fonseca, throwing his unoffending fowls into the flames. Adrian was forced by popular indignation to disband the royal forces; Fonseca and Ronquillo fled the country; the offensive seemed definitely abandoned. The few troops drafted from Africa or Sicily joined the insurgents from want of pay; the rebels seized all sources of royal revenue.

The Communes, feeling their strength, now captured Tordesillas (August 29). Padilla broke up the Royal Council, imprisoned its members, with the exception of Adrian,—too holy or too harmless to touch,—and transferred the government to the seat of the queen's residence. The mental condition of Juana gave a convenient handle to the insurgent chiefs. She was, after all, the lawful queen; as she could not possibly uphold the government, it was easy to represent her as its victim. Her mania was not sufficiently chronic or acute to make it as obvious to the ignorant as it had been to Jiménez that she was unfit to rule. It was now officially announced that Juana was set free, that she was not mad, and that she sympathised with the Communes. She was, indeed, roused by the excitement of unfamiliar scenes, amused by tournaments and festivals. This moment was the zenith of rebellion. Should Juana but sign a document, wrote Adrian to Charles, his kingship was at an end. But the queen soon relapsed into sullen indifference; neither entreaties nor threats could extract her signature. She was, perhaps, at this crisis more sane than was supposed; she refused to convert revolution into a legitimist protest.

Up to this point Charles had apparently ignored the revolution. Adrian wrote doleful letters on the hopelessness of the situation; he had no troops even to protect the coasts of Southern Spain against the Moors; the only remedy was that Charles should relinquish the subsidy granted at Corunna, and return immediately after his coronation. He laid the blame of the rebellion on his master, on his arbitrary government, on his breaches of faith to towns and nobles, on his disgraceful appointments, on the plundering of Spain by his Flemish suite. To letters so disagreeable for week after week Charles vouchsafed no reply. He would not accept the Cardinal's resignation, nor would he send him aid.

The capture of Tordesillas at length roused the royal court from its torpor. The policy of Charles or his advisers was at this moment eminently wise. Abandoning his not unnatural reserve towards the great nobles, he threw himself upon their loyalty. Going back beyond the age of bureaucracy to that of great Crown officials, he made the two titular heads of the nobility, the Constable and the Admiral, co-regents with Adrian (September 9, 1520). To other leading nobles he wrote a personal appeal, enlisting their sympathies in the cause of the young and absent king. The effect of this policy was soon to show itself. The war against the Crown was changed into a war of classes. The resistance of the nobles to the commons was becoming under all circumstances inevitable, but the king's act concentrated and legalised it—saved it from being frittered away in a hundred personal and local feuds. Henceforth, without the expenditure of a man or a ducat, the monarchy had pitted against the rebels a force for which they ultimately proved no match.

Speed and violence are essential to the success of revolution. The victory of the Communes had been so easy, so complete, that they knew not how to use it. The Junta, instead of destroying the bare remnants of royal government, respectfully memorialised the absent king. Its inaction began just as Charles was shaking off his negligence. The schedule of eighty-two petitions comprised in the memorial was in the form of those presented at each session of the Cortes. It is of high interest as setting out the shortcomings of the government since the death of Isabella, or the new aspirations of the people. This document, containing the official programme of the revolution, was probably the result of a compromise. It does not give expression to the more extreme theories of the insurgents; still less does it tally with their more violent actions. The instructions given by Valladolid to its deputies were less radical than the terms of the petition. On the other hand a draft programme of unknown origin demands that no woman, nor any prince not born within the country, should rule Castile—a provision which would exclude both Charles and his mother in favour of his brother Ferdinand.

The petition of the Junta repeated or anticipated many of the reasonable and unreasonable grievances of former or future Cortes, and these need not here be considered. The most sweeping change demanded was a drastic reform in the composition of the Cortes and in their relation towards the Crown. Each represented town should in future send three instead of two representatives, and these should be respectively elected by gentry, clergy and commons ; these deputies should be bound by the instructions of their constituencies, while death was the penalty for the acceptance of any gratuity from the Crown, direct or indirect. It was provided that the Cortes should meet every two or three years, with or without royal summons, should debate in private, and appoint the notaries who attended, and who had hitherto been the king's officials. It is noticeable that there was no suggestion for the enlargement of the representative system ; the eighteen towns still intended to retain the monopoly of the Cortes. Such was the remedy for the future. As a penalty for the past Charles was ordered to depose Adrian from the regency, to dismiss all officials who had offended the Communes, to disqualify for ever the existing members of the Councils of Castile and of State, to engage that during a king's minority or absence the regent should be a native, acceptable to the people and elected by the Council of Castile. Charles himself was peremptorily required to return, reside, reduce the expenses of his table, which were tenfold those of his grandparents, and diminish the charges of his household by dismissals and by the discontinuance of salaries to wives and children

of courtiers and others not actually in service.   Above
all, the king must marry, and that at once.

The hostility to foreigners, which had been the
immediate cause of the rebellion, naturally manifested
itself in the petitions, though it is by no means confined
to the memorial of the Junta, but is a feature in the
demands of every Cortes.   It was, however, especially
prominent on this occasion.   All offices and benefices, all
service in the army and the household, should be closed
to foreigners; precautions were taken to secure the reality
of such exclusion by a protest against the royal power of
granting letters of naturalisation.   Foreign traders were
as unpopular as foreign officials.   The Junta complained
that Castile was being drained of her precious metals,
that the price of meat, candles and shoes was trebled
by the export of cattle, sheep and pigs.   There was a
fear that Charles intended to open the American trade
to all his subjects, and that Antwerp would thus claim a
large share of it; he was therefore petitioned to maintain the monopoly of Seville.   It was claimed that
native manufacturers should have the first refusal of all
Spanish wool, and that foreign woollens should be subjected to the same strict supervision as home-made goods.

The ecclesiastical grievances of the Communes were
merely another form of the dislike to foreign influence.
Catholic as Spain was, no country more repeatedly
resented ultramontane influence.   Crown, clergy and
people had usually been united in resistance to Papal
encroachments, except indeed where the latter were
to the pecuniary advantage of the Crown.   The most
obvious distinction between the rising of the Communes
in Spain and those of the knights and peasants in
Germany was the absence of the religious motive from
the former.   And yet the outspoken objection of the

Junta to the so-called Bulls of *Cruzada* was only the war against indulgences in a slightly different form. The Communes protested, not only against the abuses of the Inquisition, but against those of ecclesiastical jurisdiction in general. Against Rome mainly was aimed the insistence upon the residence of the clergy ; the conference of benefices and pensions upon members of the Curia and other aliens had caused the ruin of churches and the decay of church services ; it was hoped to remedy this evil by the deduction of a *pro-rata* portion of the salary during non-residence ; if the king would not obtain a Bull for this purpose, the State would do so at the cost of the Church revenues. Had the Papacy at this moment been in closer union with the Crown than in fact it was, it would not have been so far a cry to schism, if not, indeed, to heresy.

The Crown was so helpless that demands upon it might be made with complete impunity. It was otherwise when the memorial of the Junta struck at the great nobles. The rebellion, as has been seen, was in its origin scarcely democratic. Yet in several towns the mob was at the very outset much in evidence, and, as time went on, the lower classes in the cloth-working centres assumed the lead. The revolt in several cities, such as Madrid, Siguenza and Guadalajara, had begun with the overthrow of the aristocratic municipalities and the exclusion of the gentry from the offices which they had before monopolised.[1] At Segovia the nobles had from

---

[1] K. Häbler (*Historische Zeitschrift*, No 95, 1905) shows that this practice was methodically adopted in all cities which were definitely committed to the revolution. The *corregidor*, the *regidores* and other royal officials were ejected, and magistrates elected in their place by a new Council to which artisans were admitted. In some cases officials who had cordially supported the movement were allowed to retain offices under the new conditions. It was to those wholly unconstitutional municipalities that the name of *comunidades* was given. Occasionally there was stout resistance by the upper classes, as at Burgos Zamora and Valladolid, and in the first two with ultimate success.

the first been threatened by the populace, whilst smaller towns which were the property of the great landholders seized the opportunity to emancipate themselves. The Junta now added to the alarm of the nobles by attacking their privileges or encroachments, by debarring them from office in the royal domain, fortresses or revenue, by assessing for taxation proprietary towns and villages previously exempt. The Crown was ordered to redeem the older assignations upon revenue, to resume without compensation grants made subsequent to Isabella's death, and at once to deprive the nobles of rents, lands and services illegally appropriated.

The nobles once in the field, events began to move more rapidly. The party of revolution was now deeply scored by dissensions, personal and political. The constitutionalists, who had led in the earlier stages, had little in common with the anarchists, who had thrust them from the van. Burgos, which lay on the northern skirts of the rebellion, had joined in it with hesitation ; it was, as always, jealous of the influence of Toledo, and in November 1520 it made its peace with the Constable. Dr. Zumel, who at the Cortes of Valladolid had incurred the displeasure of the Crown as its stoutest opponent, was now recommended to Charles as a devoted loyalist. Hitherto there had been little fighting, because the towns had no one to fight. At length a royalist force, under the Constable's son, the Count of Haro, gathered at Rio Seco, whither Adrian escaped from Valladolid. To this was opposed the main force of the insurgents at Tordesillas. Each town, however, became a local centre of disturbance, and was harassed by the hostility of a traditional noble foe. Thus the Count of Chinchon fought the citizens of Segovia up and down the very aisles of the cathedral, and through choir and cloisters.

Valladolid itself must be always under arms to beat off
the enterprising royalists of Simancas.

The insurgents were still the stronger party and the
richer ; their troops numbered three to one ; the urban
levies were stiffened by mercenaries who had drifted
back to Spain after an unfortunate expedition to the
Barbary coast.   Padilla had been superseded in the
command by the great nobleman of the party—Pedro de
Giron—in the hope, perhaps, that he would divide the
nobility.   The new general marched his troops from
Tordesillas into more convenient winter-quarters, but
during his absence the royalists surprised and stormed
the seat of the Junta in spite of the resistance of Acuña's
church-militant battalion of friars.   Several members of
the Junta were captured, and the queen was now under
royalist control (December 1520).   Giron was suspected
of treason—perhaps unjustly.   Like other leaders he had
undoubtedly negotiated, but the subsequent vengeance
of the Crown would seem to contradict the popular belief.
Finding his position intolerable he withdrew to his
father's estates, and took no further part in the rising.

The appointment of a new captain led to fresh divisions.   The moderates at Valladolid, represented now by
the members of the Junta, preferred the President, Pedro
Laso, the capable politician.   The mob, however, insisted
on the nomination of the dashing soldier, Padilla, who,
on the news of Giron's retirement, had once more led his
Toledans to Valladolid.   He whipped up the flagging
energies of the Communes, signalising his appointment
by storming the fortress of Torrelobaton—an operation
so important that Adrian once more thought that the
royal cause was lost.

The nobles, it is true, had not an easy task, for the
conflict had become a social war and spread from town

to country. The peasants began to take up arms against
their lords, while the towns organised attack on their
urban palaces; the last act of the Communes before
their final defeat was to enrol bands, to plunder the
nobles' houses. It is not surprising, if the nobles had
their waverings, their momentary longings to purchase
security for their flocks and fields and palaces by compromise. They were also much divided—so jealous of
each other, complained Adrian, that any noble would
gladly lose an eye if it cost one to his rival. The
Admiral and the Constable represented different principles; the latter was for fight—the former for compromise. The Admiral had led the constitutional opposition
on Charles's arrival in Spain; he would only act on
receiving full powers to treat; he guaranteed to the
towns concessions which met all but their most extreme
demands.

Charles in his instructions to the co-regents had
affected a consciousness of strength which he could not
have possessed. He gave them authority to summon
the Cortes, but they must make no concessions without
reference to himself, and must not abate one jot of the
royal authority. They were ordered to disperse the
Junta, and to deprive for ever of their representation
any towns which refused to send deputies to the Cortes.
Even the fighting Constable represented that extensive
concessions were inevitable, that the *alcabala* and the
subsidy must be placed on their former footing, that the
abuses of purveyance must be limited, offices confined
to natives, the export of precious metals prohibited, and
an amnesty offered. Charles had not supported his
brave words by energetic action; the Constable and
Admiral were as completely ignored as had been the
Cardinal. "I am astonished," wrote the Constable on

November 3, 1520, " to see the little attention which
your Highness vouchsafes to the interests of our kingdoms and their pacification, for neither in the shape of
money, men or artillery has your Majesty sent me any
aid—no, not even in paper and ink." If the nobles
received no resources from abroad, they found few at
home. The Communes had inveighed in their memorial
against the appropriation of royal lands by the magnates;
yet they themselves had laid hands upon lands and
mines and salt-works, had swept into the rebel treasury
the proceeds of the *alcabala* and the Bulls of *Cruzada*.

Notwithstanding their difficulties and divisions the
nobles began to prove themselves the better men. They
had more self-restraint, more guile. It was, perhaps, no
bad thing that repression and conciliation had their respective advocates in the Constable and Admiral. The
royalists, while ceaselessly negotiating, gradually increased their strength. The Admiral had practically
detached Pedro Laso and other leaders from the popular
cause before the decisive action of the war was fought.
At no period, perhaps, since early Crusading days have
the Spanish nobility displayed more ability and vital
force.

The resistance of the insurgents was now concentrated
in two distinct centres—Toledo and Valladolid. The
Bishop of Zamora, who had led large levies to Valladolid,
could not act in concert with the other chiefs, and circumstances drew him southwards. Toledo was being
almost blockaded by the royalist leader, Antonio de
Zuñiga, Prior of San Juan, with his local levies.
Moreover at this juncture the young non-resident Archbishop, Guillaume de Croy, had died. Charles's ambassador at Rome, Juan Manuel, had for months been
pressing for the punishment of the Bishop—this Second

Luther; but the Papacy had unaccountably delayed. Acuña had interest both at Rome and the French court, and now with a view to embarrass Charles, the French envoy was urging upon Leo X. the appointment of the hero of the Communes to the primacy of Castile. Marching to the relief of Toledo, the Bishop, after a severe defeat, entered the town alone and without martial following, for it was Good Friday. The people recognised him, bore him shoulder-high up the nave of the cathedral, and seating him on the throne, proclaimed him their Archbishop. Demagogue as he was, he could scarcely regard popular acclamation as a canonical election. He tried therefore to starve the Canons into ratifying the people's will, but the Chapter manfully stood the test. The scene in the cathedral produced a profound sensation throughout Spain. The classes which had led the revolution were not prepared for revolt against both Church and King, though it is true that the fighting Bishop was orthodox, and would make the sign of the cross before bringing down his man. Many of the clergy were now actively preaching peace. Outside the walls of Toledo the conflict was carried on with peculiar ferocity between the Bishop and the Prior, but the inferior dignitary proved the better soldier.

The war was decided not at Toledo, but in the North. Padilla was a dashing soldier, but no campaigner; his energies always seemed exhausted by a single stroke. He made no use of his success at Torrelobaton, and towards the end of April 1521 the Constable marched from Burgos to effect a junction with his son and the Admiral, who moved from Tordesillas. Padilla, with forces much superior to either division, failed to prevent the junction, whereupon he resolved to make for Toro, hoping to be reinforced by the Western towns, Sala-

manca, Zamora and Leon.   On April 23 the noble
cavalry, having outpaced their infantry, came up with
the insurgents.   Few skirmishes have won the reputation of that of Villalar.   Infantry struggling knee-
keep in mud against driving rain for the shelter of the
little town ahead, heavy artillery sticking in the miry
ruts, a few shots from the royalist light guns, a charge of
noble horse, a headlong flight of gunners and pikemen,
a reckless defence by Padilla and five comrades,—such
was the action which, at the cost of a single life to the
royal cause, destroyed that of revolution for ever.

On the morrow Padilla and two other leaders, Juan
Bravo, captain of Segovia, and Francisco Maldonado,
captain of Salamanca, were executed.   Before death
Padilla wrote the letters to his town and to his wife,
which are among the permanent treasures of Spanish
literature and history.   Valladolid at once welcomed the
victorious nobles, and resistance among the northern
Communes withered away.   Toledo, under Padilla's
widow and Acuña, gallantly held out, but its geographical isolation had always been the weakness of the
communal movement.   Acuña, seeing that the game
was lost, fled for France, but was captured on the
frontiers of Navarre.   Toledo capitulated in October,
though fresh troubles delayed its final reduction until
February 1522.   Padilla's widow escaped to Portugal.
She had proved herself, perhaps, the most capable of the
insurgent chiefs, and may claim to be the latest Castilian
leader of revolt against the direct Habsburg line.

The reduction of the northern Communes was followed
by an ill-timed French invasion.   Navarre was easily
overrun, but the heroic defence of loyalist Logroño saved
the frontiers of Castile.   Francis I. had intrigued with
Acuña and other rebel leaders, yet in the very thick of

the rebellion it had been recognised that a French war
would be the surest means of rallying the insurgents
round the Crown.   Had not the government's supposed
French sympathies been among the direct causes of the
outbreak?   In the Constable's army noble victors and
conquered citizens vied in patriotism.   It drove the
French back through Navarre, inflicting a severe defeat
upon them at Pamplona.   Castile was now at peace,
and could await its king's return.

If the atmosphere of Castile had cleared before
Charles arrived, the skies of Valencia were still overcast.
Civil war had in this kingdom preceded and outlasted the
rising of the Communes in Castile.[1]   It differed from the
latter in character as being essentially a social war, a
war of classes, in which the Crown became only incident-
ally involved.   The movement spread into the southern
fringe of Aragon, and reached, perhaps, its climax in the
island of Majorca.   The Valencian nobility had resented
Charles's refusal to hold their Cortes in person, and had
refused to recognise the regent Adrian as his substitute.
They soon, however, found themselves threatened by
the population of their wealthy capital.   Adrian, not
realising the gravity of the situation, gave some encouragement to the latter, and allowed the people to arm
and organise under pretext of resisting an attack from
Moorish corsairs.   An accidental spark set ablaze passions
which had long been smouldering, and the flame leaped
from the capital to the farthest limits of the kingdom.
It was an attempt to substitute a democracy for the
oppressive rule which in the eastern Spanish kingdoms
the nobility, unchecked owing to the constitutional
weakness of the Crown, had exercised over the middle
and lower classes.   The capital formed a central repre-

[1] See M. Danvila, *La Germania de Valencia*, 1884.

sentative Committee of Thirteen, and corresponding committees were elected in every Valencian town. This or some such organisation was intended to be permanent.

The control soon passed from the wealthier classes, who had a definite political programme, to the lower, whose aim was massacre and plunder. The moderates, therefore, ultimately swung back towards the nobles, who had been taken by surprise and outmatched, and thus the balance was restored. The ferocity of the conflict differed widely from the half-hearted military operations of the Castilian Communes, and it was decided by a terrible street fight within the walls of the capital. In Valencia, moreover, the cleavage between the classes was absolute, for only one small town gave any support to the nobles, and not a noble fought in the popular ranks. It is characteristic of the separatism of the Spanish kingdoms that the insurgents of Valencia received no aid from the Castilian Communes. The gentry were, however, aided towards the end by members of their own class from Murcia and Andalusia, while, after Charles returned, the Crown itself took some part in stamping out the embers.

It was probably not of design that Charles had delayed his coming to Castile. Yet it was a fortunate accident. The Crown had extinguished revolt at the cost of others; it had not incurred the personal odium entailed by active intervention. Charles could appear rather as a judge than as a party in the trial of the surviving leaders of the Communes. He had ordered 4000 Spaniards to sail for the protection of the Netherlands, and to replace these he brought with him a corresponding force of Germans and a train of fine artillery. For the introduction of this foreign force the French occupation of Fuenterrabia and the defence of Navarre gave a reasonable pretext, but the real motive was perhaps another. The passage of the seventy-four guns, small and big, bombards and falconets, across the mountains from Santander to Valladolid was an object-lesson not readily forgotten. The names of the biggest cannon still survive—the Great Dragon and the Great Devil, the Young She-Ass and the Young He-Ass, the Saint James and Saint James the Less, the Wait-for-me-I'm-coming-there. The mules that dragged the guns alone were 2128, their drivers 1064. The monarchy meant to assert itself in the face alike of its late enemies and allies. Charles had been warned from Spain not to place himself at the mercy of the nobles, who had shown some desire to reap the profits of their victory ; he had no wish to advance the class which, until the recent conflict, had been the chief danger to the monarchy.

Charles had a high ideal of kingly dignity. If in his extreme weakness he had refused to sacrifice a jot of the royal prerogative, he was unlikely in his hour of strength to condone a rebellion which had been within an ace of costing him his crown. The nobles had used their victory with moderation ; they now implored the king to grant a liberal amnesty. The loss of the Communes in their final defeat had been numerically so slight, that their power was really not quite broken. Moreover there were few noble houses in Castile of which some member was not compromised ; for families had been divided as well as cities. Most of the nobles, and above all the Admiral, had felt that the rebellion had much justification in the anti-national measures of the Crown. Charles was not cruel, but he could not easily forgive. From his amnesty less than three hundred were excluded, and few of these suffered the

penalty of death. This number was not large considering the width and depth of the revolt. But the punishment was long-drawn; the quality of mercy was unknown to Charles; just sentences must be executed
to their lawful limits. Even in the hour of thanks-
giving for the victory of Pavia, forgiveness was not
extended to families whose heads had been exiled or
ruined, and which had. lost all possibility of political
influence.

Confiscation in the case of treason was at that age
considered a regular incident of the revenue, and hence
historians have ascribed the exceptions from Charles's
amnesty to fiscal reasons. The list of the condemned
does not, however, bear this out, for the large majority
were men of no position, ranging from lawyers to
friars and artisans, while in other cases confiscation was
afterwards remitted. Padilla's widow was never allowed
to return to Spain, while the Bishop of Zamora's fate
created a European sensation. Adrian VI. had granted
him a pardon, but the trial was renewed at the instance of the Crown. At length the fierce old man,
despairing of liberty, enticed the governor of the prison
to his cell, and brought him to the ground with a large
pebble concealed in a leather bag which professedly
contained his breviary. He completed the murder
with a knife, tied the body by the leg to his bed, and
then summoned the victim's son, who only escaped
his father's fate by precipitate retreat. Acuña was
for this crime incontinently hanged by secular authority, without respect for Pope or Bishop, and it was not
at once that Charles received absolution for this breach
of clerical privilege. The Bishop's end was a dramatic
dénouement to the tragedy of the communal revolt.
The king's severity in the punishment of the rebels

and in Acuña's execution has been commonly stigmatised as a blot upon his fame, but no Valois, and
certainly no Tudor, would have so lightly chastised so
dangerous a rebellion.

The rising of the Communes cleared the air for the
rest of Charles's reign. There was no further prospect
of successful resistance to the Crown. The two parties
watched each other, and the Crown could in case of
need rely upon the vanquished against the victors. It
has, indeed, been held that such was the deliberate
policy of Philip II.'s government. Charles had not
the imagination to realise a situation from a distance,
but he had sufficient common sense to learn his lesson
when it was beneath his eyes. If he was never to be
popular in Castile, he was henceforth at least judicious.
When pressed for favours by his brother and his aunt,
he earnestly insisted that Castile was for Castilians.
He very rarely conferred Castilian benefices or honours
upon foreigners. In Aragon he was less scrupulous,
but here also he drew back in face of opposition.

The chastisement of the Valencian revolt was entrusted by Charles to his grandfather's widow, Germaine
de Foix, now governor of Valencia, who inflicted it with
cruelty. The financial aspects of rebellion here received
much attention. Even if the ringleaders were worth
only powder and shot, the strong corporate character
of the towns, with their wide territories and considerable wealth, gave the Crown the opportunities of fine
and confiscation. The loss of life and the material
ruin in the kingdom of Valencia had been enormous,
and the sequel of the civil war was even more permanently disastrous.

The popular party had, as has been seen, been
armed against the African Moors, who were believed

to have an understanding with their numerous co-
religionists in Valencia; whereas the nobles, whose
wealth depended on their Moorish tenants, were believed to be backward in defence. The actual revolt
had begun with an incident of religious savagery—an
attack upon a notorious sinner who was doing penance,
and upon the clergy who had made his punishment too
light. Thus from the very outset there was an element
of religious fanaticism, and as early as July 1521 a
Franciscan friar was crying in Valencia, "Long live
the faith of Christ, and death to the Saracen." During
the war the Moorish peasantry fought for their masters,
and whenever the democracy got the upper hand they
were either slaughtered or forcibly converted—sometimes, indeed, converted first and slaughtered afterwards.
After the suppression of the rebellion the converts
frequently returned to their former faith, but the Inquisition held that by conversion the Moors had subjected
themselves to the law relating to relapsed heretics.

Hitherto, under the influence of Adrian of Utrecht,
the Holy Office had shown singular moderation towards
the Moorish or Morisco population. The king had
given up the proceeds of confiscation to build churches
for the converts; the term within which relapsed
heretics might be reconciled to the Church was extended; the obligation of wearing the *sanbenito* after
public abjuration was no longer imposed. Adrian had
ordered that arrests must only be made on direct and
conclusive testimony, and this merciful provision, which
had been grossly neglected, was yet further insisted
upon by Adrian's successor, Manrique. Nevertheless
the spirit of persecution was still alive, and after the
Valencian civil war the idea arose of converting the
whole of the Moorish population of the kingdom. It

was known that the nobles would resist, because Moorish in contradistinction to Christian tenants paid double charges, and were restricted in their power of movement, but, by leaving these relations unaltered in the case of the new converts, it was thought that the opposition might be overcome.[1]

It was necessary for Charles to obtain a Papal Bull releasing him from his oath that he would not impose Christianity on the Moors. This was granted in May 1524, but there was in high quarters an evident reluctance to persecution, and eighteen months elapsed before the Bull was published. Meanwhile in March 1525 a great Junta was held, consisting of the Councils of Castile, Aragon, the Inquisition, the Military Orders and the Indies. Cardinal Manrique was president; eminent theologians were summoned to attend; the Emperor himself took part in the proceedings. The result of the deliberations was the declaration that the Moors forcibly baptized were Christians, that their children must be baptized, and that buildings in which Mass had once been said must never again be used as mosques. All the expert evidence—that of the Council of Aragon, the nobility of Valencia, even of the Bishop—was in favour of a merciful solution. Owing to the enormous number of the Moors affected Charles did, indeed, apply for a Bull modifying the severity of the usual procedure, but he sternly rebuked the nobles who were showing favour to the Moors.

The Commissaries sent to Valencia to execute decisions of the Junta at once found themselves involved in difficulties which had not been unforeseen. Some of them at least were men of moderation, and it is

[1] This subject is fully treated by H. C. Lea in the *Moriscos of Spain*, 1901, from which book my short account is mainly derived.

possible that the fever for conversion might have worn itself out but for the victory of Pavia. Charles now took an intense personal interest in the question. When it was urged that forced reconversion would only lead to untold trouble, he would reply that all great deeds were difficult. To his intolerance on this occasion no parallel is found until after his abdication ; he seems to have been subject to a fit of religious exaltation consequent on the unexpected mercy which God had vouchsafed in the capture of Francis I.; he believed it to be his duty to repay his debt. In November 1525 the alternative of conversion or expulsion was offered to all the Moors of the kingdom of Aragon. To discourage the alternative of exile, and to prevent the unconverted Moors from reinforcing their brethren in Africa, it was decreed that distant Corunna should be the port of embarkation. One month's grace was given to the Valencian Moors, and two to those of Catalonia and Aragon. Against the decree the authorities protested, while the more warlike Moors replied to it by taking to the Sierra. The reluctance of the local magistrates to extreme measures, and the recalcitrance of a great lord, the Duke of Segorbe, doubtless strengthened the spirit of opposition. Edict followed upon edict, but the Moors organised a desperate resistance in the mountains. Beating back their invaders they retaliated upon Christian villages, and desecrated the churches. This caused indescribable emotion among the Christian population. A crusade was preached, and the mountain district was surrounded by Christians from all parts of Spain. Again and again the local and royal troops were driven back, until at length Charles sent to their aid the German *landsknechts* whom he had brought to Spain. It is an

illustration of the poor quality of Spanish soldiery
when fighting in their own country, that the Germans
at once brought to a successful issue this little mountain war, in which hitherto half-armed peasantry had
carried off the honours.

Reference has been made to a Sicilian rising. This
was, in fact, the earliest marked event in Charles's reign
over his Spanish kingdoms. It lay, however, so far
outside the main current of his life,—it affected so little
his personal movements,—that it may be more convenient to remove it from its chronological place, and
consider it in connection with the Spanish troubles.
The disturbances began in 1516 and virtually closed
in 1518. It was only in 1522 that a threatened recrudescence brought them into any connection with
European politics. They have usually received scant
attention, but it is unjust to ignore them, because they
serve to emphasise the difficulties of Charles, while the
temper in which they were treated compares favourably
with the clumsy handling of Castilian and Valencian
disaffection.[1]

The Sicilian revolt resembles most nearly that of
Castile. As the Castilians rose against Flemish government, and as the Communes refused to recognise
Adrian's regency, so the Sicilians resented Spanish
influences and insisted that the viceroy Ugo de
Moncada's office expired with the death of Ferdinand.
It was in its origin a rising of the nobles and the
domain towns, forming two branches of the Parliament
of the realm, against a peculiarly unpopular viceroy,
who found support in the bureaucracy centred in the
Royal Council, which consisted mainly of lawyers.

[1] A detailed account of this rising may be found in *La Sicilia sotto Carlo V.*,
by I. La Lumia, 1862.

Palermo, the capital, played throughout a prominent part, through the agency both of its municipality and its mob, and exercised an influence quite peculiar over the whole island, with one great exception. The actual revolt began, indeed, with the people of Palermo, and the municipality for a time assumed the lead.

Moncada, expelled from Palermo, took refuge in Messina, the sole town which would receive him. This brisk, commercial city had long been, and was, in the coming centuries, to be the rival of the capital. Messina was almost a republic within the monarchy, but throughout it remained loyal, though split by the factions of nobles and burghers, in the hope of supplanting its ancient enemy. Elsewhere, as in Castile, municipal and fiscal officers, known to be favourable to the government, were killed or hunted out, taxes were abolished, and the town councils elected by the populace. Then the nobles obtained more influence, and a provisional government was established under the presidency of the Counts of Golisano and Cammarata. A commissioner was despatched to Brussels to express the fervent loyalty of the island, but to demand the deposition of Moncada, and the abolition of the new-fangled Inquisition, which had from the first been the object of fierce attack.

Charles cited both Moncada and the so-called Presidents to his court. With great patience he heard both sides. Moncada was not allowed to return, but was shortly afterwards placed in command of a fleet destined for Africa. The Presidents were detained under honourable pretexts. The Count of Monteleone, a Neapolitan noble, was appointed as temporary lieutenant-governor; the acts of the provisional government were annulled as unconstitutional; the suppressed taxes were restored; an amnesty was granted to all

save a few who had been guilty of the most violent
outrages (April 1517).   Thus ended the first stage of
the Sicilian troubles.   There had been much disorder,
but little disloyalty.   The motive cause had been the
personal unpopularity of Moncada, aggravated by the
novel form of Inquisition introduced by Ferdinand and
by a new tax imposed in 1514.   Charles and his
government had so far incurred no dislike.   Golisano,
the most prominent and capable figure in the movement,
died shortly afterwards fighting gallantly in the
Imperial cause at the battle of Bicocca.

Very different was the second stage of rebellion.
Monteleone, as a Neapolitan, was fully as much a
foreigner to the Sicilians as was Moncada.   He
naturally fell under the influence of the royal officials
who had formed Moncada's following, and discontent
began to revive.   One Squarcialupo, belonging to an
influential burgher family of Pisan origin, now natural-
ised at Palermo, began the attack on the government
with a few personal friends of his own class.   The mob,
after some hesitation, joined the little gang, and perpetrated a series of brutal murders.   Monteleone himself
was treated with respect, but was virtually a captive.
Once more the influence of Palermo immediately
affected the whole island with the exception of Messina ;
but on this occasion the attack upon officials and the
Inquisition was yet more violent.   There were occasional
protestations of loyalty, but there is no doubt that
Squarcialupo, relying on the distance and embarrassments of Charles, intended to drive the Aragonese
government from the island, and establish some form of
Sicilian republic.   The nobles at first looked on ; some
of them then tentatively joined the movement, and this
at once produced rivalry and division in the head-

quarters of the insurgents at Palermo; meanwhile, just as in Southern Spain, the troubles gave the opportunity for the revival of faction fights between the old family parties in the other Sicilian towns.

The reaction of the majority of the nobles against the popular aspirations proved, as in Castile, decisive. The rebellion ended much as it began. A group of nobles surprised and killed Squarcialupo in Palermo (September 1517). Charles, after some delay, despatched a considerable body of troops, and the revolt withered away. It is remarkable that the Parliament which assembled in 1518 was very bold in its demands for reforms which were all in a national sense; these comprised the monopoly of civil office and benefices by natives, the enforced residence of the clergy, the modification of the Inquisition, the formation of a Sicilian militia, the retention of the galleys paid by Sicilian taxes for the protection of the Sicilian coasts. Monteleone, now formally appointed viceroy, was instructed to meet these demands half-way. The results were in favour of the aristocracy, to whom the king owed his hold upon the island. They received additional judicial privileges in their fiefs, while the municipal government of Palermo shrank in importance until nearly the close of Charles's reign.

Sicily was not yet quite safe. There was, or might have been, a third stage of rebellion. As the former two were essentially indigenous, the third was mainly international. In 1522 the French government, and especially the French party in Adrian VI.'s cardinalate, headed by Soderini, thought to hamper Charles by raking up revolt in Sicily. The movement was a combination of *condottieri* and cardinals with Sicilian exiles and local busy-bodies. It centred in the Count of

Cammarata, one of the two original insurgent Presidents who had been allowed to return to the island. The ramifications were very wide—so wide indeed that the government could hardly fail to discover them. On this occasion there was much letting of malcontent blood, and Sicily had peace.

A comparison of the three uprisings in his Spanish and Sicilian kingdoms within five years of his accession will help to prove how complicated was the task of Charles. Spain, as Jiménez had urged, could not be ruled without a king, and yet it was impossible that the Emperor should always be resident in Spain. The rising of the Communes was the most complex of the three. The national factor had undoubtedly predominated, but the latter stages of the war had shown the existence of social cleavage between nobles and burghers, between landlords and peasantry. The economic and constitutional grievances had a strong nationalist tinge ; the protective measures demanded by the Junta were outwardly the result of the rapacity of Charles's Flemish suite ; the outcry against the subsidy of Corunna was mainly due to the belief that it would be expended on objects in which Castilians had no interest. On the other hand kings purely national had been or were to be the recipients of very similar petitions.

It would be rash to assume that foreign influences alone caused the clash between the two growing elements in the state,—the cities and the Crown. The religious factor, as has been seen, counted for little in the rising of Castile, and had a distinct nationalist character. Had Leo X. yielded to the royal entreaties and condemned the Bishop of Zamora, the Communes might readily have asserted the independence of the national

Church, and then Castilian orthodoxy might have been imperilled, for heresy treads close on the heels of schism. The quarrels at the Council of Trent in later years turned mainly on the assertion of independence by the Spanish episcopate ; nor, by way of retort, was it spared the charge of heresy. In addition to the national claims was also to be noticed now, as before and here-after, a certain secular resistance to the financial and judicial pressure of the clergy. In Spain, however, the clergy was of old so directly dependent on the Crown, that this resistance easily associated itself with constitutional opposition to the monarchy. The proceeds of the indulgence system in Spain went mainly, it must be remembered, into the coffers of the Crown. It was not quite a foregone conclusion that in any general upheaval Castile would remain Romanist; she had not, indeed, suffered so much from Rome as had Germany, but her position had some similarity to that of England.

In Valencia the troubles had been less complex. The probable opposition of the nobility to the Crown had been smothered by the fierce rising of the Communes against the nobles, and the Crown had only ultimately intervened in the cause of order. The radical changes in the constitution, demanded or effected by the revolutionary party, had been directed against the predominance, not of the Crown, but of the nobility, under the existing system. The religious motive had been prominent from first to last. It was characteris-tically Spanish and followed the lines of the social cleavage. In the people rather than among the nobility the crusading spirit survived. The people, priding itself on its pure blue blood, looked with hatred and disdain on the Jewish or Moorish taint which they traced or fancied in the gentry. The pleasant and profitable relations of the nobles and their Moorish tenants excited at once fanaticism and envy, and in the final stage of the war the Moors were attacked because they were at once infidels and their masters' loyal servants.

In Sicily the personal element counted for more than in Castile and Valencia; but the chief feature of the rising, apart from this, was its national character. Although the nobles finally decided the conflict in favour of the Crown against the citizens, and although there were instances of sanguinary struggles between local magnates and their feudatory towns, the social cleavage was not so distinct as in Castile, and much less so than in Valencia. Economic discontent appeared, but was not very prominent. The religious factor, taking the form of hostility to the Inquisition, had much more weight. There was, however, in this no taint of unorthodoxy; it was part and parcel of the national question. The Sicilians resisted the Inquisition as being an alien institution; they begged only to return to its old diocesan form; opposition had in the previous reign taken precisely the same direction in Aragon. The importance of the city of Palermo caused the Sicilian movement to assume a singularly modern type of revolution, although this may be compared to the part played by the city of Valencia, and in a somewhat less degree by Toledo. The Sicilian nobles gained more by their victory than did their Castilian and Valencian compeers, but the chief gainer was, in Sicily as in Castile, the Crown.

CHAPTER VI

Importance of a mutual understanding to Pope and Emperor—Leo X.'s
attitude during the Imperial election and afterwards—He finally
decides for alliance with Charles—His desire for war in Italy—
The resources and alliances of Charles and Francis—The condition
of Italy—The Medici and Venice—The smaller dynasties—The
smaller republics—The Orsini and Colonna, the Guelphs and Ghibellines—Italian sentiment and Italian soldiery—The weakness of
Charles in Naples and Sicily—The separation of France from
Milan by Piedmont, Montferrat, and Saluzzo.

" LET His Majesty pay more attention to a little monk
named Luther." This was the advice proffered to
Charles by Juan Manuel, Imperial ambassador at Rome,
whose duty it was to bribe or frighten the Pope from
the French alliance, which seemed ever imminent.
Charles did, indeed, pay more attention to the little
monk than Leo relished, and this perhaps contributed
to his change of policy, even though territorial considerations may have been more decisive. It is at all
events significant that, on the day after Luther's condemnation, was despatched to the Pope the draft of a
treaty which became the basis of an offensive and
defensive league. Throughout the earliest stages of
the diet of Worms the Pope's political intentions were
still obscure, and Charles thought it needful to convince
him that religious orthodoxy must be reciprocated by
political solidarity—that the Lutheran difficulty could
not be isolated from the Italian problem.

If the Emperor's aid were essential to the Pope for the suppression of Lutheran heresy, there could be no question that the Papal alliance was of paramount importance to Charles in view of the inevitable war. In Italy the Pope held the balance between Charles and Francis, even as Henry VIII. was believed to be able to turn the scale in Europe. Lord of the Papal States and master of Florence, Leo X. wielded no inconsiderable material power. To the side which he might join he gave the opportunity of the offensive ; he could bring the French to the Neapolitan frontiers, or could let the Imperialists loose on Lombardy. The Swiss were believed to be the determining military factor in the coming wars, and the cantons were expected to act in concert with the Pope. Leo, moreover, had the power of the purse. Francis, indeed, could bleed his clergy almost at will, but for Charles it was impossible to raise ecclesiastical subsidies save by Papal consent, and without such subsidies he could not fight.

Throughout the reign of Charles his relations to the Papacy were of such paramount importance that the policy of Leo X. at this crisis is worth consideration.[1] If the Crown of Aragon was to retain its hold upon Naples, the alliance of the Papacy was essential. The Papal claim to the investiture was no mere form ; the Pope's refusal could create a rallying-point for aristocratic disaffection. The nobility were always opposed to Aragonese rule, or, as tradition had it, to the actual ruler. The abandonment by Pius II. of the traditional Guelphic for a Ghibelline policy, of the Angevin for the Aragonese alliance, had determined the retention of

---

[1] Leo X.'s diplomacy is the subject of a monograph by F. Nitti, *Leone X. e la sua Politica,* 1892. See also B. Fritsche, *Die Päpstliche Politik und die Deutsche Kaiserwahl,* 1909.

Naples by Alfonso of Aragon's illegitimate issue. This lesson was remembered when the legitimate line of Aragon ousted the bastard branch. Throughout the troubled, shifty pontificate of Julius II. the constant factor was the understanding between the Pope and Ferdinand. Leo X. had been forced by the victory of Marignano into a French alliance, but had Ferdinand lived he would have changed all that, and Charles, as ruler of Naples, must needs pick up the line of Ferdinand's policy at the point where it was broken.

This reconnection would have been easy had Charles been only King of Spain, but the waters were troubled to their depths by his candidature for the Empire. It was an old maxim of the Papacy that the ruler of Naples must not be Emperor, and, if the assiduity of Maximilian in pressing his Imperial claims on Northern and Central Italy be considered, the nervousness of Leo X. for the temporal independence of the Papacy was natural. Hence Leo, almost to the last moment, had resisted the election of Charles. On the other hand Francis was far stronger, or at least could more easily mobilise than Charles, and he combined a very definite claim on Naples with the actual possession of Milan. Thus Leo had vainly groped for a candidate which should be neither France nor Spain, the possessor of neither Milan nor Naples. In despair he had made the mistake of throwing his weight on the side of France, and in the temper of Germany this went far to determine the success of Charles. No one was more interested than Leo X. in an honest national election to the Empire, and yet no one had so strenuously prejudiced its prospects. In this matter, if they had only known it, the interests of Leo and of Luther were identical. Leo X. accepted and exaggerated Machia-

velli's principle of the danger of neutrality to a weak
state. He must not only side with one or other of two
combatants, but he must drive them into war, that he
might take a side. To Leo, as to some preceding and
succeeding Popes, the danger, territorial and ecclesiastical, was an accord of the great powers. He knew,
perhaps, of the conference of Cambrai in March 1517,
where the partition of Northern and Central Italy
between Habsburg and Valois had been discussed. The
temporal power could only exist by stimulating war.
Leo's policy was the reverse of Wolsey's. The latter
hoped to retain the influence of England over Europe by
prolonging a peace of which she should be the arbiter.
The former would provoke a war in order to gain
territorial accessions which would make him independent of either foreign power in Italy.

The Pope's difficulty was to know which side to
join. It should be the weaker—but which was the
weaker? Charles's election frightened him, and he
at first urged on France an offensive quintuple alliance
in conjunction with Venice, England and the Swiss.
He finally, however, concluded that Charles was the
weaker, and thus Charles in Italy was really helped
by his misfortunes, by the rising in Spain, by the
weakness and mutiny of his Italian forces, by his total
want of funds, by the wealth and power of France.
But Leo was not content with the mere negative
security which war might give; he must add positively
to his own temporal power, and here Charles was more
generous than Francis. The latter offered to extend
the Papal territory to the Garigliano, and to confer
Naples on a French cadet who should be guided by
a Papal legate. But the ambition of the Medici lay
northwards; Leo wished for a free hand against

Ferrara, and for the recovery of Parma and Piacenza,
which had been restored to Milan after the French
victory at Marignano. All this Charles was prepared
to give. Francis, indeed, under extreme pressure,
consented implicitly to abandon his best ally, the
Duke of Ferrara, but Leo knew that he did not mean
it, and that the Venetians, allies of France, would do
their utmost to thwart it. Nor was Leo insensible to
the services which Charles might render in respect of
Luther, to the danger of whose preaching he was now
thoroughly awake.

From October 1520 Leo's hesitation was, perhaps,
only apparent, and caused by that of Charles. He
played with the French to force Charles into his alliance, and to get a safe-conduct for his Swiss mercenaries through Lombardy. These he intended from the
first to employ against the French king, but he persuaded him that they were required to protect Papal
territory from the mutinous Spanish troops who had
gathered on the Neapolitan frontier. To the moment
of his treaty with Charles in May 1521 he led the
French envoys to believe that their master had only to
hold out his hand. It was a masterpiece of deceit.

With or without the Pope war must sooner or
later come, but Leo undoubtedly forced the pace of its
arrival. The surest proof of Charles's reluctance to be
pushed into an Italian war was his hesitation to accept
the Papal offers. Over and over again Juan Manuel
was in despair at his master's timidity and change of
purpose. He told him plainly that he was driving the
Pope into the arms of France by incessant changes in
the terms of the treaty. Even when it was despatched, it
provided only for defensive alliance, whereas the Pope was
bent upon an offensive league stipulating for the com-

mencement of operations within two months, and such
an alliance Manuel on his own responsibility signed.

From this treaty Charles derived no direct gain;
indeed, its provisions made the Papacy so powerful that
it outweighed the Italian possessions of the Spanish
Crown. Charles offered Parma, Piacenza, Ferrara and the
suzerainty of Siena. He engaged to invest Francesco
Sforza with Milan and Antoniotto Adorno with Genoa,
as Imperial fiefs. These two native states, with a
more powerful Pope holding also Florence, would cover
Naples from French attack, and this might be considered a sufficient gain for Charles. But however
offensive military action might be, the Imperial policy
was defensive and conservative, for, with the exception
of the change of dynasty at Naples, it was a return
to the condition of Italy previous to the barbarian
invasions. Before this treaty was actually completed
the indirect attacks of Francis had goaded the Emperor
to retaliation. It may be well, however, before plunging
into the thick of the combat to consider the respective
resources of the combatants and the condition of Italy,
whose fate was thereby to be decided for the coming
centuries.

Leo X., whose self-interest made his researches
thorough and impartial, arrived at the conclusion that,
in the event of war between Charles V. and Francis I.,
the former would prove the weaker. This may seem
at first sight surprising in view of the enormous territories which the Emperor directly or indirectly ruled,
and the wealth which he could ostensibly derive from
Netherland looms or fisheries and the mines of the
Indies. The Spanish infantry had already made as
high a reputation as the French regular horse, and the
landsknechts, if not quite the equal of the Swiss, were

similarly organised and infinitely more numerous. The regular squadrons of Netherland horse were armed on the French model, while the martial gentry of Franche Comté, Artois and Hainault were in no way inferior to their French neighbours. The French artillery had, from its rapidity of firing and mobility, proved its superiority in the English and Italian wars ; Maximilian, however, had devoted much attention to this arm, and Charles followed in his footsteps ; the cannon turned out of the Augsburg foundry were not inferior to the French. France possessed many generals who had made a name in the Italian wars, while Marignano had given Francis a dazzling reputation ; on the other hand the spirit of Gonsalvo de Cordova lived not only in the Spanish but in the Neapolitan service, and Antonio de Leyva, the Marquis of Pescara and Prospero Colonna were no unworthy pupils of the Great Captain.

Charles could strike France at many points, but his rival, possessing the high advantage of moving on interior lines, could concentrate defence or attack with greater ease. If only for financial reasons this was of extreme importance, for Charles complained that the transport of his troops cost him a third more than his rival. The Emperor from Navarre could enter Gascony, while his province of Roussillon, lying north of the eastern Pyrenees, was geographically in France. But home service was unpopular in Spain, and Charles found that he could never muster a force respectable either in quantity or quality on his northern frontier. The French, moreover, could utilise disaffection in the recently conquered kingdom of Navarre, and its long-standing division into two factions gave them a certainty of the support of one. Into Castile, however, they could not hope to penetrate, for the difficult, barren country made it impossible to feed an army. As long as Francis I. retained the friendship of Savoy and the control of Genoa, his advantage in Italy was undoubted. To attack Lombardy the Spanish levies must painfully tramp through two-thirds of Italy, nor was it possible, as it afterwards became, to feed the Netherland forces with reinforcements from Italy. Franche Comté was neutralised by agreement with the Swiss, and on the Netherland frontier events justified the belief that the balance would be even.

War in the sixteenth century had become too expensive for the resources of any government. Notwithstanding the apparent wealth of the Emperor, Francis usually had larger available supplies. This was not only due to the recuperative powers of France, but to the absence of a parliamentary system. "How much can you raise from your subjects?" asked Charles of Francis in a moment of confidence. "As much as I please," was the reply. Very different was the case of Charles. In none of his possessions was there supply without consent; in each of his Spanish kingdoms, in each of his Netherland provinces, in each of his hereditary Austrian states, in Naples and in Sicily, there was a system of Estates in full working order, and all were jealous of their privilege of supply. The consequence would clearly be that even if supply were granted, it would never be in time, and hence the necessity of loans from the German banking-houses at a ruinous rate of interest, or in return for concessions which deprived the Crown of the few sources of independent income which it possessed. "Money, money—send me money!" was the perpetual wail of Charles until his abdication.

It was improbable that Francis I. would meet with serious trouble within his kingdom; the treason of Bourbon was due to the king's own folly, and the later discontent in Guyenne was not of grave importance. Charles V. seemed certain from the first to meet with resistance from either nobles or towns in one or other of his Spanish kingdoms, while religious dissent easily took hold on the lower classes in the Netherlands and on higher ranks in the Austrian territories. In Italy whichever party had most success would have to cope with most opposition; the Pope and Venice would resist the preponderance of either rival, and in any state over which France or Spain gained control, the defeated nation could rely on subsequent disaffection.

Nothing has been said of Germany, and yet on Germany everything depended. If Charles could only carry Germany with him victory was assured. "There is no such power as a united Germany, if only you could find it," was virtually Machiavelli's dictum. It was easy to foresee that the union of Germany was a vision of dreamland; it was of ill omen that, in spite of all prohibition, Francis from the first could levy as many *landsknechts* as could the Emperor. Of the German recruiting sergeants in French pay the Duke of Guelders ultimately came to terms with Charles, and William of Fürstemberg entered his service in the last campaign, but to the end the French king raised as many Germans as he could feed and pay.

No one could have doubted that the energies of the Habsburgs' Austrian territories would be fully occupied in checking the advance of the Turks up the Danube and its tributaries. In North Africa Charles's reign opened with a serious reverse, and there were already signs that the corsair squadrons of Barbary were but the uhlans of the sea-power of the Porte. Meanwhile Barbarossa single-handed could cope with the two score of galleys which had the impossible task of protecting the Emperor's Mediterranean coasts. It was, it is true, antecedently probable that the English would continue their traditional hostility to France, but Henry VIII., though he possessed some of the domestic instincts of the Turk, had little of the enterprise of Solyman, and half a century must pass before Barbarossa and Dragut found their Atlantic counterparts in England's pirate admirals.

Charles, like a true Habsburg, strove to extend his power by marriage. One sister, wedded to Christian II., was established as an outwork to command the Baltic; another in Portugal covered the flank of Castile. Mary and Ferdinand, married respectively to the King of Bohemia-Hungary and his sister, were pushed eastwards to bear the brunt of the Turkish onslaught. As time went on, Savoy, Lorraine, Milan, Florence, Mantua, the Papacy, England,—nay, France herself,—were to be swept within the Habsburg's matrimonial meshes. The Valois princes, killing themselves before they were ripe for marriage, had little chance against the earlier and more moral descendants of Maximilian. For the moment, however, the irrepressible French ally, the Duke of Guelders, did more than balance the kings of Hungary, Portugal, and Denmark.

The foreign invasions had rather modified than destroyed the political system of Italy. The five chief states were still separate entities, although Milan had fallen under the sway of France, and at Naples the legitimate line of Aragon had replaced the illegitimate, which had become a national Italian dynasty. The election of Leo X. to the Papacy had set Rome as well as Florence under the dominion of the Medici; but this personal union was not likely to be permanent, and there still survived at Florence a strong republican sentiment which would seize any opportunity to overthrow the ruling house. Venice, notwithstanding her losses in Apulia and Romagna, and the cession of Cremona, was still rich and powerful—the more powerful, perhaps, for being the more compact. Yet her relations to the French ruler of Milan and the Spanish ruler of Naples differed widely from her attitude towards the two states when under weaker, independent dynasties. Moreover the filching of the spice trade by Portugal was sapping her wealth, while her strength was being drained by the incessant advance of the Turk in the Levant and the Adriatic. She was therefore no longer the enterprising state which had threatened to absorb all Italy; her policy, with the exception of one moment, was, throughout the reign of Charles V., marked by cautious, tentative alliances or by obstinate neutrality. The best of manners secured for her diplomatists the best of information, and in times so tangled knowledge was no bad substitute for action.

Of the smaller dynasties many had been destroyed in the first two decades of the century, but some still survived to play a considerable part in the ensuing wars. Mantua and Ferrara were important from the strong geographical position of their capitals, situated in peculiarly fertile territories. Their rulers had inherited political wisdom of the Italian type, and considerable control over the military market; Ferrara possessed, perhaps, the best artillery in Europe. The marquisate of Mantua was an Imperial fief, and the neighbourhood of its powerful Guelphic neighbours, Milan and Venice, made Imperialism almost a necessity of existence. The position of the house of Este was more complex. Ferrara was a Papal fief; the sympathies of the house had been for half a century French, and before long the marriage of Ercole to Renée, daughter of Louis XII., seemed likely to intensify this sentiment. On the other hand Modena and Reggio, the former of which has given its more modern title to the house, were Imperial fiefs. The main factor, however, in Ferrarese policy was the ambition of almost every Pope to annex this too independent fief, and thus the duke's proclivity towards France or Spain must vary inversely with the Pope's alliance with either of these powers.

The Duke of Urbino, a Papal feudatory, might have passed without notice but for a mistaken belief in his military ability, and the temporary annexation of his duchy by the Medici, which made him the inveterate enemy of the house—a fact not without its future importance to Charles V. Two other princelings deserve a word of notice. Mirandola, a tiny state situated between Mantua and Cremona, had been celebrated only as the home of Pico, and as the scene of Julius II.'s martial enterprise. Its prince, by placing himself under French protection, became under Charles V. a source of much danger and annoyance to Milan and to Florence. On the Tuscan littoral the weakness of the Appiani, lords of Piombino and Elba, gave them a factitious importance, because, when the struggle for supremacy in the Western Mediterranean became acute, the eyes of France and Spain, of Pope and Florentines, were directed to their undefended ports.

Among the republics Lucca slept comfortably, but for intermittent nightmares, in the arms of its impassive oligarchy. Far different were Genoa and Siena, which for centuries had restlessly tossed in the fever

of faction.   Genoa had long recognised French suzerainty, and yet she claimed to be a chamber of the
Empire; practically she had fallen under Milanese control, tempered by a large measure of self-government.
The conquest of Milan gave Francis I. a doubly strong
position in Genoa, but the ruling faction governed the
city in French interests.   This advantage, however,
was lessened by the fact that no small proportion of
the leading citizens were always exiles, and therefore
enemies of the existing order.   A glance or a thought
will show the momentous importance of Genoa in a
struggle for the possession of Lombardy between the
rulers of Barcelona and Marseilles.   Siena was still
distracted by the quarrels of the *Monti*, which were
successive strata of dominant factions, social or political,
whose horizontal formation was disturbed by chronic
seismic upheaval.   This would not have mattered, but
for the situation of the state, which lay on the high-
road from Rome to Florence, and would therefore form
a convenient appanage for a Papal *nipote*, while the
rulers of Florence would gladly annex the territory of
an old enemy, and so convert a source of danger and
disorder into one of power and profit.   The Sienese
ports, moreover, in spite of Dante's gibes, were useful
in the days of galleys, and, like those of the Appiani,
might give a *pied-à-terre* either to French or Turk.

Of much military importance were the two Roman
noble houses of Orsini and Colonna, round whom were
grouped the lesser martial families of the Campagna.
The Orsini lying immediately to the north and the
Colonna to the south of Rome, both having their urban
palaces and both exercising an influence in the Conclave
or Consistory, they became the regular instruments of
the great powers in putting pressure on the Papacy.

As a rule the Orsini preserved their Guelphic and
the Colonna their Ghibelline traditions. The foreign
invasions had given a new meaning and a fresh violence
to these long-lived factions. The Guelphs were now the
French, the Ghibelline the Spanish or Imperial party.
The survival of these factions intensified the dissension, not only of Italy, but of her several states and
towns, for all local or family quarrels became sooner
or later merged therein. The history of most towns
in the Papal states during the first half of the century
proves how much of the energy of the population was
exhausted in this feud, which was a source of weakness
even in cities under the stronger rule of Milan and Venice.

Every Italian theoretically wished for the expulsion
of the foreigner; the barbarian dominion, in Machiavelli's words, stank in the nostrils of all. Yet the
dissension and mistrust which, in 1494, had brought
in the stranger was still to keep him there. There was
no hope of subordination to a common leader, or even
to common interests. On paper there was enough and
to spare of Italian sentiment, but the Italians were
at heart a material race, tempted by foreign pay and
foreign titles and ultramontane benefices. They hated,
moreover, the foreign enemy less than those of their
own state or city. Even the purer souls, such as
Savonarola and his followers, had welcomed the French
in preference to the Medici. Italy teemed with soldiers,
but their efficiency and *esprit de corps* was diminished
by the short terms of service for which they were
engaged, and, if the Venetian or Florentine militia
be excepted, there were few or no national forces.
Italian troops bore the character of being quarrelsome and
insubordinate, wasteful and conceited; but in foreign
pay they frequently did good service and worked

better in concert with Spaniards than did the Germans.
The nobility for a century and a half supplied the
Imperial, Spanish and even French armies with some
of their ablest generals. It was no mere accident that
Alexander of Parma was the greatest general of his
century. Prospero Colonna won the battle of Bicocca;
Pescara, virtually an Italian, that of Pavia. Renzo
da Ceri baffled the Imperialists at Marseilles; save for
the death of Giovanni de' Medici Rome would probably not have fallen. Francesco Ferrucci, with an extemporised corps, held his own in the open field against
the trained Imperialist forces which were besieging
Florence. The Marquis of Marignano, after good service in Germany, evicted the French from Siena.
Ferrante Gonzaga was one of Charles V.'s most trusted
generals, and Emmanuel Philibert of Savoy, trained
under his own eyes, won within his lifetime the battle
of Saint Quentin. Thirteen Italians in Gonsalvo de
Cordova's army had beaten thirteen Frenchmen in the
lists before Barletta: it would not be difficult in the
sixteenth century to select thirteen Italian generals
who could challenge an equal number of French or
Spanish officers.

The fact that Naples and Sicily were, since the conquest of the former by Ferdinand, under a single ruler
would seem to double the strength of the Spanish king
in South Italy. Yet this was not the case. Sicily,
separated from other Italian powers for two centuries and
a half, was more Spanish than it was Italian, even though
its revolution had been directed against Spanish rule.
The two kingdoms had separate viceroys, separate par-
liaments, separate courts and councils. The Strait of
Messina is hardly deeper than the antipathy which
divided the mainland and the island. They were,

however, alike in this, that the growth of the sea-power of the Barbary corsairs was ruinous to both. Communication with Spain was dangerous and difficult; the few galleys paid by Neapolitan and Sicilian subsidies were wholly inadequate to the protection of the coasts.

If Spain were separated from her Southern Italian possessions by storm and piracy, between France and Milan lay Alpine snows and Piedmontese fortresses. The weakness of recent dukes of Savoy and their close dynastic relations to the French monarchy had hitherto given free passage to the latter, but when Charles III. married the sister of the Emperor's wife this trespass was forbidden. Under all circumstances, the French in their relations to Milan were very dependent upon the favour of the mountaineers of the Valais, the Swiss cantons and the Grisons, who held the northern passes. Notwithstanding the victory of Marignano, Francis I. could not hope to hold Milan in their despite. Between France and Milan lay two small marquisates, Saluzzo and Montferrat, the names of which frequently recur in the history of Charles V. Saluzzo, nestling in the south-western angle of the Alps, had long been a bone of contention between Savoy and Dauphiné, each of which claimed the suzerainty. Its position made its favour of no small importance to invaders of Italy from Dauphiné, or to an Imperial army forcing its way into Southern France. Montferrat was curled in between Lombardy and Piedmont, and its strong fortress of Casale was invaluable to any power which had to cover Milan from a French attack through Piedmont.

Such was the Italy of which the hegemony was to be one of the chief problems of the Emperor's career. The problem was none of his own setting; it was forced upon him by his inheritance of Naples and Sicily.

These he could not hope to preserve so long as the straight Emilian road tempted the French lances towards Southern Italy, and the port of Genoa harboured the French ships whose prows were turned towards Naples. Italian liberty it was not one of Charles's tasks to kill, for it was dead a quarter of a century before his wars began. Weakened by a too luxuriant growth, it had been trampled down by the wheels of the French artillery and the clumsy feet of Swiss auxiliary pikemen.

CHAPTER VII

Opening of hostilities with France—Imperialist successes and reverses—
Wolsey's anxiety for peace—The treaty with England—The capture
of Milan and Tournai—Death of Leo X.—Election of Adrian VI.—
Papal neutrality—Papal Imperialist victory of Bicocca—Treaty of
Windsor—Death of Adrian VI.—Revolt of Bourbon—Abortive
proposals for peace—Invasion of Provence—Advance of Francis I.
on Milan—Siege and battle of Pavia—Reception of the news by
Charles—Alternative policies of Lannoy and Gattinara—Decision of
Charles—Removal of Francis to Spain—His interview with Charles
—Course of the negotiations—The question of Burgundy—Treaty
of Madrid—Release of Francis—Marriage of Charles with Isabella
of Portugal.

THE life-long conflict between Habsburg and Valois
opened with little of the pomp and circumstance of war.
Unofficial raids were the order of the day. Robert de
la Marck from his little principality of Bouillon devastated the southern borders of the Netherlands, while the
Duke of Guelders ravaged the northern provinces (March
1521). Charles suffered for the sins, not only of his
Burgundian great-grandfather, but of his Spanish grand-
sire, for Henri d'Albert crossed the Pyrenees in May
and easily occupied Navarre. The disavowals of Francis
were made only to be disbelieved; his objects were to
exhaust his rival's strength by the darts of his picadors,
to gall him into taking the offensive, and then to claim
from England the fulfilment of the treaty obligations of
1518 against the aggressor. In the second of these
three aims Francis certainly succeeded. The Castilians,

regardless of recent civil war, swept back d'Albret and his French auxiliaries, while the Count of Nassau and Sickingen brought de la Marck to his knees. But Charles was not content with the chastisement of cat's-paws. When the French crossed the Pyrenees war was declared.

How wise is Machiavelli's statement of the only true *casus belli*—"the war which is necessary is just." Yet in every century the would-be combatants have ransacked brains and pigeon-holes for justification of the combat which needed none, save the determination to fight engendered by inevitable collision of temperament or interests. This is due, of course, to an uneasy feeling that war is sinful, or at the least extravagant, and those who break moral or economic laws must plead extenuating circumstances.

Charles and Francis were doomed to fight; death alone would really part them. Yet few combatants have so elaborately set forth each trifling detail which might lighten their respective responsibility. There was, it is true, in their case a plausible reason for this elaboration in the fact that the alliance of England ostensibly depended on the most convincing proof of French or Imperial aggression. The vexed question of the policy of Wolsey and his master need not be here determined. It may be that they sincerely desired peace, spiced by chronic disputation, for this would enable England to play the arbiter. It is certain that Wolsey wished to postpone the outbreak of war from his knowledge that Charles was less ready than his rival. From the first the English government leant towards the side of Charles, and in this tendency it was strengthened by the anti-French feelings of nobility and people. The interviews at Canterbury, Gravelines and

Calais were so many stages towards alliance. Even at
Canterbury, if not before, the proposals for the marriage
of Charles and Henry's daughter Mary were already
made. As she was already promised to the Dauphin,
and Charles to a French princess, a rupture with the
father of the slighted children seemed a necessary
consequence. Nevertheless when war broke out,
Wolsey was still pressing his arbitration on the combatants, and so far imposed upon Francis that the French
king induced Scotland to make peace, thus setting
Henry free for action on the continent.

On the question of aggression Charles had the better
of the argument. Against the devastations of la Marck,
the Duke of Guelders and Henri d'Albret, Francis
could only set border raids from Guipuscoa and Luxemburg. The other grievances were more fairly balanced.
Francis complained that the Emperor, in defiance of the
treaty of Noyon, intended to marry the Portuguese
Infanta; that he denied justice to the king of Navarre,
and the homage for Flanders and Artois to himself;
that the pension on Naples was in arrear, and the
Neapolitan partisans of France deprived of their
possessions; that he favoured Milanese rebels, and had
conspired with the Electors and the Pope for the
conquest of Lombardy. Charles could urge as a set-off
to this list of charges the practice of the French king
with Ulrich of Württemberg for the invasion of Alsace,
the corruption of the Swiss, the intelligence with the
Bishop of Zamora and the Spanish rebels, the attempts
to debauch the Marquis of Pescara and the commandants
of his Neapolitan fortresses, the concentration of troops
intended to prevent his journey to Rome for coronation.

Each side had its moment of hesitation; England

made no decisive sign. Then the Imperialists entered
French soil with the capture of Pont-à-Mousson
(August 1521). In the Netherlands they invested the
isolated French fortress of Tournai, while in Italy the
value of the Papal aid was at once manifest, for operations began in or near the valley of the Po, instead of
in those of the Garigliano and the Tronto. With the
outbreak of war the very character of Charles seemed
to undergo a transformation. Contarini wrote to the
Venetian Senate that the Emperor was completely
changed; that whereas formerly he was most anxious
for peace, and would gladly listen to any one who spoke
of peace, now he was so aflame for war that none could
mention peace without his rehearsing all the times and
times that Francis had broken faith. It was a relief
no doubt that the tension was at an end. When
French troops crossed the Pyrenees, Charles raised his
hands to heaven, exclaiming,—" O God! I praise Thee
that this war has not been begun by me, and that the
King of France seeks to make me greater than I am!
Thanks be to Thee always that Thou hast given me
the means to defend myself. I hope that shortly either
I shall be a poor Emperor, or he a poor King of
France."

Disappointment followed the first successes. Bayard's
defence of Mezières demoralised Henry of Nassau's army,
and soon the French were burning the villages of Hainault and West Flanders. Charles and Francis were
both at the front, and, indeed, were never again so near
each other in the field. The Emperor only left Valenciennes immediately before the French attack, and he was
present at the siege of Tournai, though it is doubtful if
he underwent as yet his baptism of fire. In Italy also
fortune began to frown. An attempt to expel the

French party from Genoa failed; the Swiss in Papal
service were reluctant to fight against their brethren in
French pay; little impression was made on the defences
of Lombardy.   Worse than all, the Admiral, Bonnivet,
surprised Fuenterrabia, the key of North-Western Spain
(September 1521).

The Emperor's resources seemed already exhausted.
Wolsey, now thoroughly in earnest, implored him to
accept a truce.   The English minister had come to
Calais on August 2, to press his arbitration, but on the
Emperor's early successes he used his opportunity to
visit Bruges, and there concluded a secret treaty of
alliance.   Now in genuine alarm he urged an armistice,
believing the continuance of the war to be impossible.
Margaret in hot haste visited Charles and used all her
influence in the same direction.   Francis I., under threats
of English intervention, made substantial temporary
concessions.   But Wolsey's autocratic bearing angered
Charles; the Cardinal wished, he said, to do everything
out of his own head, and treated him like a prisoner.
Gattinara observed that Wolsey had expected to find
Charles the pliant youth that he had known in the days
of Chièvres, but that now the Emperor was a man, and
took no one's counsel but his own.

In Gattinara Charles's obstinacy found support.
The Chancellor drew up a schedule of seven arguments
for the truce and ten for war, and these he called the
Seven Deadly Sins, and the Ten Commandments.   To
Charles the Commandments proved more convincing or
attractive than the Deadly Sins.   Yet in November the
situation seemed so hopeless that Charles was on the
point of yielding, when of a sudden the English minister
gave way, and on November 24 Wolsey signed the
treaty confirming the previous agreement of Bruges.

Henry VIII. and Charles engaged to protect the Pope and the Cardinal Medici, to endeavour to win the Swiss, to chastise heresy. Charles was pledged to wed Mary when she reached her thirteenth year, and the Pope would grant dispensation for the marriage. Henry promised to protect the Emperor on his voyage to Spain, and the contracting powers agreed to invade France in the spring of 1523.

Never was obstinacy so fully justified. On the following day arrived the astounding news that the Papal-Imperialist forces, favoured by popular agitation, had entered Milan (November 19). Within two days of these tidings Tournai capitulated. The cantons ordered the Swiss in the French army not to fight against their compatriots in Papal service. Within a fortnight the Lombard towns followed the example of their capital; the French held only Milan citadel and a few scattered fortresses. Parma and Piacenza were surrendered to Leo X., whose fond hopes were thus fulfilled. But the chills of the Campagna are no respecters of either joy or sorrow. At Leo's hunting-box of Magliana, malaria struck him down with the brimming cup of fortune at his lips (December 1, 1521).

Leo X. had been so instrumental in forcing on a war, his relations to the all-important Swiss so decisive in determining its results, that the Emperor's fortunes seemed greatly to depend on the action of the Conclave. With his own hand he wrote to Wolsey, engaging to do everything in his power to further his election. He forwarded to him a copy of his instructions to Juan Manuel to press the claims of the Cardinal of York upon the Conclave. Wolsey, however, had no practical chance. The Emperor's promises and professed instructions were but a diplomatic compliment; his real candidate was Leo's first cousin, the Cardinal Giulio de' Medici, the soul of the Imperialist party. Giulio had too many opponents to secure his own election, but he surprised his wearied colleagues into the choice of Adrian of Utrecht.

There is little doubt that the Spanish envoy contributed to this strange election. Charles in congratulating his old tutor plainly told him that he owed his promotion to consideration for his own wishes; he dwelt on the great and noble deeds which Emperor and Pope combined could do; he warned him against the soft words of the partisans of France. The choice, however, did little credit to the judgment of the Emperor or his envoy. The sixteenth century disliked dull men with chronic good intentions. Adrian had been despised in Spain; in Rome he was to be detested. Simplicity was no virtue in a society so complex. An unpopular Pope, even if he supported the cause of Charles, could not command the resources of the Papacy, for the oligarchy of Cardinals was difficult to lead, impossible to drive.

A successful candidate rarely believes that he has been elected on any other merits than his own. In reply to the Emperor's congratulations, Adrian set aside his claim to gratitude and ascribed his own success to the purity and piety of the Conclave. Charles had been anxious for an interview with the new Pope before the latter sailed for Italy; Adrian recognised the reasons for this anxiety, and hurried his departure. Once at Rome the Pope refused material aid to his late pupil. He had no interest in terrestrial politics, no sons or nephews for whom to beg Italian fiefs; it mattered not to him who ruled at Naples or at Milan; his conscience pointed to the restoration of the faith and the union of Christian powers against the Moslem.

Had Leo X. died a month earlier, before the Emperor's success was so complete, Adrian's election would probably have been followed by the victory of France. Charles had lost the aid of the Central Italian ally which wielded the power both of Rome and Florence. Now that the Medici no longer controlled the Curia, their hold over Florence was endangered by the republican party : the Duke of Urbino returned to the duchy of which Leo X. had unrighteously robbed him. Old despot families came back to the towns of the Papal States from which Alexander VI. Julius II. or Leo X. had driven them. These Italians were actuated by motives purely personal, but any opposition to the Medici or to the late Papal rule was, by circumstance, tantamount to the revival of French influence.

It was yet more important that Adrian's neutrality entailed the defection of the Swiss. Nevertheless even this scarcely checked the Imperialist success. In 1522 Lautrec returned to Italy with a large force of these mercenaries, now in French pay, but he was beaten off both Milan and Pavia. The decisive battle was fought at the Bicocca, a country-house close to Milan (April 27, 1522). Machiavelli had foretold that the Swiss would prove inferior to good Spanish infantry, and so it was. Prospero Colonna had added entrenchments to the banks and ditches of the garden ; the pike was no match for the Spanish harquebus, and the Swiss were mowed down without ever charging home. Lautrec's ill-combined turning movement was checked by the Milanese under Francesco Sforza, who had returned to his father's duchy. The Swiss withdrew sulkily to their mountains ; all Lautrec's fortresses, except the castles of Milan and Cremona, fell, while the capture of Genoa by Colonna brought the eastern Spanish ports into easy connection with the Imperialists in Lombardy.[1]

The victory of Bicocca made its impression on the English government, and this was emphasised by Charles's visit to London, on his way to Spain. The inevitable festivities led up to the treaty of Windsor, and before he sailed, Charles was introduced to his intended bride, Mary. In July an English force invaded Picardy, while Surrey's fleet hovered off the Norman coasts. The following year (1523) was, as far as diplomacy could make it so, one of the most successful of Charles's reign. Henry VIII. was prepared for a serious invasion of France, and exercised a far from gentle pressure upon Venice. The embargo upon all Venetian property in England quickened the growing conviction of the Republic that the French was a losing cause. Imperial success would replace the too powerful French king at Milan by a weak Sforza duke; Imperial alliance would secure the Venetian frontiers from the attentions of the Emperor's restless, ambitious brother. Within one week (July 29 to August 4) treaties were signed with Venice and with the Pope. Savoy and Montferrat, Genoa and Florence, joined in the league against the French. Success followed upon success. At the close of September Adrian died, and Charles this time, in spite of renewed compliments to Wolsey, caused the election of his zealous supporter, the Cardinal Medici. The Imperial position in Italy seemed now to be impregnable.

The neutrality of Adrian had been absolutely honest, but Charles was truthful in arguing that he was play-

---

[1] For the military operations in Italy especial attention may be called to *Tratado de las Campañas . . . de los ejércitos del Emperador Cárlos V. desde* 1521 *hasta* 1545 ; by Martin Garcia Cerezeda, published by la Sociedad de Bibliófilos Españoles, 1873-6. 3 vols.

ing into French hands. It was the discovery that his most trusted cardinal, Soderini the hereditary enemy of the Medici, was abusing neutrality to encourage French enterprise on Sicily and Naples that at last drove Adrian into the Emperor's camp. This, or an unduly low standard of comfort in an unhealthy climate, was probably his death-blow. It is difficult to distinguish the pathos from the bathos of Adrian's career. He had risen from low estate to the throne of St. Peter, and none had a word against his honesty. Yet in every important capacity he had proved a failure. The failure and the success were characteristic of the age which recognised his virtue and resented his stupidity. They also illustrate a quality early noticed in the character of Charles, that he clung closely to old friends. Adrian and Chièvres were the most important factors at the most critical period of his early life ; to them, differing as they did in policy and practice, his misfortunes and mistakes have not unjustly been attributed by contemporaries and posterity. Charles in after years would speak openly of the discredit which his subordination to Chièvres had brought upon his youth, but, while resolving never to repeat his error, he warmly praised his minister's services. There is much in the Emperor's life which recalls the influence of Adrian also ; to his old tutor he not improbably owed his ideal of doctrinal orthodoxy combined with disciplinary reform, his dreams of Christendom purging itself of heresy that it might healthfully fight the infidel. Adrian's regency in Spain and his short pontificate may well have taught his pupil the inconvenience of ideals in practical politics, but disillusion is the lesson which honest, if not brilliant, pupils most readily forget.

It was not only in Italy and in the Channel that

fortune was smiling upon Charles. Francis had from
the first toyed with military and aristocratic discontent
in his rival's Italian possessions, and encouraged revolt
in Spain. This was now to be repaid in kind. The
Constable Bourbon was too powerful to be a safe or
submissive subject, but the personal insults and injuries
by which the Crown strove to humiliate him aggravated
a dangerous situation, and they were probably but
typical of those inflicted on many others who did not
enjoy the capricious sunshine of the Court. France was
seething with discontent at the Court's extravagance, at
the arbitrary taxation and the demands on human life
for a war in which neither noble, citizen, nor peasant had
any interest. In the absence of parliamentary opposition, revolt was the only remedy. Machiavelli had
written that France was always open to attack through
the medium of the great feudatories. Since the autumn
of 1522 the Emperor's agents had intrigued with Bourbon. This was not so strange as may at first sight appear.
The relationship between the houses of Burgundy and
Bourbon was long and close; it had shaken the throne
of Louis XI. The neighbouring house of Burgundy was
the natural resort of an injured Bourbon; did not even
the cadet line of Condé hereafter defy the reigning
branch from the Court of Brussels, when Henri Quatre
was king in France?

Charles hoped much from Bourbon's defection. The
Constable's price was consequently high, no less than an
independent kingdom in the centre and south of France,
and the hand of the Emperor's sister, Eleanor, the
dowager of Portugal. Had Bourbon trumpeted out his
challenge from his own huge domains, it might have
awakened many an echo throughout France. But he
delayed his manifesto too long, and when his conspiracy

was discovered, he had not the courage to hold his
ground.   Bourbon was ruined from the moment that he
fled.   Henceforth he was but an *émigré*, at most a *roi
en exil* with only a paper crown.   Nevertheless his conspiracy had one immediate effect.   Francis I. abandoned
his intended invasion of Italy in person.   Bonnivet in
his place led the French forces across the Alps ; but the
Imperial grip on Lombardy was now strong, and in the
spring of 1524 he was forced back across the Sesia.
The death-wound of Bayard during the retreat was the
one event which has rendered memorable the Italian
campaign of 1523-24.

The Spaniards meanwhile at length recovered Fuenterrabia (February 1524), but their most efficient troops
were drained to Italy, and though Charles threatened in
person to invade the South of France, he found no force
adequate to offensive measures.   In the North and
North-East of France the desultory and ineffective
fighting reduced itself to burning villages and wasting
fields and orchards.   Henry VIII. had despatched a very
considerable force, but its commander, the Duke of
Suffolk, was a brave, big-boned athlete and little more.
Abnormal talent was required for successful offensive
action in this age, when the defensive almost everywhere held the advantage.   There was, moreover, no real
sympathy between the English and Imperial govern-
ments, and this was reflected in the countless daily
difficulties arising from the liability of the Netherland
officials to provide food and transport.   Imperial diplomacy had in fact, in spite of his Italian and Spanish
successes, far outrun the military and financial resources
of the Emperor.

It might have been well for Charles had he been
earlier content with his success.   He had appeared as

the liberator of Italy, as seeking not a palm's breadth of territory for himself, but only protection for his kingdom of Naples. Hatred for the French had largely contributed to their loss of Lombardy. Francesco Sforza at the head of the Milanese militia had shared in the victory of Bicocca. Charles had kept faith with the Pope, and had substantially increased the Papal territories. He had not as yet tampered with the independence of any Italian state ; the native powers, monarchical or republican, had rallied to his side. A revived Empire, after which Dante had yearned, might seem to be bestowing upon Italy that federal unity which was suited to her temper and traditions, but which she could not herself compass.

Charles more than once had had momentary volitions for peace, due partly to financial stress, partly to the shock of the capture of Rhodes by Solyman. He had been deeply affected by the fall of the great Crusading Order, and had listened to Adrian's supplications for peace among Christian powers. Again in 1524 he made proposals, not entirely unreasonable, for reconciliation with his rival. He was not, indeed, wholly, or even mainly, responsible for the continuance of war. The refusal of Francis to surrender Lombardy made peace difficult, if not impossible. There could be no security while the French retained a foothold in Italy, and all previous sacrifices would be in vain. Francis I., a characteristic Frenchman, believed that his nation had an inalienable right not to pay the cost of an adverse verdict in the Courts of War. Wolsey had once admitted that there could be no peace until the French were extirpated. Charles's blood was now up ; he was encouraged by the alliance of England, the defection of Bourbon, the election of the Cardinal Medici. After

the failure of the tentative negotiations and after the
retreat of Bonnivet he deliberately resolved to dismember
France to such an extent as to make her harmless.

The invasion of France in the summer of 1524 had
as its programme the transference of the crown to
Henry VIII. and the creation of the separate kingdom
promised to Bourbon, consisting of his own possessions,
with the addition of Dauphiné and Provence.   Whether
Charles seriously intended the elevation of his allies
may well be doubted, but he was set upon the conquest
of Marseilles.   With the French driven from their principal port, with Marseilles in friendly hands as a half-
way house between Genoa and Barcelona, the Gulf of
Lyons would have become a Spanish lake, and the sea-
power on the Mediterranean would definitely have
passed from France to Spain.   The attempt was well
worth making, as the subsequent history of the Franco-
Turkish naval combination proved.

It was thought that the conquest of Provence would
be an easy matter.   The county had not long been
annexed to France ; the inhabitants had no good reputation for courage, for, whereas in the rest of France
every man could wield a sword, the Provençals, it was
said, could scarcely handle a knife.   The invasion,
however, had been undertaken with insufficient resources, and this was due to inadequate supplies.
Bourbon quarrelled with his colleague the Marquis of
Pescara ; the English envoy Pace had passionate scenes
with Bourbon.   The French fleet under Andrea Doria,
far superior to Ugo de Moncada's squadron, could throw
provisions into Marseilles.   The Emperor's promised
diversion in Languedoc fell through from want of means ;
the English attack on Northern France was a dead
letter from lack of will, for Wolsey was   already

negotiating with the French court. Thus Francis I. was enabled to collect the whole of his fighting force at Avignon. Marseilles, strongly defended by the Roman *condottiere* Renzo da Ceri, beat its assailants off, and in the autumn they were forced to raise the siege.

Back to Italy struggled the Imperialists by the rough road which skirted the Riviera. Their guns were taken to pieces and packed on mules; behind them and sometimes before them were the light horse of Montmorency, who was instructed to break up the roads in front of them, and head them off the pass which leads from Nice over the Col di Tenda into the plain of Piedmont. The Imperialists, however, effected their retreat by the coast road to Finale. The Spaniards holding the rear very roughly handled the French pursuers, and when once they had made good the dangerous passage through Mentone, the retreating army was virtually safe. Francis himself dashed rapidly into North Italy through Dauphiné and over the Mont Genèvre; he entered the western gate of Milan as Pescara's troops retired from the eastern gate on Lodi. The citadel of Milan only was held by the Imperialists; the plague-stricken town was abandoned to its old masters.

Charles during the late campaign had shown at singular disadvantage as compared with his French rival. The presence of Francis at Avignon had necessitated Bourbon's withdrawal from Marseilles; he had energetically carried the war into the enemies' territory. Charles meanwhile had loitered in Spain; he had fulfilled neither the military nor the financial obligations which he had undertaken. He could not now meet his rival in Italy, nor could he send aid to his retreating

generals, for the French fleet commanded the Gulf of
Lyons. Charles was not yet a soldier, but the responsibility for his apparent lethargy was probably less his
own than that of the parliamentary system which tied
him to the recalcitrant Cortes of his Spanish kingdoms.
He had learned his lesson, and could not once more set
Spanish opinion at defiance. Charles had little or
nothing to do with the coming months of trial and
triumph. If either Habsburg served to save the situation, it was rather Ferdinand than Charles.

Retiring upon Lodi, Bourbon and Pescara held the
line of the Adda. Behind them was Venetian territory still nominally friendly, while over the passes of
the Tyrol they could draw their German reinforcements.
The only other respectable Imperial force lay in Pavia
under Antonio de Leyva, and blocked the road from
Milan southwards. Francis should probably have
followed Pescara and broken up his dispirited troops
beyond all hope of rally. Naturally impatient, he
chose what seemed the more rapid course, and besieged
Pavia. His decision was not unreasonable. The garrison was mainly German, and was thought unlikely
to hold out without its pay; the occupation of Pavia
would exercise pressure on Florence and the Papacy,
for Clement VII., at the first sign of Imperial failure,
had begun to veer towards France; Pavia would serve
as a base for an advance on Naples; after all, sooner
or later it must be besieged, for its powerful garrison
could not be left in the rear of a force with a long line
of communications stretching from Naples back to Milan.
It was thus no mere accident and no fit of punctilious
obstinacy that made Pavia the scene of the war's crisis.
As early as October 29, 1524, Richard Pace wrote that
Francis was about to attack Pavia, that, if defeated, his

whole reputation was lost, if victorious his object was gained; at Pavia therefore he should be resisted to the uttermost. A few days later the Abbot Najera begged Charles not to despair of ultimate victory, for his captains in Italy were confident that the king of France would ultimately lose his credit and his army, and finally be either killed or captured, as had been predicted by astrologers and prophets.

Francis was over confident. He weakened his own army by detaching troops to attack Genoa, and he sent the Duke of Albany with a considerable force to the frontiers of Naples. This confidence seemed to be justified by the opinion of the other Italian powers, less wise than the prophets and astrologers. Venice prepared to revert to the French alliance; the Pope made a secret treaty with Francis; Ferrara and Florence, Lucca and Siena, all contributed to his expected victory. The English government shared the general opinion, but here the French success produced a reversion of feeling in the Emperor's favour. Wolsey encouraged the Venetians to stand by Charles; he showed the Pope that the French at Milan and at Naples would be his Scylla and Charybdis, that Francis would aspire to the Roman Empire, and that Clement would become his chaplain.

Meanwhile in Pavia Antonio de Leyva had fired the German mercenaries and the citizens with his own spirit, and the French assault degenerated into a wearisome blockade. Behind the screen of the Adda Pescara had reorganised his forces; Bourbon and Frundsberg had brought their levies of *Landsknechts* through Tyrol; Lannoy, viceroy of Naples, who had at one time despaired, joined them with such Spaniards and Italians as he could muster. Brushing away the

French, who were too weak to contain them, from the district of the Adda, the Imperialists advanced upon the French army, now demoralised by inaction, weakened by the despatch of Albany to Naples and the withdrawal of the Grisons mercenaries to the defence of Chiavenna. The relieving force was unpaid, unfed, unclothed, but its spirit was admirable, and during the three weeks which preceded the decisive action it gave proof of its superiority in ingenuity and courage. The French could not be tempted from their entrenchments in the great park of Mirabello ; the Imperialists must fight or starve, and so it was resolved to beat up the French in their quarters on St. Matthew's day, the birthday of the Emperor.

The dawn of February 24 surprised the attacking army while battering down the solid park wall of the Mirabello. From the moment when the French artillery began to play upon the flank of the entering host the battle was a confused *mêlée*. No two accounts of the actual operations agree. It is only possible to realise dimly the dangerous rush of the French horse, the steady fire of the Spanish harquebusiers on their flanks, the French cry of victory as the Imperialist Italians were forced back with the loss of their guns, the concentration of Pescara, Bourbon and Lannoy for one supreme effort, the sortie of de Leyva from Pavia, the flight of the Swiss and the French rearguard, and the last wild charge in which Francis was unhorsed and taken. No victory could be more complete. Spaniards and Germans had torn away the laurels which French horse and Swiss pikemen had long worn. Almost every hero of a quarter of a century of French warfare was engaged, and either killed or taken. A whole generation of French paladins was swept away.

It was for the Emperor's generals to win the victory, for Charles to use it. The lack of supply had been so complete, the appeals of his commanders so despairing, that he had anxiously awaited news of a reverse at Pavia or Naples. There exist several accounts of the arrival of the tidings of the victory, all which agree in the marvellous self-control of Charles, in the total absence of outward exaltation. He repeated, as if dazed, the words of the courier : " The battle is fought and the king is your prisoner," and without a further word retired to his room, and fell on his knees at his bedside. Only after a long interval of prayer did he ask for details of his victory. No public rejoicings were allowed for this disaster to a Christian power. On the following day Charles went in procession to the Church of Our Lady of Atocha, but the preacher was forbidden to dilate upon the triumph. " In all his good fortune," wrote the Papal envoy Baldassare Castiglione, " Cæsar has behaved with the modesty of a truly religious man." The Emperor's aim appeared to be the peace of Europe with a view to war against the Turk. Yet he knew what he wanted from the French king, and he intended to have it. The means, however, were less definite than the end.[1]

The first pair of alternatives which presented themselves were the active prosecution of the war before France could recover from her blow, or the exaction of a favourable treaty. The former was almost immediately set aside, and a truce was granted. It was impossible to lead the victors of Pavia into France.

---

[1] For the documents relating to the captivity of Francis I., see A. Cham. pollion - Figeac, *La Captivité du roi François Ier*, 1847 (*Collection de documents inédits sur l'histoire de France*). In *Documentos Ineditos*, vol. xxxviii., will be found a good contemporary memoir relating to Pavia, the imprisonment and release of Francis. the Emperor's marriage, and the siege and relief of Naples.

Every German, Spaniard or Italian in the garrison
or relieving force, animated by Leyva, Bourbon or
Pescara, had been a hero for a month or more. But
it is hard for mercenaries, fighting for a living wage,
to sustain indefinitely the heroic note without the
material accompaniment of food and clothing. If the
conquering army held together it must starve; if it
was scattered over a wider area, it fell out of hand,
and plundered the Emperor's subjects and allies. The
problem solved itself partly by desertion. The *Landsknechts* trooped across the Alps to stiffen the tumul-
tuous hordes of their peasant brethren, now in full
revolt, or to aid the princes in their extermination. It
was ill travelling over Alpine passes for respectable
ambassadors in those days.

If Charles utilised his rival's captivity to close hostilities, should the terms of the treaty be generous
or exacting? Gattinara, good Italian as he was, had
little hesitation. He urged Charles to ignore English
claims, to win the heart of Italy, to cripple France
beyond all hope of her recovery. No promise nor oath,
he insisted, would ever be kept by France; he pleaded
for good faith towards Charles's Italian allies, for the
immediate investiture of Francesco Sforza with Milan;
it was gain enough for Charles that France should be
excluded from Italy by the interests of her native states.
A similar argument was to be employed in later days
on French behalf by more than one French statesman,
by Richelieu, by Mazarin, and above all by d'Argenson.
With Gattinara, however, it was something more; he
would utilise the independence left to the several
Italian states for Christian and Imperial objects. His
was the ideal, not then unknown in Germany, and once
familiar to Italy, of superseding selfish particularism

by a higher unity, of an Imperial order not incompatible with local liberty. At first Charles seemed to listen. When Francis proposed to conquer the whole of the Venetian state for him at his own expense, he resolutely declared that he would have no war in Italy.

Lannoy, viceroy of Naples, an unsympathetic Netherlander, rating the probabilities of Italian gratitude less highly, early began to press reconciliation with France at the expense of Italy. He knew, perhaps, better than Gattinara, the impossibility of continued war, should France prove obdurate. He eagerly accepted the French king's proposal that he should be transferred to Spain that he might effect a personal reconciliation with Charles. Francis was vain and sanguine; he believed that his powers of fascination, so effective with court ladies, would prove irresistible to his inexperienced rival. His removal was, at all events, a defeat for Gattinara and the Italian party, and a victory for the French faction at the Court.

Charles rejected the policy of Gattinara. He had little imagination; he could not project himself into unknown space; he did not know Italy, for he had never seen it; he did know the current view of his Netherland advisers, the necessity of compromise with France, for this from earliest days had been impressed upon him by Chièvres. The Chancellor was out of favour, and, indeed, asked permission to resign. But Charles did not frankly adopt the opposite alternative. His demands on France were not unjust, but they were scarcely generous; they entailed ten months of wrangling which only envenomed personal and national hostilities. So too in his attitude towards Francis his professions of eternal friendship left little to be desired, and yet he used his rival's impatience of imprisonment as a lever to raise the terms of his release.

Francis had been brought to Spain in June, but not until August was he transferred from Valencia and its neighbourhood to Madrid. Even then Charles hunted tranquilly in the Segovian forest until, on the evening of September 18, he heard that the French king was dying. Then with sudden resolution he rode, almost without drawing rein, to the sick man's quarters in the Alcazar. Here he waited until Francis awoke, and then went to his bedside. The king painfully raised himself to receive Charles's embrace, saying, "Here I am, my Lord Emperor, your servant and your slave." Charles replied, "Not so; you are my good friend and brother, and I hope that you will always be so." He begged the invalid to keep his spirits up, and to think only of getting well : when his sister arrived peace would soon follow and Francis regain his liberty, for Charles demanded only what was reasonable, and the king, doubtless, would not fail in doing what was just. During the next day's visit Charles used equally fair and loving words, and left the patient with his health miraculously improved. It is possible that Charles was really moved by his first interview with Francis, and that he made the verbal promises to which the latter afterwards testily referred ; as far as the evidence goes, however, the consolation was confined to diplomatic generalities.

As the Emperor left the sick-room after his second visit, he met on the stairs, Margaret of Angoulême, who had come to conduct the negotiations for her brother's release. Margaret had just lost her husband, and the mission of the young widow inspired the English ambassadors with terror, lest she should woo the

Emperor for herself, and his sister, the queen-dowager of Portugal, for her brother. They had solemnly warned Charles not to receive her, for she would only confirm her brother in his obstinacy. "Besides," they added, "being young and a widow, she comes, as Ovid says of women going to a play, to see and to be seen, that perhaps the Emperor may like her; and also to woo the queen-dowager of Portugal for her brother. . . . Then as they are both young widows, she shall find good commodity in cackling with her to advance her brother's matter; and if she finds her inclined thereto, they will help each other."

The envoys were nervous without need. Charles kissed Margaret and granted her private interviews, but not all her charms could abate the conditions of release. He was not insensible to women's physical attractions, but throughout his life, with the possible exceptions of his aunt Margaret, his sister Mary and his wife, they never influenced his policy. Margaret returned without bringing her brother back "to rescue all his servants and subjects from limbo and the shades below." When news reached Charles at Toledo, that Francis was near his end from a relapse, he did not at once again take horse, but confined his sympathy to the pious ejaculation,— "The Lord gave and the Lord has taken away." There was some slight reason for this disregard of the cry of Wolf, for Margaret in a note to her brother begged him to wear a feeble and distressful countenance in the presence of Alarcon, his guard, for his debility would fortify and advance her mission.

These royal interviews are not without their personal interest, but the real negotiations were conducted neither at the bedside of Francis, nor in a *tête-à-tête* with Margaret. The kernel of these negotiations was

soon detached from the husk.   The Chancellor paraded,
only to waive, the antiquarian claims to France itself as
forfeited to the Empire under a bull of Boniface VIII.
to Provence as having passed with Naples to the crown
of Aragon, to Languedoc as being an old possession of
this crown, to Dauphiné as a province of the Empire.
It was only decent to enlarge upon the pretensions of
the English ally and the rewards due to Bourbon.   The
former at least presented no serious difficulty.   The
English envoys pressed for resolute action, for the
dethronement of Francis I. in favour of Henry VIII., or
at least for the cession of the old English provinces.
Charles offered to continue the war, if Henry would
pay the costs, and if Mary were at once sent to Spain.
Neither side was serious.   Although the English
Council was divided and some members wished for the
complete humiliation of the traditional enemy, yet it was
known that Wolsey had quite deserted the Imperial
cause, and that he was discussing with France and the
Italian powers the means of resistance to the Emperor's
menacing authority.   English operations during the
war had been throughout half-hearted and ineffective.
In the time of Charles's greatest trouble Wolsey had
been cold and sulky, "like women," wrote Margaret to
Charles, "when they feel that they are in the wrong."
By the close of June peace between France and England
was practically concluded.   Charles felt little obligation to
consider the extravagant English claims, but Bourbon's
reward was a less easy question.   He now, perhaps, really
wished to add the old Imperial provinces, Dauphiné and
Provence, to the Constable's own possessions, and to
convert them into a kingdom, that Bourbon might be
a fitting husband for Queen Eleanor.   Yet this desire
was subordinate to more immediate wants.

The French government from the first accepted as inevitable the abandonment of all Italian claims, and made little difficulty in relinquishing the suzerainty of Artois and Flanders.   Galling as this last concession was, it was of little actual detriment to France, while it relieved the Netherlands of no inconsiderable vexation. Under the modern system such suzerainty was chiefly valuable as an exercise for legal ingenuity, and as a pretext for picking quarrels.   The kernel of the negotiations was the claim for the duchy of Burgundy, with its annexes Mâcon, Auxerre, Auxonne, and Bar-sur-Seine. This was no mere antiquarian pretension.   Burgundy was the cradle of the Emperor's forefathers, the home of the order of the Golden Fleece.   Charles was still rather a Burgundian than a Spaniard, and his paternal inheritance was still nearest to his heart.   In the numerous draft proposals for peace, made early in 1524, the burden of each was the recovery of Burgundy in exchange for Milan.   He regarded the duchy as his lawful heritage, filched from a defenceless girl on the tragic death of Charles the Bold.   Legally he was probably in the right, and he had an eminently legal mind.   His claim to Burgundy was at least as strong as that of Francis I. to Milan.   He was entirely honest in his repeated statement that he was only utilising his victory to demand his own.

For Burgundy the French negotiators fought desperately.   Whatever were the rights and wrongs, no Frenchman could willingly surrender the wealthy duchy which would place an enemy more formidable than Charles the Bold within striking distance of the capital. France is not always modest in the hour of victory, but, however crushing her defeat, she professes an imprescriptible claim to territory which she has once possessed. The "not a stone of our fortresses or foot of our land" of Jules Favre had its antitype in the "not an inch of French soil" of Francis.

As a compromise, the French proposed that the case should be submitted to a court of law, and that, if Burgundy were assigned to France, it should form the dower of Eleanor whom the king should marry. Charles would not yield on Burgundy, but Eleanor's refusal to be twice married at her brother's will, and to accept the rebel French noble if she could wed his king, perhaps favoured the final settlement.

Charles had an advantage in his prisoner's character. Francis was a bad subject for prison life, even though comfortably lodged and reverently treated. He was too selfish and too sensitive to sacrifice himself for his kingdom. Should, however, he abdicate or die, the fruits of his capture would be lost. France had not been demoralised by her disaster, and the energy of her regent had prepared her against attack. The Emperor's troops in Italy were dwindling, their generals wrangling; every Italian State was heaving restlessly under the incubus of the unpaid soldiery. Ferdinand, who, true to himself, had advised enterprising measures against France, was crippled by the dangerous Tyrolese rebellion. Thus it was that on January 13, 1526, the treaty of Madrid was concluded.

By the terms of the famous treaty Francis resigned all claims to Milan, Genoa, and Asti; he ceded the suzerainty of Flanders, Artois and Tournai, restoring places taken on the Netherland frontiers; he engaged to persuade the Estates General and the Parliament of Paris to assent to the cession of Burgundy, or, failing this, to return to the prison to which two of his sons should be sent as hostages; a French fleet should escort

Charles to Italy for the purpose of his coronation; a
French army under the king in person should co-operate
in a crusade against the infidel, and in the suppression
of Lutheran and other pernicious sects.   Francis
abandoned his ally the Duke of Guelders, and renounced
the claims of the house of Albret to Navarre.   To
Bourbon was promised the restoration of his estates, but
Charles made no further stipulations in his favour.   It
was, however, understood that the Constable should
receive the duchy of Milan, while Louis XII.'s daughter
Renée, poor shuttlecock tossed from prince to prince,
was suggested as his bride.

On the morrow of the treaty an altar was placed in
the king's room.   Here, after mass was said, Francis
swore upon the Gospel to keep his oath.   Lannoy
asked him for his word of honour as a knight.   Francis
with bared head laid his hand in Lannoy's, and promised
on his word as a gentleman to return to prison in six
weeks, if all the conditions were not fulfilled.   Francis
lied and he had meant to lie, for on the previous day he
had, in the presence of the French ambassadors, renewed
a protest made in August, that he was acting under
compulsion and vile duress, that the treaty reduced
France to slavery, that he would never sacrifice the
rights of the French crown.

When the last arrangements had been made,
Emperor and King spent five days together in true
brotherly intercourse.   At parting they stood alone
man to man before a roadside crucifix.   Here Francis
renewed his pledges under pain of being held a miserable
scoundrel.   Charles assured him that he had never
hated him, but that if he broke his word to Eleanor, he
could never forgive him, and would strive to wreak his
vengeance on him, wherever he might be.   Every one in

Europe knew that the king was on his road to France
and perjury. On March 17 Francis leapt from his boat
into the French water of the Bidassoa, waded to land,
and, springing on his horse, exclaimed, "Now I am
king, I am king once more." Charles had let slip his
chance. He had lost that one August day which
Lannoy, in announcing the victory of Pavia, had
declared comes to a man once and once only in his life.

The situation had been peculiarly difficult for the
young ruler, and it had therefore brought into prominence features in his character and political methods
which will reappear. He was confident that time
would work in his own favour, and time did, indeed,
force Francis to nominal submission to his will. Time,
however, also bred ferment in Italy and Germany,
which more rapid action might have checked. Charles
did not logically adopt either of the alternatives before
him. He borrowed from each, thinking that he would
steer most safely in mid-channel. His mind was rather
that of the lawyer than of the diplomatist; he looked
more to his rights than to his interests; his pretensions
were more lawful than expedient. Alike in victory and
danger he gave proof of an imperturbable temper; he
refused to be either elated or flustered; he only gave
vent to wrath, if this were likely to serve his purpose.
Men and nations began to fear the impassive youth
who went mechanically on his way, untempted and
unpushed from the path which he had chosen. Friend
and foe alike began to forebode the revival of a universal Empire which the hybrid Cæsar, without a
nationality, almost without a language of his own,
seemed born to rule.

The halcyon days of peace were destined to be few,
but they were appropriately spent in preparations for

the Emperor's wedding. The wealth of matrimonial alternatives had been not the least of his embarrassments, but recent events had simplified his choice, which finally fell upon the Portuguese Infanta, Isabella. This marriage was a salve to the irritation which the wounds of civil war had left. In spite of almost inveterate antipathy between Spaniards and Portuguese, there has always existed a sentiment of peninsularity, an indefinite yearning towards union under one form or other. From the first his people had pressed upon Charles the attractions of the Infanta, and had emphasised their dislike to his English entanglements. To the Cortes of 1525, who repeated the national desire, the reply of Charles was frank and round :— He could not meet his obligations to the English Crown without either the English dowry or a Spanish subsidy. The Cortes liberally padded their horn of the dilemma, and there was no further obstacle to the marriage, beyond the decent disputation as to settlements. Charles was not without romance, but it was not worn upon his sleeve, still less did it tingle in the fingertips that held his pen. He confessed to Ferdinand that his matrimonial motives were the dowry of a million ducats, and the possibility of leaving Spain under his future wife's guardianship. To marry a wife because she is likely to be useful in your absence is rather sensible than sentimental. Some ten proposals or engagements had knocked off the tender bloom of sentiment. There is little doubt that Charles regarded the future Empress as a valuable member of the family federation ; she would rule Spain, while he would be the travelling director of the Habsburg syndicate. In a measure he was right ; Isabella was not the usual nursery princess, but a women of twenty-three, with ripe judgment and the business capacity of a sixteenth-century Portuguese. Probably the tardily-developed youth did not, and could not, realise as yet the spell which the small, thin figure, the clear, white complexion, the sound head and the true heart, were to exercise. Reasons financial and political were long forthcoming to explain Charles's reluctance to leave Spain. It is remarkable that his absences during his wife's lifetime were short, while after her death Spain only saw his face for a year or so, until he returned, no longer king, to die.

The wedding was made an opportunity for visiting Southern Spain. The marriage took place in Seville, which was by far the finest town in Spain (March 1526), and thence Charles visited Cordoba and Granada. Within the precincts of the Alhambra he began to build the splendid palace, the unfinished walls of which the visitor still sees. He had as yet never been in Italy, but this building proves that he could to the full appreciate the subtle beauties of Italian architecture, even as in later years he could insist on the pre-eminence of Titian's art in portraiture. Charles throughout his life was never able to do as he would like. Even Castile had no real capital, for Valladolid could hardly be reckoned such. Wherever the royal palace was, there would be the centre of the united kingdoms. To Spain above all European nations could be applied the principle of *nouvel empire nouvelle capitale*. Philip II. fixed his affections on the grim northern hills; Charles would command the sunny *Vega* of Granada. Had his wishes been fulfilled, Spanish history might have taken a very different direction. He never again had leisure to bask on the Alhambra Hill; he had but a single honeymoon.[1]

---

[1] For Charles V.'s marriage and his visit to Southern Spain the letters of Baldassare Castiglione are of much interest. See *Baldassare Castiglione: His Life and Letters*. By Julia Cartwright (Mrs. Ady) 1908.

To the erection of the new palace was applied part of the sum obtained from the Moors of Granada for a modification of a new order of the Inquisition, which Charles suspended during his pleasure. Only recently he had shown excessive severity against their Valencian brethren, but, as was seen later in the case of German Protestants and Italian rebels, personal contact served to mitigate his rigour. The fit of religious exaltation was now over, and the Pope was at this moment peculiarly troublesome. Obstinate and positive as Charles was, he had an open ear for profitable compromise.

CHAPTER VIII

Panic in Italy after the French defeat—Danger of Clement VII.—
Dreams of Italian independence—The Morone conspiracy—Milan
capitulates to the Imperialists—Moncada and Colonna surprise
Rome—Overtures for peace between Pope and Emperor—The
march of Bourbon upon Rome—Storm and sack of the Holy City—
The responsibility of Charles for the tragedy—Indignation in
Spain—Ideas of the secularisation of the Papacy—Indecision of
Charles—The treaty with Clement VII.—European combination
against Charles—French successes in Italy—Siege of Naples—
Helplessness of Charles—Weakness of Papal policy—Failure of
the French at Naples—Imperialist victory of Landriano—Treaties
of Barcelona and Cambrai—Visit of Charles to Italy—His coronation at Bologna—Departure for Germany.

THE removal of Francis from Italy to Spain had provoked a panic among the Italian states. Hitherto the
Emperor's movements had been conditioned by those
of the enemy. He had striven to preserve the friendship of successive Popes, because this was essential to
the security of Naples; he had driven the French from
Lombardy, because this was their base of operations
against South Italy. Francesco Sforza had been allowed
to take virtual possession of his father's duchy, although investiture was still delayed. In Genoa and
in Siena one time-honoured faction had been suffered
to replace another, but no effort had been made to
change the constitutions of these republics. Yet Italy
was nervous at the growth of the Imperial power; she
already had her grievances theoretical and practical.

In Maximilian's time it had seemed not unlikely that the Emperor might revive at least the financial claims which the dust of centuries had so long concealed. If Maximilian once came to Italy, wrote Machiavelli, not all the leaves on all the trees, if turned to ducats, would satisfy his needs; nor could Italy, as Germany, pay an Emperor with diets. Charles had levied heavy contributions for his wars against the French, and the precedent might readily ripen into custom. More destructive to Italy's comfort and prosperity was the quartering of German and Spanish troops on town and village. Even Adrian VI. had complained that Charles's generals had treated Papal cities as conquered lands, while the towns of Sforza's duchy had received scant respect. Yet all this could be attributed to the immediate exigences of war; Charles himself had from Spain indignantly denounced the misconduct of his troops. It was now feared that Francis would use his personal influence upon Charles to purchase peace for France at the price of Italian independence.

Of all Italy's princes Clement VII. had most to fear.[1] The Medici had hurried the emperor into war; he had endowed them richly with its spoils. To him Clement VII. owed the tiara; without Imperial favour the family could scarcely have maintained its hold on Florence. Yet in the hour of stress the Pope had first professed neutrality, and then deserted to the French. He had encouraged his cousin Giovanni to join Francis with his Black Bands before Pavia; he had allowed and probably prompted the Duke of Albany's passage

---

[1] For the connection of Clement VII. and the Emperor, see R. Grethen *Die politischen Beziehungen Clements VII. (zu Karl V.*, 1887. See also C. Randi, *La guerra di sette anni sotto Clemente VII.* (*Arch. della Soc. Rom.* VI., 3 and 4).

through the Papal States to Naples ; recruits had been
levied for French service in Papal territory. A secret
treaty had been made between the Pope and France
as early as November 1524, but it was not so secret
that the Imperialists did not know it. In December
Charles had instructed his envoy, the Duke of Sessa,
to dissimulate with the Papal ministers : the time
would come for strict settlement of accounts. In
January Sessa forced Clement to a confession of his
French alliance. Three weeks before the victory of
Pavia Charles had spoken plainly to the Florentine
ambassador : "I am expecting bad news both from
Milan and Naples, but I care not the least in the
world. I shall go to Italy, and have a fairer opportunity of obtaining my own and of taking my revenge
on those who may have wronged me, and most
especially on that villain Pope. Some day or other,
perhaps, Luther may become a man of worth." The
Venetian envoy, Contarini, rightly thought this language worthy of much consideration, above all as
coming from the Emperor, who was very reserved in
speech. It was, indeed, the most noteworthy of all
Charles's utterances with respect to Pope and heretic.

It is small wonder that, on hearing of the French
disaster, Clement became "as a dead man." Yet
Charles treated him with moderation, using his victory
as an opportunity of reviving the old alliance. There
was, however, in Italy a genuine desire to have done
with the foreigner, to restore the independence which
before the fatal year 1494 she had enjoyed. Patriots
saw a prospect of salvation in the French defeat and
the exhaustion of the victors. Girolama Morone,
Chancellor of Milan, gave a definite direction to general
disgust, and political shape to patriotic yearnings.

Ludovico Sforza had been instrumental in robbing
Italy of her liberty; his son should now be foremost
in its recovery. Once more the Sforza should rule
in Milan, the Medici in Florence; the forces of Rome
and Venice were almost unimpaired; from Naples the
illegitimate, Italianised line of Aragon had disappeared,
but could not a substitute be found? The need of the
Italians was a general, and the best general in Italy
was the Marquis of Pescara. The Aragonese house of
d'Avalos had been settled in Italy for well-nigh a
century; Pescara's father had been the one prominent
Neapolitan noble who had remained faithful to his
king in the tragedy of 1494; he had followed him into
exile, and had fallen in the act of restoring him.
Pescara's own brilliant courage and conduct had been
the chief factor in the victory of Pavia; yet he had
been robbed of its rewards by Lannoy, ruined by his
self-sacrifice in paying the Imperial troops from his
own resources, refused the modest guerdon for which
he had petitioned. Could not Pescara himself, virtually
an Italian, the husband of Vittoria Colonna, a Roman
of the Romans, be won by the prospect of the crown
of Naples? Who could more fitly succeed the dynasty
which Charles's grandfather Ferdinand, with more than
his normal perfidy, had cheated of its kingdom?

Clement VII. listened to the overtures of Milan and
Venice. Negotiations had been opened with France,
England and the Swiss. Pescara entered into confidential communication with Morone, his personal
friend. Could he but be tempted, the game was won.
But his sense of military honour, or his Spanish origin,
outweighed his grievances and his Italian traditions.
Faith unfaithful kept him falsely true. Pescara betrayed and seized Morone. The troops which he had

unostentatiously concentrated occupied the Lombard
towns (October 1525). The Italian movement, as an
independent enterprise, was over; henceforth it was
merged in a European combination against Charles.

No sooner was Francis I. released than he repudiated
his obligations. All Italy had foreseen this and rejoiced at this striking illustration of Machiavelli's
chapter, "How far princes should keep faith." Clement
VII. at once rejected the Emperor's liberal proposals,
armed his fortresses, and took into his service the naval
condottiere, Andrea Doria. The Imperialist troops were
disorganised by want of pay, disheartened by Pescara's
mortal illness, endangered by the hatred of the
maddened population, hampered by the necessity of
besieging the citadels of Milan and Cremona which still
held for Sforza. If these fortresses once fell, Italians
believed that the hourglass of liberation had run down.
Francis I. was readier to break his word than to face
the consequences of the breach. What were Milan and
Cremona in comparison with the beast of the forest and
the beauty of the Court? Not until May 22, 1526, was
the league of Cognac formed between France, the Pope,
Florence, Venice and Francesco Sforza.

On Henry VIII. was bestowed the title of Protector
of the Holy League. Wolsey sedulously whipped up
the flagging patriotism of Rome and Venice. He
prated to Italian envoys of Italian liberties. He protested that Charles wished to make himself master of
the world, and the Pope his chaplain—a favourite
phrase: cost England what it might, he and his master
would not tolerate the Emperor's monarchy. Henry
VIII. in person assured the Venetian ambassador that he
would not fail Italy. It seemed indeed that the Tudor
king had a genuine interest in Italian independence;

while negotiating with Louise as Regent he had
insisted that Francis should abandon his claim to Milan
in Sforza's favour, contenting himself with the expulsion
of the Habsburg. The English government fanned the
Italian flame, but declined to burn its fingers. The
Defender of the faith was Protector of the Holy League ;
the defence and the protection were on a par.

The professed object of the allies was the peace of
Christendom, but the very formation of the league was
a challenge to a European war. A place was, indeed,
left for Charles V. if he would put Sforza in possession
of Milan, leave the Italian States as they stood at his
accession, visit Rome for his coronation with such
escort only as the Pope and Venice pleased, pay all his
debts to England within three months, and release
the French princes for a ransom. If Charles refused,
and it was certain that he would refuse, the contracting powers agreed to expel the Imperialists from
Lombardy and Genoa, and then from Naples. France
once more claimed a foothold in Italy, for Sforza consented to marry a French princess and cede Asti to
the king, while Genoa now again should fall under
French suzerainty. To the Pope was left the decision
as to Naples, but the problematic king would accept
bankruptcy with his crown, for he was pledged in
advance to pay a large pension to France, to provide a
wealthy principality for Henry VIII. and reward Wolsey
with a substantial lordship. Francis brutally left Italy
to her fate ; for more than a year he never moved, and
by that time two of the signatories of the league had
fallen. Either he wished the Emperor and the Italian
States to exhaust each other, that he might then impose
his yoke, or else at Italy's expense he hoped to recover
his sons by composition with the Emperor. To release

his sons he was ready, it was said, not merely to marry Eleanor, who was in the prime of her womanly beauty, but any hag of a hundred years or an Imperial mule.

Clement VII. was learned, clever, respectable, and industrious, but he had little enterprise and less decision. The Papalists from the South, the Venetians from the East, had closed round the small Imperialist force which, in the midst of the huge, hostile city, was clinging desperately to the siege of Milan citadel. In vain the peasantry of Lombardy and Piedmont murdered stragglers and cut down companies; in vain the populace of Milan stormed outposts, and seizing the Cathedral, clanged its bell for war; in vain the Venetians, surprising Lodi, crossed the Adda to join the Papalists. On July 6, 1526, the general of the allies, the Duke of Urbino, attacked the besieging force and was beaten off. He waited for the arrival of the Swiss, intending to attack again on the 25th. He was just a day too long; the citadel had but rations for four men left, and was driven to capitulate.[1]

Sforza had fallen; it was now the turn of Clement. All Imperial ambassadors and officials had told Charles that it was impossible to resist the league, that he must divide it by making terms with France, or by winning the roving affections of the Medici. Charles was too proud to condone his rival's perjury, but he went to the utmost limits of concession to the Pope. Clement's friendship was, indeed, an absolute necessity, not only in view of Italian, but of German and Spanish interests, and for the defence of Austria and Hungary against the advancing Turk. If the Pope's statement to a French

[1] Attention may be called to two monographs on military events between Pavia and the Sack of Rome : A. Professione, *Dalla battaglia di Pavia al sacco di Roma*, 1890, and A. R. Villa, *Italia desde la batalla de Pavia hasta el saco de Roma*, 1885.

envoy may be believed, Charles offered to invest Sforza
with Milan after a merely formal trial, to abandon the
Duke of Ferrara to the Pope's greed and vengeance, to
concede entire control over the Church in Naples, and
so close a quarrel of a century past and several centuries
to come, even to submit to his arbitration the dispute
with France.

Clement's constitutional irresolution infected his
antagonists; Charles was by nature and circumstance
addicted to alternatives. He was now ringing the
changes on force and friendship. If, he wrote, conciliation proved impossible, his envoys might try the effect
of fright. This course was now being urged alike from
Genoa and Rome. "All the harm that you can do to
the Pope," wrote Lope de Soria, "is lawful, considering
his ingratitude, and want of respect for the service of
God and Christendom. . . . You alone can punish him.
You ought to refuse the obedience of your dominions,
and call out all your vassals against him, as a warning
that Popes should not usurp the authority of Emperors
nor form leagues against them." From Rome, Secretary
Perez advised Charles to make war in grim earnest
on the Pope, for all the people of Rome were ripe for
revolution against Papal rule. The theologian, Pedro
de Urries, recommended from Genoa, that Charles should
nominate the Cardinal Colonna captain-general, and
send him to take Rome and all the neighbouring
fortresses; which done, he should appropriate one-third
of Church revenues for a term of years, and impound
the income of the Cardinals who followed Clement.

The theologian's advice was probably in part anticipated. The Cardinal Pompeo Colonna who, as a staunch
Ghibelline and for personal reasons, was Clement's
determined enemy, had long offered to turn him out of

Rome and overthrow the Medicean government at
Florence. Ugo de Moncada, the violent, unscrupulous
envoy extraordinary whom Charles had sent to Rome
when threats might become the alternative for concessions, now let Colonna work his will. After a trumped-
up treaty, which caused Clement to disband his troops,
the Cardinal and the envoy let loose their soldiery
from the Alban hills upon the capital. Not a Roman
hand was raised to defend the Pope, who had taxed his
subjects almost to starvation. The Imperial eagles
floated over the Vatican ; from his shelter in the castle
of St. Angelo Clement could watch the plunderers
issuing laden from his palace (September 20, 1526).

If Colonna's raid was a rehearsal of the tragedy
shortly to be staged, it was also a Spanish-Italian adaptation of that Franco-Italian drama which, at Boniface
VIII.'s expense, a French envoy and another Colonna
had long ago acted at Anagni. For two trumpery
Ferrarese townships the Pope had finally broken
with the Emperor. It was a grim practical joke on the
temporal power which the Papacy had so laboriously
amassed at so great a sacrifice, that a member of the
Holy College, proprietor of a dozen half-savage villages,
should drive the Holy Father from the Vatican, and
loot his furniture. It was all the grimmer, since at the
very moment of Colonna's attack, the Pope was discussing the news of the Hungarian defeat at Mohacz,
which laid central Europe open to the Turk. Pope and
Sultan were already the enemies of the Emperor and his
brother. The Porte was the strenuous sword, the
Vatican the somewhat ineffective shield, against which
the official champion of orthodoxy must arm.

Moncada, full of apologies for the outrageous conduct
of his troops, visited Clement in St. Angelo, and

extorted a pledge that the Papal troops should be withdrawn from the army of the league in North Italy.
Secretary Perez wrote to Charles, advising him to
disclaim all responsibility for what had happened.
Charles assured the Pope and the European princes that
the "disagreeable incident" was due to the unpremedi-
tated action of undisciplined troops and against the
will of their commanders; that he would have given
anything that so gross an outrage should not have been
inflicted by troops under a captain of his own. He had
not probably foreseen or desired the actual pillage of
the Vatican. Now, having frightened Clement, he
once more tried to win him; but a breath of good
news from North Italy turned the Papal weathercock.
Clement seized the opportunity to wreak his vengeance
on the wrecked Colonna villages, and even inflicted a
reverse on Lannoy's Neapolitan troops.

The viceroy, a pupil of the policy of Chièvres, was
too timid, not sufficiently sanguine for a season of storm
and stress. Disbelieving in the possibility of victory,
he pandered to the Pope's illusions by offering terms
unreasonably good. These Clement at length accepted,
but the solution of the Papal-Imperial problem had
already passed into hands of a rougher and readier type
than those of a depressed viceroy, an over-sanguine
Pope and an absent Emperor. Clement and Lannoy
might haggle over conditions and securities, but meanwhile the Germans, who with Frundsberg had opened
new passes from Trent to Brescia, and the Spaniards,
who under Bourbon had starved on the exhausted fields
of Lombardy, must be paid and fed. When once
these two forces were suffered by the passive generals
of the League to unite at Milan, the Pope's fate was
sealed.

There was really no longer such a thing as the liberty of Italy, as an ideal for which to fight. Italy was a geographical, a sentimental, but not a political expression. A Colonna in Imperial interest had humiliated the Pope. The Duke of Ferrara, a Papal feudatory, forced from his traditions by the intrigues of successive Popes, saved the German invaders from extinction by giving them supplies and lending them his fine artillery. A ball from a Ferrarese gun wounded to the death the first of Italian soldiers, Giovanni de' Medici. The Venetians, rightly mistrusting the Pope's steadfastness, ordered their general, the Duke of Urbino, to limit his action to the defence of the Republic's territory, against which the starving Imperialists would turn if Clement deserted the Italian cause. Urbino, the victim of the territorial ambitions of the Medici Popes, was unlikely to abandon his natural caution in Papal interests. So intent was Clement on temporal gains, that he refused to cede to the allied general the usurped possession of San Leo, a township on a hill-top inaccessible from anywhere. The government of Florence had as much to fear from revolutionists within as from Imperialists without. Italian kites and crows were squabbling, when from Germany and Spain eagles and vultures had gathered to their prey.

The Imperialist army in the North was in full mutiny, and clamoured to be led to Rome. Frundsberg in attempting to control his *landsknechts* was struck down by apoplexy at the drum-head. Bourbon threw in his lot with the mutineers; a discredited adventurer, he had spent his fortune on the army, and through the army must re-make it. The whole force of 20,000 men or more, mad with hunger and suffering, staggered blindly down through Italy.

Florence was too strongly held to be attacked; the peril of Rome became immediate. In vain Lannoy pleaded his convention with the Pope; too late Clement sold Cardinals' hats to provide for the defence. Renzo da Ceri, indeed, the skilful defender of Marseilles, manned the walls with such mercenaries as he had. Urbino was shadowing the mutineers at a respectful distance. The Imperialists had abandoned their artillery at Siena; they had neither food nor transport; a single check and the whole force must be extinguished.

In a thick mist on the morning of May 6, 1527, the attacking force flung itself upon the western walls of Rome. Bourbon, seeing his men waver, sprang upon a ladder to scale the wall; with his foot upon the second rung he was shot down, but his example saved the day. The mutineers poured into the Borgo. The Pope with the more fortunate of his Cardinals narrowly escaped to the Castle of St. Angelo; in the space of three *credos* more he would have been caught. No geese cackling in the mist had saved the Vatican; no Horatius held the bridge across the Tiber; the college of Cardinals styled itself the Senate, but such Senators did not for a moment awe, or, indeed, await the barbarian host. Rome palpitated with horror while the international medley of Germans, Spaniards, and Italians, with all the discipline of expert mutiny, stood at ease in the *piazza* Navona and other squares until the signal for the sack was given.

The long-drawn agony of the ensuing weeks needs no fresh description. Rome after all only endured what a hundred towns and villages less holy had more undeservedly suffered. The ladies of Rome were no chaster, her nuns no more saintly, than those of Borgo San Donnino. Cardinals and prelates were no

more susceptible to shame and torture than the humble
priests and friars who in many an unknown village
had been the victims of Lutheran *landsknechts*. Long
before the reign of Charles the Spaniards had earned
an unenviable notoriety for their uncanny skill in the
discovery of hidden treasure. The horrors of the sack
of Rome were but the concentrated essence of the
sufferings of Italy for which the first French invasion
of 1494 must be held responsible.[1]

How far is the tragedy of the storm and sack to be
debited to the memory of Charles? It has been seen
that his starving army was in a chronic condition of
mutiny; that Bourbon himself could only retain a
measure of control by sharing in its passions. Communications between Spain and Italy were so slow and
difficult that events refused to wait upon despatches.
The war of pamphlets and recriminations had little
synchronism with the clash of arms. The proof of this
is easy. A Papal brief of June 23, 1526, detailing the
Emperor's enormities, reached Granada on August 20.
The Emperor's elaborate Apologia covered the whole
field of Papal offences from 1518 until the date of its
presentation. It well deserves a place among the
weightiest instruments in the armoury of Ghibelline
polemics. Of this, moreover, Charles was conscious,
for he had it simultaneously printed in Spain, Germany and the Netherlands, and reprints were rapid.

---

[1] The accounts of the sack of Rome are too numerous to be mentioned here.
Attention may be called to another of A. R. Villa's useful monographs, *Memorias para la historia del asalto y saco de Roma*, 1875. Among contemporary
descriptions recently published are the *Relation inédite de Jean Cave*, in
Mélanges d'archéologie et d'histoire publiés par l'École française à Rome, vol.
xvi. (also published separately), and *Il diario di Marcello Alberini*, 1521-36,
printed by D. Orano in *Arch. R. Soc. Rom.* 1895 and 1896. Some letters are
printed in *Hist. Jahrbuch*, 1891. See also H. Schultz, *Der Sacco di Roma* ;
Karls V. Truppen in Rom. (*Hallische Abhandl. zur neueren Geschichte, xxxii.*,
1894).

This defence was with much solemnity delivered to
the nuncio on September 17. On the next day he
gave the nuncio a more conciliatory letter, while on
October 6 was composed a missive, not to the Pope,
but to the College of Cardinals, in the name of the
Empire and all Christendom, begging them to hinder
the Pope in his godless intentions, and to further the
meeting of a Council which, in their default, the Emperor would summon on the strength of his Imperial
authority. These three documents were delivered in
Rome on December 8, long after the pillow of Papal
policy had submitted to and rebounded from the
pressure of Moncada's fist. The correspondence, of
high theoretical interest, had absolutely no influence
upon the sequence of events.

It is clear therefore that the responsibility of
Charles, or rather his intentions, must be carefully
checked by dates. He was necessarily some three
months behind time in his information as to the
military situation and the condition of his army,—an
all-important question. He was playing a game or
several games of chess blindfold with an interval of
from two to three months between the moves. It is
not therefore surprising if the Emperor's despatches to
the viceroy and to Bourbon contained inconsistencies.

Charles did not know that Bourbon was definitely
on the march for Rome until Rome had fallen. Yet
Bourbon, until the moment of his arrival at the
Milvian bridge, was anticipating his wishes. As
Charles had authorised Moncada to use the Colonna
for putting pressure upon Clement, so now he had
ordered Lannoy to amuse the Pope with truces, until
Bourbon could dictate terms under the walls of Rome.
He warned Lannoy not to trust the Pope, for those of

Rome would never do any good or virtuous action, unless reduced to the last extremities; he must cut his straps from another's hide—draw money, that is, from his nearest neighbours for the maintenance of the troops; Florence as well as Rome deserved some chastisement; in treating of peace with Clement, it was essential to make so safe that one would not always have to begin again at the beginning. On March 31 he wrote to Bourbon that he must be quick with his game, which was being too slowly played; he must employ his army to enforce a good peace, or at least a good truce. On April 23, a fortnight before the sack, in sending Bourbon powers to treat, he instructed him to keep them secret, for it was much better that Pope and princes should realise that he was marching to impose peace by force. Charles, in fact, looked to conciliation effected under a show of force, but the Spanish veterans and Lutheran *landsknechts*, with whom the decision lay, had other views than a full-dress parade under the walls of Rome.

It is impossible to defend the political morality of Charles in these two dark years, but his forbearance had been great, and greater still his provocation. Neither friend nor foe could trust Clement, who was, not only faithless, but irresolute. The other constituents of the Emperor's problem were Francis I. and Wolsey. This much may be said in his favour that he only accepted the alternative of an Italian war under compulsion, and that he had, not only a theoretical, but a practical and personal interest in the projects for a Christian war against the infidel. The secret instructions of December 13, 1526, to the Spanish envoy in England prove that Charles was already prepared to suspend the prosecution of his claim to the duchy of Burgundy, to place the portion of Lombardy which he occupied in the hands of Bourbon, until the guilt or innocence of Sforza were decided, and to reassure European and Italian princes that his intended visit to Rome for his coronation involved no designs on Italian liberties.

The news of the sack of Rome reached Spain when the festivities for the birth of the Infant Philip were going merrily forward. It is often said that Charles at once suspended them. On the contrary he gave as an excuse for their continuance the expense which the nobles had incurred therein; he took a personal part in every joust or game. He quickly, however, found that public opinion was deeply stirred by the Pope's misfortunes. The Archbishop of Toledo and the Duke of Alba openly remonstrated; many grandees thought that the festivities should be suspended, lest they should be ascribed to improper motives. Bourbon's death delighted all the Court with the exception of the Flemings. His obsequies were indeed celebrated in the Emperor's presence for five days, but when Charles effusively assured the nuncio that Bourbon was the involuntary plaything of his army, few believed it; Spaniards abused Bourbon as the deepest-dyed villain that had ever lived.

Having tested public opinion, Charles countermanded the festivities, and the Court went into mourning. A little later he wrote a circular letter to the crowned heads stating that he would rather not have conquered than win such a victory. Again and again he assured Pope and Cardinals that the tragedy was beyond his knowledge and against his wish. Nevertheless he was resolved to make his profit out of the stroke of fortune which had placed his enemy at his mercy.

As to the exact extent to which he should press his advantage Charles was genuinely irresolute. Among Spaniards and in his own court opinion was divided. Imperial agents, Spanish or Italian, who had lived long in Italy were convinced of the rottenness of the present Papal system; they urged that all the recent wars were the result of the policy of the Popes, who had fomented discord among the powers to divert attention from the abuses of the Curia. To them the sack of Rome was a judgment from the justice-seat of heaven. If there was with them any hesitation as to the extinction of the temporal power, it arose from the fear that France and England might set up national patriarchates, and Spain be saddled with the expensive luxury of a puppet-Pope. The Spanish troops in Rome, with all their zealous Catholic training, had shown no more respect for sacred things and holy persons than had the Lutheran *landsknechts* who counted it for righteousness to scourge the whore of Babylon.

In Spain the court party which followed the Chancellor Gattinara was Erasmian; its most notable representative, Alonso Valdés, was Erasmian and something more; he was a protagonist in the long strife between the temporal and spiritual power, to which his pamphlets form no mean contribution.[1] The fact that there was a quarrel of some standing between these Erasmian secularists and the friars aggravated the division on the present situation, which supplied either side with arguments and illustrations drawn from life. In spite of the benevolent tolerance of liberal opinion by the Inquisition at this time, the friars dominated public opinion to a great extent; it

---

[1] For the Emperor's defence see E. Boehmer, *Bibliotheca Wiffeniana*, vol. i., 1874.

is probable that the clergy refused a grant in Cortes because the Emperor might employ it against the Pope.

Charles himself halted between two opinions. His first envoy to the Pope, Pierre de Veyre, was instructed to make claims which would have reduced the temporal power to the shadow of a shade. On his steps, however, closely followed the Emperor's confessor. Quiñones is described by a plain-spoken English envoy as " a whoresun flatteryng fryar," but he had told Charles with no adulatory phrases that if he did not make haste to do his duty towards the Pope and make good the grievous wrongs inflicted, he could no longer call himself Emperor, but Luther's captain. It was said in Spain that Quiñones had instructions to release the Pope and restore all his fortresses. The Venetian ambassador at Valladolid hit the nail hard upon the head. "The Emperor," he wrote, "is by nature slow, and in the present situation is very doubtful what he ought to do. On the one hand it seems to him fair to release the Pope, while on the other he does not feel sure of securing his Holiness's friendship even if he does so " (August 1, 1527).

The conflict of opinion among Charles's advisers was necessarily serviceable to Clement. In the treaty of November 26 the conqueror's more extreme pretensions had disappeared. The Papal States were restored with the exception that Ostia, Civita Vecchia, Civita Castellana and Forlì, were to be occupied as securities, while hostages from the Medici family and the College of Cardinals were given as pledges for the payment of a sum of money to satisfy the troops. In the earlier stages of the quarrel the Emperor had made much insistence on a General Council, sometimes as a means of reconciling the European powers, sometimes with the wider aim of purifying the Church on Erasmian lines, and of reconciling the dissidents to a more liberal system. In the treaty the subject of the Council reduced itself to vague generalities.

Moncada regarded the Emperor's concessions as dangerously generous. Civita Castellana was not surrendered, nor was the Pope's ransom paid in full. But Clement was an inconvenient prisoner; there were fears that the soldiery might offer obstacles to his release. It is possible that the Imperialist officers deliberately looked the other way when the Pope in disguise slipped through the Vatican gardens, and escaped to a tumbledown palace at Orvieto (December 6, 1527). Here, before long, he was protected from Imperial molestation by the French advance.

The temporal power of the Papacy had been in real danger. In Italy there was a general belief that its days were numbered. Even the lower classes, writes Varchi, thought that, as pastoral staff and sword went ill together, the Pope would once more return to his office as mass priest at St. John Lateran. For such a revolution Charles was too conservative and too irresolute. He let slip his chance of recovering Rome and Italy for the Empire, even as he had abandoned his project for dismembering France. "Your majesty is on the straight road to universal dominion," cried Gattinara in triumph, and the kings of France and England echoed the cry in fear. But Charles was not marching along the road; he was merely marking time, while his enemies at leisure blocked the way. "We must not have to begin all over again," had said Charles himself. Yet this fresh beginning was very near at hand, nor in the Emperor's reign was there

any ending. The Augean stables had been cleansed,—
nay, gutted,—but the old steed and the old stablemen
were reinstalled.

The capture of Rome, followed by Clement's capitulation, was for Charles a Pyrrhic victory; the total
loss of Italy seemed likely to be its sole result. A
week before the tragedy the kings of France and
England had concluded the alliance of Westminster,
which they had long negotiated. They agreed to send
an ultimatum demanding the release of the French
princes on payment of a ransom. Francis, braving
the Emperor's vengeance for his abandonment of
Eleanor, was prepared to accept the hand of Mary
Tudor, rejected of the Emperor, either for himself or
for his son. Wolsey and his master proposed to move
every stone in the cause of the Holy See, and for the
prevention of a universal monarchy. In August the
treaty of Amiens knit together the two crowns in a
project for offensive war.

Henry VIII. had every reason to render service to
the Pope, whose wrongs might well induce him to
consent to his ally's divorce from the aunt of his
enemy. Although, however, his envoys made their
way to Rome with infinite difficulty, the thoughts
of the king were fully occupied by Anne Boleyn. The
martial zeal of Francis was more practical. Even
before the treaty of Amiens war had been opened on
his side, though without declaration, and in the autumn
Lautrec took command of the French forces co-operating
with the Venetians and Milanese. His vastly superior
forces soon pinned Antonio de Leyva to the walls of
Milan, though he had wrought miracles with but 6000
unfed, unpaid men. Every power in Italy turned
against the Emperor. The Duke of Ferrara reverted

to the traditional French alliance; Florence, controlled
by the anti-Medicean party, threw herself into the
arms of France; even Savoy and Mantua deserted.
Above all Genoa, at the appearance of the fleet of
Andrea Doria, now a *condottiere* in French service,
fell away from Charles. In vain de Leyva looked for
the advance of the Imperial troops from Rome. These
were now a disorganised mob of brigands, decimated
by their own excesses, exhausted by the recurrent
delirium of plunder. No general dared assume command. Lannoy, when he visited Rome, had almost
to remain in hiding; he too was now dead. Not till
January 1528 was the Prince of Orange induced to
place himself at their head.

In this month Lautrec started on his march for
Naples, and it was only then that the heralds of the
French and English kings brought to Charles the formal
declaration of war. The challenge was the origin of
a serio-comic episode in Charles's history. He repeated
to the French herald a message despatched to Francis
from Granada when his breach of faith was first made
known:—" Your king has done a sorry, dastard deed in
breaking his word to me, and this I am ready to
maintain, my person against his." Francis did not take
up the challenge with marked alacrity. After nearly
five months he retorted in Granvelle's presence that,
if it were asserted that he had ever done anything
unworthy of a gentleman of honour, the Emperor lied
in his throat; he begged that he would write no more,
but fix the time and place. To this Charles sent a
written reply that the place should be decided by a
court of honour, but ironically suggested the Bidassoa,
on whose waters Francis had regained his liberty. On
this self-same river the Imperial herald was kept waiting

for seven dreary weeks, and only on September 9 was allowed to appear before the king.   Even then Francis would not receive the letter, but shouted him down with cries of " The safe-conduct and the place."   The herald, losing his head, retired, his mission unfulfilled, his letter still in hand.

With this farcical scene the would-be melodrama ended.   While the principals were wrangling, the Imperial and French armies had been, without any safe-conduct, fighting, and hill and plain round Naples had been the field.   In that very month of September the French champions had to admit defeat.   Charles had probably been in earnest.   He reproached his herald for accepting the customary guerdon, and for not throwing his challenge, according to instructions, at the French king's feet.   He wrote to Ferdinand in July that it would be from no fault of his own if the fight fell through.   In Spain he threw himself upon public feeling, printing his case and begging for the advice of the Council of Castile, the Archbishop of Toledo, the great nobles and the towns.   Their answers may still be read : they usually deprecate the personal encounter with much contorted argument and sound common sense.[1]   Wolsey's pious wish had proved a prophecy :—
" I truste to God these yong corragious passions shall be finally converted into fume."

The year 1528 was pregnant with the fate of Italy and Charles's fortunes.   Had Lautrec shown more dash, Naples must have fallen.   The delay just saved the Imperial cause.   Yet the French general for long met no resistance.   The Abruzzi, always hostile to the actual

---

[1] Correspondence relating to the challenge will be found in *Documentos Ineditos*, vol. i.   In the same volume are printed the letters of Ugo de Moncada to Charles until his death before Salerno.   Salinas gives a full account of the challenge.

ruler of Naples, rose in revolt; the nobility of the kingdom once more gave proof of its Angevin sympathies.
Although Orange and the new viceroy, Moncada, contrived
to draw or drive their troops from Rome, they strove in
vain to save Apulia.   Desperate letters reached Spain
from Italy, that nothing but a miracle from God could
save it from falling into the Frenchman's hands.
Gattinara was told that the Spanish government took
no thought for the needs of them who daily offered up
their lives; there was no rescue unless Charles or his
brother came.

By the end of April Lautrec had shut the Imperialists up in Naples; they dared not arm the people for
fear of disaffection.   Starvation stared them in the face,
for the French and Genoese fleet, blockading the bay,
cut off all hope of supplies from Spain or Sicily.   In
making a desperate effort to meet a Sicilian convoy,
Moncada's fleet was annihilated in the gulf of Salerno
by Filippino Doria.   The viceroy was killed; the Spanish
seaman, experienced as he was, was no match for the
Genoese.   The Venetian fleet, fresh from conquests on
the Apulian coasts, now rode with the French and
Genoese squadrons before the town.

This then was the result of all the Imperial victories
in Italy.   Milan and Naples, two huge disaffected
cities, were virtually the only posts held for Charles,
and this by miserably insufficient bands of starving
mercenaries.   Yet their conduct might well have modified Machiavelli's opinion of the worthlessness of
mercenary troops.   Very moving are the forlorn letters
of their leaders to the apparently apathetic Emperor.
De Leyva wrote from Milan, even in 1527, that Charles
must not build upon his luck, for God did not work
miracles every day; that his troops were without pay

and ammunition ; that they were still fighting and had
no fear, and yet the end must needs be death by
hunger : not a letter, he added, had been received for
four months. In Naples the Spaniards and Italians
gave up their pittance of wine that the Germans might
not lack it. The Germans, when Orange told them
that they too must live on bread and water, replied that
none should say that such a noble town was lost for
want of wine. Mercenaries of the three nations bound
themselves by oaths not to desert each other. Orange
in his despatches dilated on the valour of his troops,—
" Yet, Sire, neither they nor I can do more than the
possible ; if we have to hold out beyond this month, the
end will be very near. Therefore, Sire, do not forget
us."

It seemed, indeed, as if Charles had completely
forgotten Italy, that he cared nothing for his promises,
his generals and his troops. He was, in fact, deficient
in imagination, and he had not yet been in Italy ; he
did not possess the power of realising what he had not
seen, although he quickly adapted himself to a foreign
environment with which he was brought in actual contact. He was not, however, so apathetic as he seemed.
The difficulty of communication between Spain and
Italy can scarcely be exaggerated. The consequences
of the loss of Genoa were now realised to the full ; the
power of the sea had passed to France ; Spain could not
safely float a galley on Mediterranean waters. To send
Spanish drafts to Italy was to court certain capture.
Charles was compelled to warn his aunt Margaret,
Ferdinand, and the Milanese and Neapolitan governors
that they must rely on their own judgment and their
own revenues ; the units of his too extensive Empire
were in confessed isolation.

Charles was, moreover, entirely without resources.
In 1527 the Castilian Cortes had refused supply on the
ground, it is said, that the war was against the Pope;
the Aragonese in 1528, as often, proved recalcitrant.
Not a ducat could be raised from Italy or Germany,
Charles did, indeed send letters of exchange to Italy,
but who could cash them? The only banking centres—
Venice, Florence, Genoa—were all his enemies. His
letters prove that he was relying on the negotiations
with Portugal for the mortgage of the Moluccas, but he
sorrowfully confessed that "he had reckoned without
his host," that "if he had to deal with people who had
a little sense, the affair would long ago have been
settled, but the Portuguese were mere merchants, always
trying to beat him down."

Spanish agents in Italy had long insisted that the
situation could only be saved by Charles's presence.
Apart from the impossibility of leaving Spain, it was
clearly unlikely that, even if he started, he could reach
Italy. He therefore in the late autumn of 1527 threw
the burden upon Ferdinand, imploring him to take or
to send a German army to the relief of Naples. But
the Ferdinand of 1527 was not the Ferdinand of 1526.
He was no longer merely the Emperor's vicegerent in
Germany, his brother's *alter ego*, but the King of
Hungary and Bohemia. He had other problems to
solve, his own duties to fulfil. Zapolya was contesting
Hungary with him, the Turk would soon be at his gates.
He did indeed despatch in May 1528 the zealous
Imperialist champion, Henry of Brunswick, but the
wild *landsknechts*, for the most part Lutherans, only added
to the detestation of Imperial rule in Northern Italy, and
to the famine which was devastating even prosperous,
victorious Venice. Germans, with the honourable

exception of those in Naples, would not face starvation. The force which was to relieve Naples could not even cross the Adda under the fire of the batteries of Lodi, and in August straggled, famished and mutinous, back to Germany.

In his early troubles Charles always found dependable allies in his ostensible enemies. Clement VII. was yet more irresolute than Charles, for he was irresolute not merely as to means but as to ends. Francis I. was yet more apathetic than Charles, for it was not merely that his sympathies were dormant, but that they were actively engaged elsewhere,—to the last pretty woman that attracted his roving, vulgar fancy,—to the last forest that offered a good head of game. Against such enemies Charles's patience and decision as to ends were valuable auxiliaries. A power substantially strong, yet unable to rapidly realise its strength, could afford to act on the phrase, which was for ever on the lips of Italian statesmen, and which, writing of weak and would-be neutral states, Machiavelli so emphatically condemned. Charles could venture to enjoy the benefits of time (*godere il beneficio del tempo*).

Had Clement VII. decided to ally himself with France, the fate of Italy would probably have not been happier, but it might have been very different. At Orvieto Clement was in no personal danger from the Imperialists, for the French swept past Rome to Naples. It seemed certain at first sight that he would renew his relations with the French crown, begun when its prospects of success were far less radiant. But Clement, although a speculator, was rarely sanguine; it was his nature to lay against the favourite. Apart from this, his position was really intricate. For the independence of the Papacy it would be a gain that the Emperor

should cease to hold Milan and Naples. The alliance of
France would save him from all danger of a General
Council, for which he had an insuperable repulsion. He
would have been more or less than human if he could
have forgiven the outrages inflicted by the Emperor's
troops. Charles himself, while professing to regret the
unfortunate incident or accident of the Sack of Rome,
had utilised it to the full, and insisted on holding the
military keys of the Papal States. But Clement was
first Medici and then Pope, and as Pope he placed his
territorial Italian ambitions high above the spiritual, or
even the European, interests of the Papacy. His first
aim would be to restore the Medici to Florence, but then
Florence was under French protection. The very
general of the army of the League, the Duke of Urbino,
had been the victim and was still the enemy of the
Medici. In the general disturbance Venice had seized
Ravenna and Cervia, while the Duke of Ferrara reoccupied
his Imperial fiefs of Modena and Reggio, but Venice and
Ferrara were staunch allies of the French king. And so
in spite of French persuasions Clement VII. sat motion-
less on his rail at Orvieto, and well was it for him that
he so sat.

Francis I. had arrears of pleasure to make up, and
his finances were in a condition little better than those
of Charles. Until it was too late he did nothing to
make victory certain by reinforcing Lautrec in front of
Naples. Lautrec himself alienated the Neapolitan nobles,
and in the summer of 1528 Neapolitan towns began to
pass over to the Emperor. But worse than all was the
alienation of Genoa and of Andrea Doria by the French
king. He imposed a French governor and a French
garrison upon the city, depriving her of her free constitution ; he refused to Andrea Doria the reasonable

reward of his services ; against the warnings of the Pope and Trivulzio he converted Savona into a rival port. Charles had for more than a year attempted to win Doria, whose fleet suddenly left the Bay of Naples in July, and, appearing off Genoa under Imperial colours, forced the French garrison to capitulate in September.

Thus the sea power passed from the French king to the Emperor, and with him it remained, save when the union of the French with the Turkish-Algerian squadrons gave Francis a momentary superiority off the Provençal coast. The importance of Doria's change of sides can scarcely be overestimated. His price was, indeed, the independence of Genoa, but this was little more than nominal. She was for centuries the bank of the Spanish kings, and the water-gate to Italy. Even before the French loss of Genoa the Bay of Naples was open, and supplies poured in for the starving garrison, while the French rotted away from plague, malaria and famine. The death of Lautrec, the capture of Navarro, the capitulation of the whole French army, followed fast upon each other (August–September 1528).

Both combatants were by this time absolutely exhausted. After the Duke of Brunswick's retreat Francis had sent Saint-Pol to drive Leyva from Milan and march on Naples. But the Spaniard made up in skill for his inferiority in numbers. He surprised and beat Saint-Pol at Landriano, as the latter was struggling to thread the passes between Lombardy and Genoa. This battle (June 1529) was fought out between only 8000 and 12,000 men, but it determined the fate of Lombardy for many a generation. Neither Charles nor his successor had ever seriously to defend Milan against French attack. Few such insignificant battles have had more permanent results.

The Pope had already sent the Bishop of Vaison to make his peace, and on June 29, 1529 the treaty of Barcelona was signed. By this it was stipulated that the Pope should recover from Venice Ravenna and Cervia, and from Ferrara Modena, Reggio and Rubiera : the Medici should be restored to Florence, and Alessandro marry the Emperor's bastard Margaret. The Pope consented to invest Charles with Naples and to demand no tribute, to give his troops free passage through his territories. Pope and Emperor together would decide the fate of Milan, the source of all evil. It is noticeable that the subject of a Council had dropped out of sight. The assurance of the Imperial envoys at Rome that their master would not press it, had decided Clement to negotiate for peace. Charles and Ferdinand now pledged themselves to subdue the heretics, if they would not obey the Pope. Clement in return promised to lay his ban upon all who aided the Turk and tempted him into Europe ; he granted Charles and Ferdinand a quarter of the ecclesiastical revenues of their dominions to be employed against the Turks, and absolution to all those who had outraged Rome and its territories, on condition that they would march against the infidel.

This "Eternal Peace" between Pope and Emperor might seem, as has been said, the revival of the mediæval ideal, the blotting out of some two centuries. In fact it was a temporary expedient, a working compromise between two essentially modern powers, to satisfy immediate needs in which there was little that was ideal. Clement wished to recover Italian townships and to be rid of the terror of a Council ; Charles must needs have money, and it was urgent that he should visit Italy. There might be antiquarian talk of infidel and heretic, but Solyman and Luther were

modernity itself, to be combated only by the most
modern weapons of diplomacy or war. Sentiment did,
indeed, in one respect affect the agreement between
Charles and Clement. On July 16 the Pope, under
the Emperor's pressure, transferred the divorce of Henry
VIII. to Rome. This caused a new schism in the
Church and completed the breach in the Anglo-Burgund-
ian alliance. Great, however, as were the results to
Charles's successors, he was personally not much affected.
Catherine died before the next French war broke out,
and this made it the easier for her nephew to pursue the
prudent policy of protest, beyond which he did not
mean to pass. An English envoy early in the day had
shrewdly said that Charles had seen two sisters (the
queens of Denmark and Hungary) deprived of their
kingdoms without avenging them, and was not therefore
likely to go to war for Catherine. Few men will court
ruin for an aunt. Peace with France closely followed.
On August 3, 1529 was signed the treaty of Cambrai,
which the Emperor's aunt Margaret and the king's
mother had for some months been negotiating. It was
in the main a recapitulation of the treaty of Madrid,
but Charles did not insist on the cession of Burgundy
nor on the complete reinstatement of Bourbon's heirs.
His claims to Burgundy, Macon and Auxerre were
reserved for friendly and judicial settlement; Charles
never surrendered them, and in later years warned
his son to maintain them, but not to make them a
casus belli. Francis I. abandoned all his Italian claims
and Italian allies, even engaging to compel Venice to
disgorge Ravenna and Cervia on the Pope's behalf. So
also in Germany a free hand was given to the Emperor
to deal with heretics and enemies as vengeance or mercy
prompted. In exchange for an enormous ransom the

French princes were released; the marriage of Charles's
sister Eleanor was at length completed, and henceforth
he had a spy or an ally on his rival's throne; he might
almost claim that France had become a member of the
family federation.

Charles had at last been able to sail for Italy. He
put in at Monaco and at Savona, where he heard of the
conclusion of the treaty of Cambrai. The entry of his
fleet into the port of Genoa on August 12 was a right
royal sight. The Imperial galley was rowed by two
hundred liberated slaves, for Andrea Doria had urged
that it did not become so great a king to be rowed by
convicts. Her sails were of black and yellow damask
bearing the Emperor's device, her ropes were all of
silken cord. As she swept into the harbour, every ship
lowered her sails to the water, the cannon roared, and
every voice kept shouting—"Carlo, Carlo! Impero,
Impero! God bless and preserve the King of the World."
A wooden platform, two hundred feet in length, had been
built out from the mole, and here the *Signoria* of the
city met the Emperor as he landed, clad from head to
foot in white, and followed by his three companies of
German, Spanish and Flemish guards.[1]

Although the mountains which encircle Genoa might
echo the salvos and cries of joy with which the Emperor
was welcomed, yet his advent caused terror in the
miserable land of Italy, already unnerved by war,
plague and famine. Milan and Venice made some
hysterical show of resistance, but the Turkish advance
upon Vienna was in itself · sufficient to make the
Emperor adopt a friendly attitude. He had, he said,
none of the desire for universal lordship which his

---

[1] A graphic account of Charles's visit to Italy may be found in *Cronaca del
Soggiorno di Carlo V. in Italia dal* 29 *Luglio* 1529 *al* 25 *Aprile* 1530, published
by M. Romano (Hœpli, Milan).

enemies ascribed to him ; he did not covet an inch of land that was not his own. Italy was highly strung and susceptible of alternating moods; her forebodings easily made way for panegyric.

From Genoa Charles journeyed to Piacenza, where he received the treaty of Cambrai for signature. At Parma he was greeted by the news of the Turkish defeat before Vienna, and thence he travelled by Modena and Reggio to Bologna, entering this second capital of the Papacy on November 5, a fortnight after the arrival of Clement VII. The original programme had been that Charles should visit Naples and then be crowned at Rome. Ferdinand, however, was loudly calling him to Germany. Clement was privily pushing him in the same direction, for, as he explained to anti-Imperialist friends, in Germany he would get rid of all his money. Thus it was agreed that the coronation must take place at Bologna. Experts persuaded the Emperor that place was not of the essence of the ceremony, although the Romans vowed that they would not style him Emperor of the Romans but of the Bolognese, which made him very angry. Here, however, it was that Charles received the iron crown of Lombardy, and then in the Cathedral of San Petronio the Pope placed upon his head the crown of the Empire (February 24, 1530). For Clement this can have been no pleasant task :—"The Pope," wrote the bishop of Tarbes, "tried to show the Emperor the best cheer possible ; but I think he never in his life performed a ceremony which touched him so near the heart, nor of which less good is likely to come to him. For several times when he thought no one saw him he heaved such sighs that heavy as his cope was, he made it shake in good earnest." There was a presentiment among the people that

Charles would be the last Emperor crowned in Italy.
and so it proved.

The Emperor's biographer, H. Baumgarten, as Ranke
before him, has noticed that Charles was surrounded,
not by German princes, of whom only one was present,
but by Italian, Netherlandish and Spanish nobles; the
Empire was no longer German; the world dominion
of Charlemagne was revived. Yet it is scarcely needful
to return to Charlemagne. Dante's lofty Henry, the
first Emperor of the line of Luxemburg, which that of
Habsburg had succeeded, had been escorted to his
coronation, not by Germans, but by Italian Ghibellines,
and the nobles of the Franco-German borderlands from
the Channel to the Savoyard passes. Charles was the
personification, not of the universal Empire, but of the
combination of elements opposed to the pushing power
of France. The hero of the hour was the gouty veteran,
Antonio de Leyva, defender of Pavia, borne on a green
velvet chair behind the roll of the Spanish drums. The
ceremony was military rather than political or religious.
Fourteen guns with their complement of tumbrels headed
the procession. Through the city filed three thousand
landsknechts, seven abreast, with banners flying and
drums beating, and then in fives, three thousand Spanish
harquebusiers, and three thousand Italians, the very
pick of Italy. In the square round the Cathedral these
troops deployed, guarding the mouth of every street
that led to it. And hither the Emperor himself had
followed, truly as the very sword of God, escorted by
the light Italian and Albanian horse.

With the coronation the task of Charles in Italy was
not quite complete. He had received the Duke of
Milan to his favour, had compelled the Venetians to
accept his not too onerous terms, had forgiven the

Dukes of Ferrara and Urbino, and reconciled them with their suzerain the Pope. Florence, however, was still obdurate, refusing to receive the Medici. This had been no quarrel of the Emperor's. The Medici had been expelled when Clement was his enemy. On the news of the Sack of Rome the Florentines had risen and driven from the city the Papal *nipoti*, Ippolyto, bastard of Giuliano, and Alessandro, putative bastard of Lorenzo, Duke of Urbino. But the extreme democratic party which had wrested the government from the moderates had then revived the French sympathies of Savonarola, and republican Florence was therefore a source of danger to the peace of Italy and to the emperor's safety. Charles besought the Pope to be merciful, to spare his own city from destruction, to reduce the quarrel to the proportions of a financial bargain. But Clement VII. had from the first been very obstinate, declaring that he would sooner be the Emperor's chaplain or his stable-boy than forego his rights. Charles confessed to Ferdinand that he could not desert the Pope, and that the Pope held him to the terms made at Barcelona. As early as September the Prince of Orange had invaded Florentine territory, but the brave city did not capitulate until the following August.[1] Long before this, in the

---

[1] The correspondence of Charles and the Prince of Orange, who commanded the Imperial troops before Florence, is printed by A. Bardi from copies or very full abstracts preserved at Brussels, *Carlo V. e l'assedio di Firenze (Arch. Stor. It.* 1893). U. Robert has published the Emperor's letters and instructions from the originals, most of which are at Vienna, *Philibert de Chalon, prince d'Orange, 1502-30 (Boletin de la R. Acad. de la Historia,* July 1901 to September 1902). The correspondence is of first-rate value on all questions connected with the settlement of Italy at this critical period. With regard to Florence it is made clear that Charles wished at once to be loyal to his engagements to the Pope, and to come to an amicable arrangement with the city. He was prepared even to negotiate behind the Pope's back for a preliminary understanding, and ordered Orange to delay his march. It must not be assumed that Charles was acting from humanitarian motives. The instructions given to Vaury on October 9, 1529, and the letter to the Prince of the same date prove that he was mainly

April and May of 1530, Charles had crossed the Brenner, and was striving to repeat in Germany the triumphs of his Italian visit.

actuated by the Sultan's westward march. He said plainly that the Pope's obstinacy with regard to Florence and the Duke of Ferrara would hinder the settlement of Italy, and imperil the orthodoxy and the very existence of Christendom; he would even compensate the Pope by slices of Milanese territory. Charles, in fact, needed Orange's army and the largest sum which could be extracted from Florence for the defence of the Austrian frontier. Salinas, however, who was with Charles at Bologna, and Orange both dwell on the impossibility of getting the Spaniards to face the Hungarian campaign. Those who were with the Emperor marched off to Florence, partly from this cause, and partly to share in the expected sack; those before Florence mutinied or deserted from fear of being ordered against the Turk. It is noticeable that in the Florentine question, as in Charles's eagerness to hurry on the coronation, the subject of German heresy is merely touched; the real issue is resistance to the Turk. The Emperor's wish for compromise at this moment, and his later desire to mitigate Clement's vengeance go far to prove that Florence owed her misfortune not to the alien and hybrid house of Habsburg, which restored prosperity with a legitimate line of Medici, but to an amalgamation of bastards or extremely dubious scions of that family.

CHAPTER IX

Germany since 1522—The Council of Regency and its financial proposals
—The Knights' war—Defeat and death of Sickingen—Collapse of
the Council of Regency—The Edict of Worms a dead letter—
Proposals for a General Council—Difficulties and imprudence of
Ferdinand—The Peasant Revolt—Responsibility of Luther—Vary-
ing character of the revolt—Attitude of the towns towards it
—Its suppression—Comparison of the German and Spanish risings
—Effects of the revolt on Lutheranism—Charles loses his opportunity—Lutheranism finds support with the Princes—The diet of
Speyer of 1526—Death of Louis of Hungary at Mohacs—Election
of Ferdinand in Bohemia—His contest with Zapolya in Hungary
—Effects of his new position upon his policy—Luther finds refuge
in territorialism—Organisation of Lutheranism—Diet of Speyer of
1529 and the Protest—The Zwinglian movement—Philip of Hesse's
connection with it—Luther and non-resistance.

WHEN Charles left Germany for Spain in 1522 the two
problems in the immediate future of the Empire were
the fortunes of Lutheranism, and those of the new
Constitution, of which the Council of Regency was the
centre. Would Lutheranism be stamped out by the
execution of the Edict of Worms, would it degenerate
into anarchism, or would it associate itself with some
form of political order? Would the artificial Constitution maintain its existence against the natural, elemental
forces, and, if so, would it be the instrument of the
monarchy or the oligarchy—would it be the protector
or destroyer of the reformation?

To Charles some central authority was essential at

the present crisis, for he could not as yet trust Ferdinand, whom he had left as Stattholder in the Empire.   His choice of the Count Palatine Frederick as President of the Council was a good one ; the Count was popular in the Empire and devoted to Charles ; he was, thought Aleander, the nicest and kindest and most sensible gentleman, not only in Germany, but in the world.   The Council took itself quite seriously, proposing reforms to check excessive luxury and curtail the commercial monopolies of the great trading syndicates.   Success, however, depended, not on activity of legislation, but on the command of funds for the maintenance of order and the payment of the Council and Chamber of Justice.   Poverty was to prove the first of the new Constitution's infantile maladies.

The Council's financial proposals comprised as alternatives a revival of the poll-tax termed Common Penny, the taxation of clergy and the appropriation of annates hitherto paid to the Papacy, and an import duty collected at a line of custom-houses along the Imperial frontiers.   The fermentation among the peasantry, already manifest, rendered the Common Penny a dangerous expedient ; the second alternative required the Pope's improbable consent ; against the Imperial toll the towns vigorously protested.   A town deputation sent to Valladolid (August 1523) urged that their quota of taxation was already out of all proportion, that the toll would ruin their commerce, and especially affect the Emperor's hereditary States, Austria and the Netherlands.   It was hinted that the Council of Regency was an unnecessary expense, and that the Chamber with a strong Stattholder would meet all requirements.   It has been believed that Charles welcomed this attack upon the Constitution, but neither his correspondence nor his later conduct bear this out; what, indeed, was he to substitute for it? He was, however, accustomed to the urban point of view; he was by education a free trader; the aid of the great bankers was essential to him, and it was they who were mainly affected by the proposals for the toll and the abolition of monopolies. Thus Charles ultimately declared against the toll, while he shelved the question of monopolies: he suggested to the deputation that the towns must recoup him by an ample subsidy, and rated them for their alleged Lutheran proclivities.

From lack of funds the Council of Regency was already ineffective, and the so-called Knights' War added to its disrepute. The knights had long been the curse of Germany. Created by the long internal wars of past centuries, they were reduced, when these ceased, to preying on society or their subjects. Their continued existence on the old lines was incompatible with modern life, with commercial and territorial interests. They were of all others the declining class, the hardest hit by the rise in prices. Possessing neither knowledge nor capital they could not compete with the city merchants, who were now giving attention to scientific agriculture and forestry, grape-growing and market-gardening. Yet in spite of their falling incomes they pressed the citizens hard in luxury and dress; most of their livelihood, wrote a Venetian envoy, went down their throats. Their relations with their peasants were strained, for they had commuted labour for money rents, and then with rising prices found out their error, and either exacted higher rents or fell back upon the customary services. Many of the knights were miserably poor, owing in great measure to the constant subdivision of property. They were often distinguished from the peasants only by class and privilege, and for this very reason their pride and exclusiveness were on the increase, for their caste was all that was left to them; they would rob and murder a wealthy citizen, but nothing would induce them to marry his well-dowered daughter. The lawyers had supplanted them in lucrative magisterial appointments in the towns; the princes were ousting them from the chapters which had formerly been the provision for younger sons. Driven to extremities, many knights made their living on the highway, maltreating their merchant victims, and often priests, with great cruelty, and in return finding short shrift, if they fell into the power of the burgher forces.

The decadence of the knights was not quite universal. Some were adapting themselves to modern environment, and were becoming an important constitutional element in the territoral Estates. Others, of whom the type is George Frundsberg, were making fame and fortune as professional *condottieri*; European complications were restoring their old occupation in another shape ; they were assuming a position resembling that of the Italian *condottieri*, or of the English gentry in the Hundred Years' War. Unless, however, they made foreign war their regular occupation, as did Frundsberg, their new character as professional soldiers made them the more dangerous in their old *rôle* of brigands. Towns and princes had easily resisted the old-fashioned knights, but could they resist the modern type, which had learnt combination, and which could bring into the field some 10,000 trained troops with all the modern appliances of warfare ?

The chief of this dangerous class was Franz von Sickingen.[1] On the one hand he was the recruiting-

---

[1] See H. Ulmann's *Franz von Sickingen*, 1872.

sergeant of the Rhineland; his geographical position made him important; he had coquetted with Francis I., and then made safe the election of Charles V. by over-awing the Electors at Frankfort; he had then joined in Charles's first campaign against France. Yet Sickingen's life was as a rule more in the old style, modified by the introduction of all modern luxuries, for he lived as a prince in great state. His troops were enormously expensive to keep together, and if he disbanded them, his consideration was gone. They could only be supported at the expense of the towns and the less powerful princes, and thus he had had his feuds with Worms, Metz and Frankfort, and had even harried Lorraine and Hesse. The part played by Sickingen at the diet of Worms has already been described. The ideas of a reformed Church and Empire had given new aspirations to the half-ambitious, half-discontented elements which surrounded him. He was the last man to possess doctrinal proclivities or intellectual tastes, but the link between the social, religious and intellectual movements was his literary lieutenant, Ulrich von Hutten.

No sooner had Charles turned his back upon Germany than the vague unrest among discontented, unrepresented classes took definite directions. The first to move were the knights of Western Germany. Sickingen had in his day waged many a private war, but his raid upon the Electorate of Trier was felt to have unusual importance, alike from his connection with the Lutheran party and with the Emperor. He relied upon Lutheran sympathies within the walls, and upon the antipathy of the Suabian and Franconian cities to one who was at once prince and priest. On the other hand Sickingen was the Emperor's stipendiary; the Archbishop had been the avowed friend of France, the only consistent opponent of Charles's candidature, and thus Trier might easily become, like the neighbouring Sedan, a hornet's nest in the very fence of Germany.

The Council formally ordered Sickingen to retire, but the Emperor was believed to dislike the Council, and Sickingen contemptuously brushed aside the mandate. Charles, he said, would approve the accomplished fact; he would be rid of an enemy, and the resources of his chief recruiting-sergeant would be trebled.

Had Charles been resident in Germany it is scarcely possible that Sickingen would have moved, or at least his movement would have been checked by organised Imperial opposition.   As it was, the Council, without men or money, was paralysed by an experience so novel.   Western Germany, however, had its old rough and ready methods for meeting a crisis.   Voluntary leagues, whether of class or locality, for commerce or defence, were formed with the rapidity engendered of necessity and practice.   While Trier was strongly held by the stout-hearted Elector Greifenklau, the Elector Palatine and Philip of Hesse combined for his defence. Sickingen's defeat and death did not satisfy the princes; they determined to read the knights a lesson, and wreaked their vengeance on the Franconian gentry who had not been directly concerned in the raid.   At this moment the Council intervened, but only to find itself as superciliously treated by the princes as by the knights.   The princes went their way and broke for ever the power of the knights as an independent force in German politics.

It could be clear to no one how Charles's course would be affected by this sudden squall which had swept over Western Germany.   The independent action of the princes had enhanced their reputation, and this very independence was the chief danger to the monarchy. As against the separatist tendency it could be of no advantage to the absent monarchy that the authority which represented it had been twice publicly flouted, even if its form was not entirely palatable to Charles. The flower of the fighting gentry had been destroyed— that very force which had intimidated the princely opposition to his election, and upon which he relied for his war with France. It had been destroyed, more-over, by princes who had shown, or were soon to show, their sympathy towards France. On the other hand Sickingen's fall seemed a decisive defeat for Luther. The knights had constituted themselves Luther's cham-pions; Sickingen was his sword and Hutten his pen. The raid was a bold stroke for secularisation, for the liberation of Germany from the priesthood. The Pope rejoiced greatly at Sickingen's defeat. The Venetian Contarini described him as "a lordling, chief of the Lutherans, highway robber, head of the poor gentry, the enemies of a peaceful life." Sickingen now was dead; Hutten, a penniless refugee in Switzerland, was soon to die. Lutheranism, indeed, suffered a double defeat, because Sickingen in falling helped to pull down the Council, the sympathies of which were, rightly or wrongly, believed to be with Luther. Yet it was scarcely a Catholic victory, for of the three allied princes two had at Worms openly favoured Luther.

The Council was now attacked on every side,—by the victors of Sickingen, by the Suabian League, by the towns, which resented its economic proposals, by the princes, with whose particularist tendencies it might interfere, by Ferdinand, who hoped to become king of the Romans on its ruins. Its president deserted;

its members were unpaid; its only sympathisers—an ill-assorted pair—were Frederick of Saxony, whose darling scheme it had long been, and Charles, who saw nothing to replace it. After an agreement in 1524 that the Emperor should bear half the expenses of the Council and the Chamber, the former was removed from Nuremberg, an Imperial centre, to Esslingen in Württemberg, under Austrian control. The Council was no longer the acting government of the Empire; it dragged out its anæmic existence until its unregretted death in 1531.

Within three years the elaborate paper-constitution of 1521 was in shreds. The Edict of Worms seemed also likely to become waste-paper. Luther was preaching again at Wittenberg, and the government had to content itself with the Elector's assurance that he could not help it. After all, Luther was a moderating influence as compared with those who, during his retirement, had replaced him. The triumph of Charles at Worms had been purely personal, and it vanished with his person. The succeeding diets had little will or power to execute their predecessor's resolution. Neither Chierigati, who represented Adrian VI. at the diet of 1523, nor Campeggi, who was sent by Clement VII. to that of 1524, received any satisfaction. The former was told that the enforcement of the Edict would cause bloodshed and revolution, the latter that the Estates would execute it as far as possible, but that the real remedy was a free General Council in Germany, preceded by a discussion of the religious question by laity and clergy. On both occasions the nuncio was reminded that the German nation had received from the Pope no reply to the Hundred Grievances which had been formulated at Worms.

Neither in the Electoral nor in the Princes' College was there a professed Lutheran, and yet it was already realised that the new religion could not be stamped out owing to the agitation among the people. The moderation of the recess of 1524, which had been drafted by the majority attached to Rome and sealed by Ferdinand, was not due, wrote the Saxon minister to his master, to goodwill, but to the fear of the princes for their skins. In the towns Lutheranism was open and unabashed; in Augsburg and Nuremberg Campeggi was rudely treated, and Lutherans preached without let or hindrance in the diet's face. Ferdinand confessed to Charles that among a thousand Germans scarce a Catholic could be found. There was wild talk of transferring the Saxon Electorate to the Catholic ducal line, or even to Ferdinand himself, but in truth no one dared touch Luther or his master.

Charles was as indignant as the Pope at the ineffective recess of 1524. He had come round to Gattinara's view as to the expediency of a General Council, but that the diet should officially propose it was an impudent interference with both Pope and Emperor. He declared that he would not and could not suffer the previous religious discussion which had been suggested; it was an unheard-of measure that the German nation should alone undertake to change the primeval ordinances of Christ's Church, which not all Christian princes in conjunction with the Pope could alter. Under pain of ban and double ban, and loss of all rights and privileges, Charles ordered the Estates to enforce the Edict and have done with proposals of Councils and other deputations. This was an astoundingly strong commentary upon a formal recess of a diet, sealed by the Emperor's representative, and

thus possessing full constitutional validity. Nothing
proves more conclusively how strong Charles's personal
animus still was against "the inhuman and unchristian
Luther who, like Mahomet of yore, would make himself big in the eyes of men."

The more zealous Catholics in Central and Southern
Germany were not altogether neglectful. They began
to combine in groups for rendering mutual aid in the
execution of the Edict in their territories, and for the
reform of the territorial clergy. To Ferdinand and
the Bavarian dukes the Pope granted a liberal share of
ecclesiastical revenues. But both in Tyrol and Lower
Austria Ferdinand found active resistance; he had
hitherto shown none of his future moderation and
capacity. Forgetting his brother's experiences in
Spain, he was forcing Spanish ministers upon territories
accustomed to free institutions and peculiarly averse
to foreign interference. The Tyrolese refused taxes
unless he resided in the province, and this he dared
not do for fear of revolution at Vienna.

In the autumn of 1524 the Imperial forces had
failed before Marseilles, and Francis I. was on his
way to Italy. At this crisis Germany was in a
turmoil. Central authority was at an end, the spirit
of particularism never so strong. The Emperor's agent,
Hannart, dwelt on Ferdinand's imprudence, and prophesied for him the fate of his brother-in-law of Denmark,
who had lately been driven from his throne. "Every
one," he wrote to Charles, "will have things done after
his own taste; no one will allow any meddling with
his own house and lordship." Charles had alienated
the more influential princes by his inability to pay
debts or pensions. He cancelled his sister Catherine's
engagement to the Elector Frederick of Saxony's nephew

in favour of the King of Portugal, not from ill-feeling, but in accordance with the long-standing policy of the Castilian Crown to preserve a dynastic connection with the neighbouring kingdom. Eleanor had lost her elderly husband, and her younger sister must marry his son and successor. This, however, was scant consolation to the Saxon Elector, who naturally cried out against the breach of faith. Francis I. meanwhile was intriguing with towns and princes. Many said that the Empire could not exist in Charles's absence, and yet, if he came to Germany, Spain was surely lost.

At this moment, while Ferdinand was sending every available man over the Alps to save the garrisons of Lodi and Pavia, a peasant revolt broke out in the Austrian Rhineland. Misunderstood and underrated at the first, it spread during 1525 over the greater part of Germany. The causes, social and economic, were various in different localities, and some of them were of long standing. Serious peasant revolts are seldom due to great distress; they are more often the result of economic grievances arising from an enhanced standard of comfort. In South-west Germany, where the revolt originated, the peasantry probably were or ought to have been well-to-do. They had meat to eat and wine to drink; they imitated their betters in increased expenditure on clothes; they would fain abolish the outward signs of class distinction. In such cases burdens which have survived or have been reimposed appear the more intolerable.

The rise in prices which had partly caused the economic distress and consequently the movement of the landed gentry, exercised its pressure through them upon the peasantry, among whom complete freehold tenure was very rare. The distinctions of tenure were numer-

ous, and the lawyers were striving to eliminate these, to
the benefit, perhaps, of the serf, but to the disadvantage
of the upper strata of peasantry.   There was in places a
tendency for hereditary holdings to sink to life-holdings,
and life-holdings to tenancy at will ; there was arbitrary
raising of rents to meet the rise in prices, there were
attempts to enforce labour services long since commuted.
The mania for hunting had caused greater severity in the
game laws, the deprivation of many privileges in wood
and water, and damage to crops which now had a higher
market value than of old.   The rapid enclosure of the
waste also added to popular indignation, even though
the waste may have lain unused.   There was doubtless
in many instances real distress.   The increased standard
of comfort had led to a habit of borrowing, and the
mortgage interest was eating up the annual livelihood to
be derived from the peasant holding.   In certain districts
the peasantry were suffering from over-subdivision of
their properties, and yet the attempt to check this led
to the creation of a landless proletariate.   Colonisation
had long ceased ; the towns, when possible, checked the
inrush from the country, and hence resulted over-popula-
tion and lowering of wage in face of a rise in prices.
In North-east Germany the peasants were more than
elsewhere at the mercy of their landlords, who were here,
under pretext of bad cultivation or failure of service,
absorbing peasant properties to round off their domain.

Thus in many cases the burdens of the peasantry
were really increased, while in others the customary
burdens appeared more onerous, because under modern
conditions of agriculture they were really more inconvenient.   Other grievances were rather of a political or
judicial character, though their sting was still economic.
The decline of the local courts led to the haling of jury-

men, witnesses, plaintiffs and defendants to distant courts
where procedure was lengthy and unintelligible. Germany was known as the milch cow of the Papacy, and
the financial pressure on the higher ranks of the clergy
reacted on the lower, and ultimately on the peasantry ;
a see, for instance, which changed hands rapidly incurred
an expenditure on annates which its ordinary revenue
could not meet. The custom, moreover, of provisions
and reservations imposed upon the country a priesthood
which was not of local origin, if it were not actually
alien, and this added to the unpopularity of tithe.
Hence therefore arose the agitation against the greater
and lesser tithes, the labour-rents, moderate as they
usually were, the marriage licenses, the heriots, and in
favour of local courts, abolition of game-laws and election of the parish clergy.

Agrarian risings had been frequent since 1431, and
had increased in frequency and intensity until 1517.
The earlier had a distinctly Hussite tendency ; the religious element was, indeed, usually present, the free
gospel being a common catchword, while priests and
friars were often involved in them. The programme was
usually extreme, rising from the abolition of tithes and
the demand for a state-paid clergy to division of goods,
extinction of nobility and clergy, and the absolute equality
of all men. The town proletariate had frequently taken
part in these movements, demanding abolition of guilds
and companies or the limitation of their profits, and the
fixing of wages and prices by popular representatives.
Less seldom the risings had a political complexion ; one
of the latest and most dangerous recognised no officials
but Emperor and Pope, who alone held their offices from
God : there should be no more war among Christians,
the men of martial tastes must be led by the Emperor

against Turk or infidel. The social and religious sides of popular ferment found a meeting-point in the cry for the plunder or extermination of the Jews, for Christians are apt to atone for their own extravagance by pious execration of the too accommodating Hebrew.

As the crisis approached the fermentation increased. While the peasant was depressed by the lawyers, he was exalted and idealised by the more romantic humanists and by the religious reformers; they saw in him the survival of mediæval, pious German simplicity, the future salvation of the state. Science and prophecy were enlisted in the peasant's cause. Astrologers and prophets predicted a general revolution for 1524, and in such cases prophecy is apt to aid its own fulfilment.

That the malady, which had long been endemic in certain districts, suddenly became epidemic and universal was due to the preaching and writings of Luther and of the followers who outpaced him. Luther's Freedom of the Gospel was expected to bring liberty from all bonds, social and political. Religion provided the justification and the formulæ for revolt, and the fever-heat for fighting. It gave here, as elsewhere, to inarticulate discontent a war-cry and, in part, a programme. The new doctrine seemed a panacea for all evils; the pure word of God of the preacher was to the German peasant of the sixteenth century the counterpart of the philosopher's doctrine of the rights of man as understood by the French peasant of the eighteenth.

Luther was unable during his retirement from Wittenberg to control the movement which his preaching had started. His return to the University scattered the extremists throughout Germany. Preachers such as Carlstadt and Münzer had many imitators. Even the Gospel was soon left behind, displaced by the intelligence of the individual. The poor man was now God's officer on earth ; to the people all was clear that to the learned was obscure; the Pope was Anti-Christ, and Emperors and princes little better. The new culture soon shared the fate of the old religion; men of learning were deceivers and deceived, the Universities temples of Moloch, riches, power and education things of naught.[1]

The wires of revolution are usually pulled partly by the unemployed and partly by the busybodies. Men of position and intelligence were going the round of country inns, dressed as peasants, holding books upside down, sitting with their feet on the table. A favourite theme was the autonomy, social and religious, of the commune, then that of the individual, and above all the moral superiority of the peasant and his monopoly of the future. The professional agitators were some of them Christian Socialists, others Nationalists, who in abhorrence of foreign religion and foreign luxury harked back to the primitive simplicity of German communal life. The spontaneity of the outbreak may be ascribed mainly, as in the English peasant revolt of 1381, to the action of two wandering classes, the preachers and the soldiers. Roving priests and friars were found agitating in secular costume. The swaggering *landsknecht*, corrupted by alternations of wealth and starvation, and graduated in all schools of mutiny, at once excited envy and stimulated discontent in his native village. When fighting began the actual leaders were unfrocked clergy, unem-

---

[1] It would be impossible here to give any account even of the recent bibliography on this subject. English readers may be referred to the admirable chapter in L. von Ranke's *History of the Reformation in Germany* (translated by S. Austin). A Socialist point of view is taken by E. B. Bax, *German Society at the close of the Middle Ages* (*The Social Side of Reformation in Germany*), 1894, and *The Peasants' War in Germany* 1525-26 (*The Social Side of the Reformation in Germany II.*), 1899. A recent work which emphasises the religious aspects of the movement is *Der Deutsche Bauernkrieg* by W. Stolze, 1907.

ployed soldiers, innkeepers, discontented gentry and disaffected officials of ecclesiastical princes.

The immediate occasion of the final outbreak, late in 1524, was a personal grievance. But, as the causes were general, within a few months it spread far and wide. It assumed, however, very different forms, being in the South-west almost purely economic and in Central Germany almost purely religious. Nevertheless the cry for the rights of the Free Gospel was never entirely absent, and this gave a common basis. Thus the Suabians, whose demands were most directly economic, stated, at the close of their Twelve Articles, that if any were not in accord with the pure word of God, they were *ipso facto* withdrawn.

The attack was in the first instance mainly directed against the lesser nobility and the upper clergy, especially against the sees which combined temporal and spiritual power. Thence the movement spread to the subjects of the princes, but, except in cases of religious exaltation, it was not here so vehement, while the princes, whose pecuniary interests were less directly attacked, were usually more willing to compromise. There was little sign of hostility towards the Emperor. In districts of Central Germany the programme was an hysterical nihilism veneered with theocracy ; here, in the catastrophe of all existing authority, civil and ecclesiastical, the Empire would have suffered as one institution among many. The more moderate insurgents hardly touched constitutional questions beyond demanding reforms for local judicature, and election of the clergy by the parish. In Franconia, however, and Tyrol there were ideas of political reconstruction. These were in the former extremely radical, but Teutonic radicalism has often a soft corner for archæology. The peasants,

as the knights before them, had an ideal of the Empire
as a saviour of society : the intermediate hierarchy swept
away, the Emperor should rule a nation of prosperous
peasants with their communal representative institutions : the princes would at most fall into line as
Imperial officials.   How far this scheme was ever formulated—how far it was a mere revival of the idyllic so-
called Reforms of the Emperors Sigismund and Frederick
III.—is still disputed.   But the Imperial idea had some
hold upon the popular imagination, and it is just possible
that a resident Emperor with the imaginative force of
Sigismund, or even of Maximilian, might have turned
it to account.   Charles, however, was non-resident and
non-imaginative.

In Tyrol the revolutionary programme was more
within the range of practical politics.   After Maximilian's
death the movement towards parliamentary government
—that is, towards the supremacy of the gentry and upper
clergy—was inevitably to the disadvantage of the
peasants, even though they had in the Tyrolese estates
the privilege of representation, elsewhere extremely rare.
The peasantry had little love for Ferdinand, who was
for them a Spaniard, but they had idolised Maximilian,
and were loyal to the Habsburgs.   Fiercely antagonistic
to the clergy, carrying their excesses as far as the
massacre of nuns, their political education gave to their
political demands moderation and good sense, usually
lacking.   Here too the aim was to eliminate intermediate
authority and to bring the communes into immediate
contact with the prince.   Thus, while Ferdinand had
to fight the latest and, perhaps, the hardest with his
peasants, the result was a compromise to their permanent advantage, whereas in Germany generally the
contest ended in bloodthirsty suppression, which for

long alienated the lower classes from the old authorities
and, in some measure, from the new religion. The
larger towns stood studiously aloof from the conflict.
They had too much interest in order to further revolution. On the other hand, were not the clergy, the
gentry and the princes at once the enemies of town and
peasant? The cities were themselves seething with ill-
defined discontent, partly religious and partly economic.
The movement might easily have spread from country
to town, and set ablaze every city in Central, Western
and Southern Germany. Thus the larger towns, to
propitiate their lower classes, did not always dare to
refuse munitions and supplies to the insurgents.

There were exceptions to the abstention of the towns.
The rising may almost be said to have begun in the
Austrian Black Forest town of Waldshut and the small
Imperial towns of Suabia, but here interests after all
were mainly agricultural. A truer exception is found
in Central Germany, where the revolt, from its centre
in Thuringia, spread to Meissen, Hesse, Brunswick and
the neighbouring bishoprics. Here it was most purely
religious, most revolutionary, most bloodthirsty, and
also most urban; it was in fact the rehearsal of the
later Anabaptist drama played at Münster. It had been
preceded by an epidemic of communism. The town of
Mühlhausen then became the centre, and it was, indeed,
with some difficulty that the peasants were persuaded
to ally themselves with the town. The town council
was overthrown, and a knight of the Teutonic Order
proclaimed pure communism and the extinction of
nobility and luxury. The preacher Münzer was influential in these districts, and the movement assumed a
theocratical character—that of the monarchy of saints
and prophets. Münzer was the Moses, the Gideon, the

avenging sword of the Lord. The doctrine of the
Dominion of Grace reappeared in a crude form : all
powers temporal and spiritual had sinned and so forfeited
their privileges : all magistracy was against the faith.
Münzer is said to have persuaded his followers that there
was a general rising against authority throughout
Europe. The rule of the Saints implied the extermination of the sinners. The insurgents, their appetites once
whetted, could not be controlled ; they entered the
important university city of Erfurt and sacked the
churches and parsonages. Münzer was an incompetent
leader, but this form of revolt would have been infinitely
dangerous, had it spread to the Rhine cities and the
Netherlands.

If in a few instances the lower classes turned against
the municipal government, in others more important
the cities themselves utilised the disturbance to attempt
to shake off the sovereignty of their bishops. Such
was the case at Worms, while Matthias Lang, Archbishop of Salzburg, the adviser whom Charles had
inherited from Maximilian, was besieged in his castle by
two distinct armies of his townsmen and his peasants.

The revolt ran the usual course of agrarian outbreaks.
Notwithstanding years of warning, nobles and princes
were taken by surprise. The gentry suffered from
contagious panic ; ten fire-eating nobles, it was said,
would fly at the very sight of a peasant. Even the
more powerful princes, such as Mainz, Baden and the
Elector Palatine, were forced to negotiate. There were
the usual cases of brutality on the part of the peasants,
which were held to justify indiscriminate retribution.
But when the gentry recovered their nerve and combined under the princes and the Suabian League, the
peasants were outmatched and beaten in detail. By

the close of the summer of 1525 the rising was suppressed in Central and Southern Germany, although
in the Suabian and Tyrolese provinces of the Habsburgs
it lingered until 1526.

Charles had no share in the suppression of the Peasants'
Revolt. The brunt was again borne by private associa-
tions of princes and by the Suabian League. The latter
had, indeed, been hitherto regarded as a Habsburg instrument, as the cleverest and most durable of Maximilian's
experiments. At this crisis, however, the League had
fallen much under the influence of the rival power,
Bavaria, because the able Bavarian Chancellor Eck had
been the life and soul of resistance to the peasants.
Indirectly Charles's victory of Pavia had contributed to
the result. Many of the *landsknechts,* returning from
Italy, threw in their lot with their own class. But
they were, after all, mercenaries, and the bulk of them
were enrolled by the princes or the Suabian League,
thus adding to the rapidity of the decision. Moreover
the collapse of French power defeated Ulrich of
Württemberg's attempt to recover his duchy with the
aid of the peasantry and a considerable Swiss force.
The presence of an organised army in the heart of the
disaffected districts might have modified or delayed
the result. But the Habsburg victory intimidated the
Cantons, who recalled their men ; they were in no mood
to risk their immunity from Imperial interference for
oppressed peasantry and an exiled tyrant.

For the second time within Charles's short reign a
terrible revolt had been suppressed by the agency of
others. Charles did not even incur the odium of the
judicial penalties which followed the massacres perpetrated in hot blood. This inaction of the Crown was
one of the few resemblances between the German and

the Spanish risings. The knights, indeed, were in
origin not unlike the gentry who in some cases headed
the Castilian movement, but in the latter case they
were urban, and acted less as the representatives of
their class than as the spokesmen of their towns. In
the last stages of the communal revolt there were,
indeed, symptoms of a social war between the gentry
and their peasants, and such the Valencian movement
actually was; but here again the attacking party was
not agrarian but urban. The fact that the great cities
in Germany stood aloof from both the revolutionary
movements, subject to the exceptions above mentioned,
marks these movements clearly off from those of Castile
and Valencia. Again in Castile national feeling was
omnipresent; in Germany, if not entirely absent, it
was not prominent. On the other hand the religious
element, almost lacking in the Castilian rising, in
varying degrees affected every issue of the German.
Neither knights nor peasants professedly or actually
attacked the Crown, but the Castilian communes, whatever might be their professions, made a direct onslaught
on the government of Charles. The differences then
between the Spanish and German disturbances are very
wide; this much, however, they have in common, that
in each case the victors were the greater nobles, the
class from which, as King or Emperor, Charles had
most to fear.

Charles had not understood the Peasant Revolt;
he regarded it as purely a Lutheran rising, *un mouve-
ment des Lutheriens.* He showed no appreciation of
the social or economic questions involved. He knew,
in fact, nothing of the agricultural life of Germany,
so far removed from the economic problems of the
great Netherland cities whose interests he zealously

promoted.   Only by degrees did he learn the needs and hardships of a poor agricultural population.   But Charles was not alone in regarding the revolt as a religious revolution.   It was the general view throughout Germany, and the peasants' defeat might well have sealed Luther's fate.   He had at first preached a wholesome moderation to both parties, but then, in terror at the threatened overthrow of all order, had thrown himself with unseemly violence on the side of authority, and had hounded on the nobles to the extirpation of the wretches who had misunderstood his far from obvious meaning.   This did not save his reputation. Moderate men realised that those had spoken true who had foretold that emancipation from ecclesiastical authority was but the prelude to political anarchy. The patriot Humanists had become aware that Luther's doctrines were leading, not to the unity of Germany, but to its disruption—that learning was withered rather than stimulated by absorption of violent theological ingredients.

The strongest force in Germany, the princes, had combined to stamp out revolt; the Emperor's brother had borne his full share of the burden ; the towns had at least not dared to declare for the peasants.   Now therefore was the time to root out Lutheranism, and to restore the authority of the Church.   Charles wrote to Ferdinand that he would at once be crowned at Rome and hasten to Germany to complete the holy work.   Speed, he urged, was the essential, and here he was in the right.   There was just a moment when, had Charles visited Germany in all the fresh glory of Pavia, he might possibly have carried the nation with him in reaction towards Catholicism and monarchy.

Without the Emperor no decisive steps seemed

possible. The princes had shown more zeal against
the peasants than on behalf of the existing Church.
While the attack was directed mainly against ecclesiastics, the nobles had looked on, many believing that
the spoils of victory would be ultimately theirs. Ferdinand himself had evinced a spirit of encroachment
on Church property. Austrian banners had waved
over Füssen, a town belonging to the see of Augsburg.
He rejected the demand of the Tyrolese Estates for
the incorporation of the sees of Trent and Brixen,
but he virtually occupied the latter. Above all both
Ferdinand and the Bavarian dukes cast greedy eyes
upon the great archbishopric of Salzburg, which owed its
preservation rather to the jealousy of the rival princes
than to their protection. None but a master-hand
could have combined the jarring interests of the
princes in defence of the old order; nought but
genuine religious zeal could have rekindled love for
the old religion.

The moment was lost. The continuance of the
revolt in the Austrian territories weakened Charles's
power in Italy, while the European combination against
the victor of Pavia fettered him to Spain. The more
eager Catholic princes, the Electors of Mainz and
Brandenburg, Duke George of Saxony and Duke
Henry of Brunswick, despairing of immediate aid
from the central government, had recourse to the
old expedient—a private league. A similar attempt
by the rich ecclesiastical princes of Southern Germany
was hampered by the dissensions between Austria
and Bavaria. These Catholic unions provoked a
counter association. Frederick of Saxony was dead.
Although Luther's protector, he was never himself a
Lutheran, but his brother and successor John had

early accepted the new doctrines, and was in league with Philip of Hesse, who had now declared for Luther.

This was a more formidable combination than might appear. John had not the statesmanlike abilities of his brother, but the quality which the Lutheran cause needed at this crisis was disinterested enthusiasm, and this the new Elector brought to it. To his consistency and outspoken courage the Reformation owes one of its largest debts. While John of Saxony provided character, Philip of Hesse supplied talent. Hesse was not a first rate state, but its ruler had youth, ambition and military prestige gained at the expense of Sickingen and the Peasants. He had, perhaps, inherited a strain of Slavonic genius from his masterful Mecklenburg mother. He was at all events totally unlike the other German princes of his day, and his policy was to be rather cosmopolitan than German. Small of stature, but great of heart, restless and highly-strung, pleasant and persuasive, supple and versatile, he tossed aside as prejudices what others might term scruples. In government he was the most autocratic of German princes, allowing neither Council nor Estates to thwart his plans. In religion also he showed his independence, rejecting the mysticism and conservatism of Luther for a system akin to the more logical and radical views of Zwingli. Philip alone of the princes courted and won the sympathy of the Imperial towns, although as yet they hesitated to declare themselves. Before long a group of smaller North German princes joined the Lutheran ranks, and also the powerful city of Magdeburg, in defiance of its suzerain, the Elector of Mainz. Far away in the extreme North-east Albert of Hohenzollern, Grandmaster of the Teutonic Order, in 1525 abjured his religious vows, and converted his religious office into an hereditary duchy under Polish suzerainty.

Thus just at the moment when Lutheranism seemed scotched by the defeat of the knights and killed by the suppression of the peasants, it found new life in the strongest element in Germany, the princes. For Charles the most immediate consideration was this, that, while he was entering on a new war against an Italian league supported by France and probably by England, the enormous fighting power of Germany was neutralised by leagues and counter-leagues. Nor was this the worst, for the princes might readily merge their mutual religious antipathies, not as yet clearly defined, in common opposition to the Habsburgs. There was a general belief that Charles intended the election of Ferdinand as King of the Romans. Against this the very three princes who had defeated Sickingen again combined; there was even some idea of proposing as a rival candidate the elder Duke of Bavaria. Of these three princes the Elector of Trier at least was French to the core, while the French court was dangling commercial privileges before the eager eyes of the Imperial towns. It was small wonder that in January 1526 Ferdinand had implored Charles to come at once, for otherwise Germany would go to ruin.

Under such circumstances met in August the diet of Speyer, which proved to be of such momentous importance in German history.[1] This importance was foreseen by no one. The diet was merely an adjournment of a former meeting which had been a failure; it was itself but thinly attended. The Elector John of Saxony was as yet the only representative of the new

---

[1] For this diet see W. Friedensburg, *Der Reichstag zu Speier 1526* (*Jastrow's historiche Untersuchungen*, Heft 5, 1887).

doctrines in his College; the Catholic majority in the College of Princes was, owing to the large ecclesiastical element, overwhelming. Nevertheless the feature of the assembly was the prominence assumed by the Luthern princes, especially Philip of Hesse, and by the town deputies; its result was entirely favourable to the Lutheran cause. The zealous Catholics proposed that the Edict of Worms should be reaffirmed and seriously executed. The town deputies rejoined that the very attempt would cause the renewal of the disturbances only just suppressed. It must be remembered that their own teeming populations still formed an intact reserve for the forces of revolution. Many of the princes were unwilling to face a fresh struggle; many more, Catholics as they might be, had no friendly feeling for the Church in its existing state, and less for the Pope, who had ignored the demands for reform pressed by Catholic Germany.

At this juncture Ferdinand intervened. He produced instructions, written by Charles in the preceding March, insisting on the simple, unconditional execution of the Edict, but engaging to urge the necessity of a Council upon the Pope at an early date. To this it was answered, truly enough, that Charles did not and could not know the circumstances and the temper of Germany; that he had no impartial sources of information; that, above all, since the letters were written, the situation had entirely changed, for the Pope was now at open war with the Emperor; what then would be the value of his persuasion on the Pope to remedy the wrongs of Germany by a Council?

In this state of feeling the committee which had the task of drafting the recess was necessarily subject to the influence of its more Lutheran element, and its proposals, slightly modified, formed the celebrated recess of the diet of Speyer. This ordinance provided that the Word of God should be preached without disturbance, that indemnity should be granted for past offences against the Edict of Worms, and that, until a Council should be held in a German city, each Estate should so live as it is hoped to answer for its conduct to God and to the Emperor.

This recess strongly marks what may be termed the suspensive period of governmental action in relation to heresy, although it is not quite the beginning nor by any means the climax. The diets of 1523 and 1524 had shown this tendency, and even that of Worms was to some extent suspensive, for action was deferred until Luther could explain himself. There is, however, this great difference, that at Worms a definite and proximate limit was imposed upon suspension, whereas now the Council which was to be the *terminus ad quem* seemed as likely as not to be held on the Greek Kalends. This suspensive policy is characteristic of the national treatment of the subject ; it retains its place even in what is regarded as the final settlement arrived at in the Religious Peace of Augsburg of 1555.

Suspension was not only suited to the national temperament and the existing condition of Germany, but to the character and circumstances of Charles. It is true that the recess was in direct contradiction to his instructions, but many a man writes a decided letter when he will not take decisive action. Several of Charles's most resolute instructions conclude with the postscript that they are to be used or witheld according to circumstances ; the responsibility, that is, was transferred from his own shoulders to those of others. The nature of Charles, as he himself confesses, was slow and irresolute; he would often, as his later life will prove, clutch at an excuse for avoiding a decision as to the precise means for compassing his ends. For Charles time was not an enemy but a healer. But, apart from character, how could he possibly resent the decision of the diet? Had he not said in 1525, "Either to-day or to-morrow Luther will be a man of worth"? In his irritation at the Pope's unfriendly attitude, he again exclaimed, "This is no time to talk of Luther." Even while the diet was debating the Emperor's instructions at Speyer, at Granada his councillors were discussing the wisdom of making some concessions to the heretics. To reduce the Lutheran towns and princes the whole force of German Catholicism would be required, and this at a time when the situation in Italy could only be saved by pouring German *landsknechts*, whatever was their religious denomination, across the Alps.

No one, perhaps, realised at first the full import of the recess. Wrongly enough it has been treated as giving a legal basis for the foundation of Lutheran churches, for the independence of the territory in matters ecclesiastical, for the principal, in fact, of *Cujus regio ejus religio*. Such an inference was never intended by the diet, and, as has been seen, the recess was in direct contradiction to the Emperor's commands. No Lutheran prince or town could doubt what his or its responsibility towards the Emperor implied. At most the act was merely provisional and suspensory: it could give no guarantee for a new constitutional principal, for the foundation of churches outside the limits of the old Papal-Imperial system, for wholesale alienation of property which the law of the land was pledged to protect.[1]

---

[1] T. Brieger in *Der Speierer Reichstag von 1526*, 1909, returns to the view of Ranke that the Recess did give a legal basis to the Lutheran Churches.

Nevertheless it is practically true that the recess of Speyer was a starting-point for the formal and deliberate organisation of Lutheran churches. Lutheran princes and divines soon realised the possibilities of the phrase, "Responsibility to God and to the Emperor." In this they found not only one duty involved but two, and these were contradictory. Inclination and interest soon taught the lesson that obedience should be rendered rather to the celestial than to the terrestrial power. Here then lies the real importance of the recess,—not in its intention but in its consequences, and hence if it were necessary to count the more important diets on one hand, that of Speyer would find a place with that of Worms of 1521, and with the three great diets of Augsburg of 1530, 1547 and 1555.

Ferdinand had effectually wrangled with the diet for an adequate grant to meet the Turkish advance. On the second day from its dissolution his brother-in-law Louis, King of Hungary and Bohemia, lost his life in the miserable defeat of Mohacs (August 29, 1526), and Solyman advanced to the Hungarian capital. The king's death was an event momentous to the Habsburgs, then and for all time. He left no children, and his natural successor was his sister, Ferdinand's wife, Anna. The Crown of Bohemia was, however, in such a case regarded as elective, and there was no lack of candidates. Among these were the Kings of France and Poland, the houses of Austria, Bavaria and Brandenburg, and both lines of Saxony. The contest was soon seen to lie between Ferdinand and one of the two Bavarian dukes. For generations it had been a maxim of Bavarian policy to recover the lost position in the Slavic Mark, or at least to thwart Austrian influence in Hungary and Bohemia. Success at length seemed near, for the Bohemian magnates feared that under Austrian rule the widowed queen Mary would have full scope for her ability and autocratic instincts. Had one of the Bavarian dukes succeeded, their power would have outweighed that of Austria, and it is scarcely possible that Ferdinand would have been elected as King of the Romans.

In spite of probabilities the skill of the Austrian envoys won the day, and Ferdinand was unanimously chosen (October 13). Though careful to safeguard his wife's hereditary claim he professed to rely on the neighbourhood and long friendship of the Austrian and Bohemian dynasties, and he was liberal in his promises to maintain the national privileges, It is characteristic of Charles's caution that in sending Ferdinand the Imperial investiture, he advised him to suppress it, if the Bohemians objected to the Imperial claim, or if there seemed reasonable doubts of its validity. The German provinces of Lusatia, Silesia, and Moravia, attached to the crown of Bohemia by a personal tie, recognised Ferdinand and Anna as hereditary rulers.

It seemed improbable that the crowns of Bohemia and Hungary should remain united. The Bohemians preferred a separate king who would not be involved in the ruinous expenses of Turkish wars, while no love was lost between Czech and Magyar. Before Ferdinand could seriously press his claim to the Hungarian crown, the hatred of German influences decided the election of John Zapolya, the Woivode of Siebenbürgen, the wealthiest native magnate. In Hungary, however, the hereditary principle was somewhat stronger than in Bohemia, and Ferdinand could represent himself as legitimate king in his wife's right, and brand Zapolya as usurper. Yet his practical authority was confined to the semi-German strip of territory round Pressburg. The Turks had now withdrawn with the plunder of Matthias Corvinus's great palace; Zapolya reigned undisputed over Magyar Hungary, the province of Slavonia giving him its adhesion, although Croatia declared for Ferdinand. Ferdinand's election at Pressburg by a group of nobles on December 17, 1526 seemed to count for little ; his rival received the congratulations of the Pope and was recognised by Venice, he was in close relations with France and with the Bavarian dukes; every enemy of the Habsburgs smiled now and hereafter on Zapolya.

Once more the ability of the Habsburg agents, and above all that of his sister Mary, stood Ferdinand in good stead. Mary had for a time despaired and begged for her recall; Charles implored his brother not to risk a contest which might lead to a catastrophe, and to a union of Zapolya with the Turk. A humorist at Zapolya's election said that his head was too small for his crown, and so it proved. While he wasted time in proposals for arbitration, Ferdinand gathered a small but efficient force, the Hohenzollerns both of Brandenburg and Franconia giving the Habsburg yeoman's aid at this eventful crisis. Zapolya was driven from Hungary to Siebenbürgen, and even there could make no stand. He was to give trouble enough in future, but his defeat caused Ferdinand's general recognition.

With but a trifling effort Ferdinand had attained the aim of generations of his Habsburg forefathers. No one, however, could have prophesied the continuance of the personal union of the three nations. Few principles, apart from national antipathies, had been involved. Ferdinand had, indeed, urged the value of the aid which the Imperial house could give against the Turks, but it

was mainly a matter of buying this man or that by this
office or that benefice.   If the elections were accidental,
their consequences were of essential import.   Ferdinand
was now head and shoulders above any German prince ;
his relation even to Charles was changed, since he had
become a king in his own right with separate interests
of his own, and with only a complimentary dependence
on the Empire.

As Ferdinand was a zealous Catholic, it might seem
that the increase of his power and dignity would injuri-
ously affect the struggling Lutheran fortunes, but the
contrary was the actual result.   In Bohemia Ferdinand
had by the constitution to recognise the parity of
Catholicism and Utraquism, although both parties
desired the exclusion of Lutheran doctrines.   In the
German crown-lands, however, where he had been most
loyally received as hereditary king, Lutheranism was
spreading, and he was forced to give a careful answer
to a petition which was virtually in its favour.   In
Hungary the bishops had opposed Ferdinand's election,
because Lutheranism was rife among the German population, and his sister Mary was suspected of heretical
leanings.   But in Hungary also heresy now spread fast,
even among the nobles.   Ferdinand could not risk a
religious war in either kingdom.

Of late Ferdinand's gaze had been directed towards
Italy ; he greedily coveted the duchy of Milan.   Henceforth it was turned mainly towards the East.   To meet
the Turk he must conciliate the sympathy of Germany ;
to raise powder and shot and *landsknechts* he must
deal tenderly with Lutherans; the campaign against
heresy must become subordinate to the crusade against
Mahomet.   The change was not all at once.   Ferdinand
long looked yearningly towards Milan ; he long out-

paced Charles in demands for action against the Lutherans. But the change inevitably came, and Ferdinand was to prove a moderating rather than an existing influence in Charles's councils.

While Ferdinand was occupied with his new kingdoms, Charles was spending his whole force in holding his Italian possessions, new and old, against the Pope and France. For three years Lutheran Germany could mould to her will the plastic recess of Speyer, and she lost no time. Luther, shrewd and versatile as he was passionate and stubborn, saw his opportunity, and threw his whole energy into the service of the princes. If his doctrines were to survive, they must be associated, not with the declining, but with the rising element, the territorial state. He had once for all had his fright; he was by nature too conservative, and also too sensible, to be logical or consistent. He had done with the priesthood of the individual, the absolute liberty of conscience, the entire freedom of religion from the state, the election of the ministry by the congregation. Obedience to authority was now to him the first and great commandment. Henceforth the territorial prince must be the guardian of doctrine, the chastiser of dissent, the fount of ecclesiastical justice, the steward of church revenues, the patron of church benefices. To ecclesiastics might be left the definition of doctrine and the organisation of discipline, but both must be so distinct that the secular power could know what it was to punish or protect. Hence Luther was forced to formulate his doctrine and his ritual. The vague and limitless possibilities which had appealed to the imaginative German intellect had passed into dreamland or Anabaptism. Luther was twitted, not without some reason, with having become a Pope. If the new Church

must be in close interdependence with the State, its
methods must imitate those of its great predecessor.
From this resulted, quite apart from Luther's own
belief in each of his own opinions, the necessary
crystallisation of Lutheran doctrine and discipline. It
was, perhaps, to the advantage of Lutheranism that
this process of cooling-off separated it from the fluid
elements of Anabaptism, some dangerous, some innocent,
which still found channels through the length and
breadth of Germany. The exclusion of Zwinglism was,
indeed, another matter, but of this hereafter.

The princes were not slow to reap where the reformer
sowed. Their harvest consisted in patronage, in revenue,
in extended jurisdiction. In Lutheran states the religious unity between the prince, the gentry and the
middle classes, gave a new force to authority, while
the Catholic lords had everywhere to dread the active
or passive hostility of their subjects : even Bavaria,
untouched by the Peasant War, was now, as Ferdinand
wrote to Charles, deeply tainted. So bold had Lutheranism become that it assumed the offensive, and a little
war-cloud scudded across the land. Philip of Hesse, too
readily deceived by false information as to a Catholic
combination, threatened the territories of the neighbouring bishops. He was only held back from action by the
Saxon Elector under Luther's influence. But even when
the clumsy forgery was conclusively exposed, Philip
blackmailed the bishops for the expenses incurred in
threatening their extinction. The power of persecution
had already passed to the new religion.

If Lutheranism was growing stronger, so was Charles.
In 1529, triumphant over the Pope and France, he
ordered Ferdinand to hold a diet at Speyer, and there
annulled " of his Imperial and absolute authority " the

clause of 1526 on which the Lutherans had founded their independent churches : it had been, he wrote, the cause of misunderstanding and abuse.[1] Ferdinand showed unusual energy in persuading the Catholics to attend the diet, and the bishops had at length awoken from their lethargy. Yet as king of Hungary Ferdinand needed Lutheran men and money to stem the Turkish advance, while the Catholics were none too willing to admit the Emperor's full and absolute authority. Thus the Emperor's proposals were softened down, but in spite of this the recess gave evidence of a marked reaction. The Edict of Worms, indeed, had disappeared, but the majority declared against any fresh novelty, any further dissidence, while it insisted on the concession of tolerance to Catholics in Lutheran countries.

To this enactment the reply was the celebrated Protest, which for all time has given its name to the party, and to many others who have not deserved or have not desired it. The Lutheran minority insisted that an ordinance which had been unanimously enacted could only be unanimously rescinded,—a political principle hereafter reasserted, and not, perhaps, without some show of constitutional precedent. It was, however, more essential that emphasis was laid on the unfortunate dualism of responsibility to God and Emperor : it was argued, as in the old days of conflict between Emperor and Pope, that in things religious the terrestrial power was subordinate to the spiritual : that the conscience was bound first to God and only in a secondary degree to the temporal power. This was not, however, the assertion of the rights of the individual conscience, but of what may be termed the territorial conscience. The Lutherans would give no ear to suggestions for univer-

---

[1] See J. Ney, *Geschichte des Reichstags zu Speier 1529*, 1880.

sal toleration: within the territory the subject must in
things religious conform to the opinions of the temporal
power; *quot regiones tot sententiae* might be the logical
result.

The Protest was signed not only by Lutheran princes,
but by fourteen towns at the head of which stood
Nuremberg, Ulm, Strassburg and Constance. Nevertheless, in addition to long-standing jealousy, there was
a dangerous rift in the solidarity of reform. Religious
dissent had closely followed the lines of class distinction;
reform had developed itself separately in the princely
territories and the cities. This was due to the growing
influence of Zwingli in South Germany. The history
of this reformer has only an indirect connection at
one or two decisive moments with that of Charles.
His defeat and death were, indeed, the facts of his
career which affected the Emperor most immediately.
Zwinglism, however, had an important bearing on
the relations of Lutheranism to Charles at the crisis
when he came to Germany to solve once for all, as he
thought, the religious problem.

As Luther had adapted his reform to the circumstances of the princely territory, so Zwinglism was from
the first fashioned on municipal lines. It asserted the
autonomy of the congregation, which Luther had dis-
carded, and was thus well suited to an urban political
system. Luther had refused to apply his early revolutionary principles to civil life; even in ecclesiastical
matters he became conservative. For Zwingli the
political aspect was, perhaps, the most important. He
was essentially radical and logical, drawing his conclusions unsparingly from his premises, sweeping away
mediæval ruins as cumbering the ground on which
he would erect his modern fabric, breaking with all

tradition, treating Emperor with as scant respect as Pope.

The South German cities, full of eager, earnest spirits, caught at a system politically and intellectually suited to their needs. They, more than the princes, had suffered from ecclesiastical pretensions and exemptions. Zwingli would not merely supply them with a purer oil, but would give them new lamps for old. Once again Swiss influence was on the point of dominating the towns of South-western Germany : Strassburg hardly differed in character from Basel, Constance had entered into a league with Zurich. This attraction of German to Swiss towns would inevitably bring the former into the stream of international politics—into relations with France and with the Swiss ally and enemy of the Habsburgs, Ulrich of Württemberg.

If Swiss influence would have drawn German cities into a camp hostile to the Habsburgs, it would also have estranged them from German territorial princes. In the long conflict between princes and towns, the former had always been haunted by the fear that the cantonal system would prove contagious ; the Swiss, after all, were traditionally opposed to the Habsburgs, not as Emperors, but as Suabian territorial magnates. The spread of Zwinglism, therefore, would have been fully as dangerous to Lutheran princes as to Catholic Emperors. Hence it was that, but for one man, reforming princes and reforming towns would have turned their backs upon each other, and the second position might have been one of clash rather than of avoidance. The one man was Philip of Hesse, Charles's most dangerous opponent. Personally interested in theological controversy, Philip was not so completely under Luther's spell as were John of Saxony and his son John Frederick. His keen, quick intellect appreciated Zwingli's logic : the Hessian Church was within an ace of being organised by the French minister, Lambert, on Zwinglian lines. A Zwinglian Hesse might well have taken the place which a Calvinist Palatinate afterwards occupied. Philip was as geographically near to the Swiss and French frontiers as John of Saxony was remote. He had none of the traditional Saxon reverence for Emperor or Empire. German peace and unity were little to him in comparison with an active, aggressive European combination, which should include all elements hostile to the Habsburgs,—provided that the Habsburgs were for the moment the obstacle to his intellectual leanings or his political ambitions. Philip had, indeed, declined the perfunctory French offer to make him King of the Romans, but he intrigued industriously with French and Swiss, with Ulrich and Zapolya ; he was hand in glove with Bavaria in opposition to Ferdinand. His clear head, however, taught him that political combination mainly depended on religious concord, and hence he moved heaven and earth, if not Acheron itself, to bring Luther and Zwingli to agreement.

The hope of this accord was shattered by the growing conservatism of Luther. Frightened by the new spirit of revolution, doctrinal and political, he shrank back upon the principle of authority ; he extended to the Catholic Emperor the obedience which he had claimed as being the due of a Lutheran prince. He taught himself to believe in the gentleness of Charles ; he preached to princes on non-resistance, as he had once preached to peasants. It is true that he was not always thoroughly consistent, that his stubborn resistance to the Emperor's will in matters spiritual did at times modify his attitude of non-resistance in matters political.

Yet none the less this attitude was to be of incalculable benefit to Charles during the coming fifteen years. Meanwhile in the face of Luther's rejection of union with Zwingli, it was a truly great feat that Philip had succeeded in subordinating religious difficulties to political necessities, and had persuaded the Zwinglian towns to join with Lutheran princes in the Protest. The two most powerful and most antagonistic classes of Germany had united in bidding defiance to the Emperor on the eve of his arrival in the very plenitude of his power.

CHAPTER X

Charles in Germany—His favourable reception—Death of Gattinara—
Diet of Augsburg—The Lutheran Confession and Catholic Confuta-
tion—The legate Campeggi—Moderation of Charles—Recess of
Augsburg—Ferdinand's election as King of the Romans—Charles's
ministers, Cobos and Granvelle—Mary of Hungary appointed regent
of the Netherlands—The League of Schmalkalde—Policy of Bavaria—
Comparison between Charles and Ferdinand—The Turkish danger—
The convention of Nuremberg—Advice of the Confessor Loaysa—
Reasons for the Emperor's truce with Lutheranism—Charles marches
to meet Solyman—Charles's failure in Germany.

NINE wonderful years had ripened the reserved youth
of whom men wrote upon the walls at Worms, "Woe to
the kingdom whose ruler is a child." He had beaten
and taken the King of France, bent the Pope to his will,
and made Italy recognise him as its paramount power.
Would it not be a lighter task to restore the monarchy
in Germany, and to drive back into the Church's fold
the little flock of bewildered, wandering sheep? Charles
was very much in earnest; he had abandoned the idea
of coronation at Rome, and hurried it forward at Bologna,
in order to hasten his visit to Germany. His arrival
would surely produce a decisive crisis in the fortunes
both of monarchy and religion.

If Charles had changed, so also had his German kingdom. He was to find that another world had shaped
itself. Instead of a renegade friar applauded by an
undisciplined rabble of discontented gentry, there were

now organised territorial churches which had cast off all connection with the Papacy, which had their own definite doctrines, their ministry, their education, their charities. They had appropriated the revenues of sees and monasteries within the territory, had excluded the authority of the great ecclesiastics in whose dioceses they might be, had forbidden the very exercise of Catholic ritual. There was now little uncertainty as to the limits of the two religions—little hope that palliatives would assuage the religious fever. The two parties stood over against each other, watching, fearing, threatening.

Charles travelled over the Brenner when the Tyrolese mountains were in their full spring beauty. It was his first experience of the Alps, and his first visit to the Austrian possessions of his house. Detailed descriptions of the journey may be derived from the letters of the Venetian envoys and agents who accompanied the Emperor, and from those of the Papal legate Campeggi. The Tyrolese gave the beloved Maximilian's grandson a hearty welcome. There were the usual reviews, in which the splendid mountaineers who had already paid their full toll of blood on Italian soil, paraded and stormed mock castles. The pleasure portion of the journey culminated at Innsbruck, described by one of the Venetians as quite a little town. Here Charles proved to the committee of reception that, though Emperor, he was still human, for " he made as though he would kiss the younger ladies, but disengaged himself as soon as might be from those of riper years."

Once in Germany Charles patiently prepared his ground. He could be genial and winning when he pleased, and he practised his powers of attraction on the Bavarian dukes. He could confidently count on George of Saxony, on Henry of Brunswick, and on the Elector of Brandenburg.   In the previous year at Speyer the prince-bishops had seemed roused to the defence of their religion and its revenues.   In Switzerland Zwingli's political and religious reforms had endangered not only the Catholicism but the livelihood of the Forest Cantons, for he had denounced the demoralising system of mercenary service.   Thus the Habsburgs could at last reckon on the friendship of the fighting element among their traditional foes.   It seemed a happy augury that Charles's luckless brother-in-law, Christian II. of Denmark, was received back into the bosom of the Church. The repentant exile might exercise all a pervert's power of propagandism upon Scandinavian and North German heretics.   It is true that Charles in his heart of hearts placed little reliance in his sister's husband, who was as light-of-love in his doctrines as in his indiscretions.

Although the Emperor was thus taking a survey of the forces of Catholicism, peace was at present in the air.   In his very summons of the diet from Bologna, he had prayed both parties to put away all that was not right, and then join in one true religion.   Justus Jonas, writing to Luther on May 4, had said that nothing could be more kindly or gentle than the Emperor's citation.   He believed that not only would Charles hear the Lutheran case, but would earnestly seek the ways of concord : all men were saying that he would give a gracious hearing to both sides, and do nothing that smacked of tyranny.   The Lutherans themselves seemed prepared to meet the Emperor half way.   The Saxon Elector had striven to gain touch with Ferdinand.   Melanchthon, his chief theologian at Augsburg, was prepared to go to the utmost limits of concession in the cause of peace.   Luther, being under the ban, could not enter the Imperial city, but even he was prepared to take a kindly view of Charles.

While Germany was expecting Charles the cause of peace suffered a rude shock in the loss of Gattinara, who died quite suddenly as he was preparing to join his master. The Lutherans regarded the old Erasmian Chancellor as the most friendly of all the Imperial Councillors; they extolled him as the Ulpian of the new Justinian. Gattinara was bent on preserving peace within the Emperor's own dominions; in his hatred for France he was the advocate of generosity to Italy, and of compromise in Germany. The Roman party was of course accused by the Lutherans of a death so conducive to its policy of violence. Sudden death is not unusual in the case of hard-worked men of seventy-seven, but it was ascribed to the "usual Italian weapon, to some Venetian juicelet."

Charles emphasised his personal orthodoxy by arriving at Augsburg on the eve of Corpus Christi.[1] This feast was from the first days of the Reformation the Lutheran's red rag, the very symbol of superstition. Campeggi rode into the town side by side with Ferdinand and behind the Emperor. He had not dared to bless the people for fear of scandal. The princes, indeed, who had ridden out to meet the Emperor bowed the knee when the legate raised his two fingers, but even then the Elector of Saxony stood upright and rejected the Papal blessing. Charles himself created a favourable

---

[1] Among recent monographs on this diet are the following: F. W. Schirrmacher, *Briefe und Akten zu der Geschichte des Religionsgespräches zu Marburg und des Reichstags zu Augsburg 1530*, 1876. H. Virck, *Melanchthon's politische Stellung auf dem Reichstage zu Augsburg 1530* (*Zeitschrift für Kirchengeschichte*, 1887). J. Ficker, *Die Konfutation des Augsburgischen Bekenntnisses*, 1891. T. Brieger, *Beiträge zur Geschichte des Augsburger Reichstags 1530* (*Zeitschr. fur Kirchenges.*, 1891). Campeggi's despatches may be read in H. Laemmer, *Monumenta Vaticana*, 1861.

impression.   He was reported as being well made,
browner than when at Worms, while a little beard
covered his long chin.   In the evening occurred the
first wrangle.   Charles asked as a favour that the
Lutheran princes should join in the solemn procession.
Not content with refusing, they emphasised refusal by
coarse abuse of the Emperor's faith.   Ferdinand cried
with rage, but Charles preserved his conciliatory
demeanour; he probably did not understand all that the
Germans said.   On the following day he braved the
comments of Lutheran princes and Zwinglian towns-
folk, walking for two hours behind the Host in the
blazing sun of June, bareheaded and clad in a brown
velvet tunic.

The Lutheran princes were now asked to silence
their preachers during the short space of the diet.   On
their refusal Charles suggested that both parties should
request their preachers to avoid contentious topics—a
petition that was at once rejected.   To this dispute
apparently belongs the tale, somewhat variously told,
that George of Culmbach cried that he would sooner have
his head cut off than abandon his convictions, to which
Charles smilingly replied in broken German, "No, dear
prince, not head off, not head off."   Taking heart of
grace, the Emperor finally ordered that none should
preach save by his own license, for in Augsburg as an
Imperial city it was within his province to regulate the
public worship.

When the diet met, the royal speech first urged the
necessity of an aid to check the Turkish advance, and
then the settlement of the religious troubles.   The
Lutherans insisted on the reversal of this order, and
thus it was that the Confession of Augsburg, couched in
studiously moderate terms as the justification of their

belief, was read aloud before the Emperor in the chapel of the bishop's palace, and the Latin version handed to him. This was followed by a fresh presentation of the Hundred Grievances of the German Nation, and by a detailed statement of the complaints of the laity against the clergy.

The answer to the Confession was the Confutation composed by the leading divines of the Catholic majority. Charles returned this to its authors five times, that it might be stated in a less hostile tone. Even then it was sufficiently long and strong to be, in the words of a stout Protestant, a cause of boredom, disgust and nausea to the more sane among the audience. The Emperor and the diet, despairing of agreement between the theologians, appointed as a last hope a committee of fourteen princes, priests and theologians, seven from each religious party. The object was to arrive at some agreement that might leave a minimum of disputed topics for a General Council. The attempt necessarily failed, although each side showed in this a greater willingness for compromise.

Theological controversies did not occupy the whole time of the Emperor and the princes. A Venetian visitor reported that Charles and Ferdinand enjoyed themselves vastly in banqueting, dancing and shooting; they seemed to care little who was Lutheran and who Catholic; indeed, a great Lutheran gave a dinner-party to the Emperor, in which above the guests' heads were to be seen the portraits of Luther and his wife, and one Philip Melanchthon. It was believed, he adds, that differences would be plastered over, and laid to rest until a Council, and all this that Charles might get an aid against the Turks, and secure the election of Ferdinand as King of the Romans. Besides feasting

there was much intriguing. The divisions among the
Protestants gave Charles some hope of breaking up the
party. Melanchthon studiously avoided Bucer; Philip
of Hesse refused to attend the sermons of the Saxon
divine, Agricola. The outspoken hostility of Luther to
the German Zwinglian towns made Imperial intrigues
within their walls the easier. The dualism between
capital and labour found its reflection in religion.
Individual princes had their temporal interest in winning
the Emperor's favour for the investiture of fiefs. The
towns generally distrusted the doctrinal loyalty of the
princes; the Strassburg envoys evidently feared that
Charles would succeed in detaching the Saxons from
their co-religionists.

As a rule negotiation and intrigue were good-
tempered, but there was a momentary outburst of
passion when Philip of Hesse slunk away at nightfall
in express violation of the Emperor's command. He
left, indeed, a message that he was called away by the
illness of his wife, but consideration for his lawful
spouse was not the distinguishing feature of Philip's
character or conduct. There were of course alarmist
rumours in abundance, with plenty of long ears to listen
and untied tongues to wag. The Lutheran princes
were warned that Charles meant to lay violent hands
upon them. Very prevalent was the notion that he had
ordered the Imperial army to march from Florence upon
Germany. Credulous Catholics had their nerves set
throbbing by the news that Philip of Hesse was bringing
the irrepressible peasantry to join the Augsburg proletariate in an attack upon their persons. Most men were
disposed to underrate the genuine desire for political
peace even among those who were most determined on
doctrinal dissidence.

No one desired peace more than Charles, and the chief enemy of peace was the Papal legate. Campeggi in his confidential letters to the Curia kept reiterating that force was the only remedy. He confessed that his persuasive powers had had little effect upon the Emperor. He now tried to bribe Melanchthon by prospects of Papal favour, now stimulated the orthodoxy of the absolutist Bavarian dukes by a grant of patronage which would enslave their clergy, now stifled the demands of the Catholic princes that the grievances of Germany should find redress. Well knowing how to court the favour of his master, he forwarded to Rome a schedule of reasons for refusing a General Council, and if this were too hazardous, another array of pretexts for delaying it until the Conciliar craze had passed. The most dangerous enemy of Charles was not Luther but Campeggi, and it is more than probable that Charles knew it.

At a critical moment the legate found allies in the German Catholic controversialists. Aleander complained later that, either of design or from national clumsiness, their too fiery pamphlets had ruined all hope of agreement when on the point of its conclusion; they had called Melanchthon the standard-bearer of heresy, and vilified the very princes who were negotiating for peace.

When the committee of fourteen failed to find a compromise between the Confession and the Confutation, Charles had no option but to accept the latter as the exposition of his own faith. At this the Lutherans were disappointed and aggrieved. They had hoped that he would act as an independent arbiter between the two religious systems. Yet had Charles so acted, and had his sentence differed a hair's-breadth from the

opinions which Luther at that crisis held, it is un-
questionable that no Lutheran, except perhaps Melanchthon, would have accepted it. On this point the
Catholics were more straightforward ; they stated from
the first that they could not bend to the Emperor's
arbitrage, for he was not the judge of Catholic doctrine
but its champion. Melanchthon, the one Lutheran who
really craved for concord and would have sacrificed
something to obtain it, incurred the violent abuse of his
party, nor has his reputation ever quite recovered.

It may now well be believed that Melanchthon was
over eager to surrender all which stood in the way of a
peace which was in itself impossible. Union and
disunion did not depend upon the minutiæ of this
doctrine or of that. Neither the attitude nor the
moral condition of the Papacy rendered reconciliation
practicable. It may be admitted that the diet of
Augsburg was one of the supreme moments of Lutheranism—that princes and towns did indeed sacrifice
something for conscience' sake. Yet conscience took an
unpleasingly aggressive form in the shrieks of Lutheran
against Zwinglian, in the bandying of abuse between the
champions of combat and the partisans of peace. Luther
directing or abusing the Lutheran disputants from his
retreat at Coburg was less the hero of the hour than
Charles, who day by day bore the turmoil and the
tedium, flouted by Protestants, thwarted by Catholics,
yet never losing his composure, never forsaking his
conciliatory attitude.

Luther himself has admitted the affection which
Charles inspired. The pages of the very *Corpus
Reformatorum* still dub him the best and most merciful of rulers. Melanchthon wrote to a friend that more
marvellous and glorious than all the Emperor's successes

was the control of his temper : never a word nor an action could be criticised as in the least overbearing : there was no greed, no sign of pride or cruelty. "In this religious question," he continued, "in which our adversaries with wonderful art strive to exasperate him against us, he has always heard us in a judicial spirit. His private life is a perfect model of continence, temperance and moderation. Domestic discipline, which of yore was most rigorous among German princes, is now only preserved in Cæsar's household." After all Charles's ideal was lofty. He was striving not only for the unity of the church, of which he was the sword-bearer, but was compassing the union of the nation. Germany, rent by religious quarrels, seemed likely to be further torn asunder by French and Turks and Swiss. In the great European conflict she had ceased to reckon. Her enormous strength was neutralised by her divisions. In every principality and town there was hatred and persecution.

The recess of Augsburg, in accordance with the views of the Catholic majority, finally re-asserted the principle of the Edict of Worms. There were, however, two notable departures from the Emperor's previous policy. He now himself adopted in a modified degree the suspensive expedient which had marked the diet of 1526. Six months' grace was given to the Lutherans wherein to reconsider their determination : within that time, if they abstained from aggression, they were safeguarded from the penalties of the law. Furthermore Charles had now convinced himself of the necessity of a General Council, although he had not as yet committed himself to the principle that it must be held in Germany. Hitherto he had either raised objections, or had treated the question as a mere diplomatic counter. When in

1529 his envoys at Rome found that the very suggestion of a Council hampered negotiation, they frankly
abandoned it, whereon Clement VII., rising from his
seat with a gesture of relief, assured them that henceforth agreement would be easy. But from the diet of
Augsburg onwards Charles rarely ceased to place the
immediate summons of a Free and General Council in
the forefront of his demands ; he was honestly persuaded
that it was an essential requisite to reunion.

Thus in the course of this important diet Charles
very tentatively adopted the three methods which for
the next fifteen years he was to try in turn—comprehension, suspension, Council. Of the ultimate appeal
to arms there was at Augsburg just one hint. Tender
as Charles was with the princes, he was rougher towards
the towns. Many of these showed Zwinglian inclinations, but few would give their adhesion to any definite
formulæ. Four towns alone—Strassburg, Constance,
Lindau and Memmingen—presented their confession of
a Zwinglian tinge, known as the *Tetrapolitana*. An
Emperor was wont to regard the Imperial cities as more
immediately subject to his control—as being to him, as
Emperor, what the towns of a territory were to the
princely ruler. Dissent therefore might pass for rebellion, and Charles was additionally irritated because
Augsburg itself flaunted its Protestantism in his very
face. When therefore many of the towns refused
assent to the recess, he exclaimed that he would sooner
die than suffer such disobedience. He saw, he is reported to have said, that they wished to teach him a
new faith, but it was a matter not for lessons but for fists,
and they would soon see who was the stronger. From
under the brown velvet sleeve, just for a moment, the
mailed fist peeped forth.

The diet which Charles had summoned in the plenitude of his power proved barren of results. Yet it is
full of interest as illustrating his methods and constitutional ideas. Whether in ecclesiastical or secular dis-
cussions there is no trace of the "Modern Monarch,"
no hint at arbitrary or novel measures, no gleam of
original or creative genius. His aims were eminently
conservative, and when he moved forward, he borrowed
from the ideas which had already become the currency
of the religious question. The hasty phrases which flew
from Spain to Germany, and which "of Imperial and
absolute authority" annulled the recess of 1526, found
their substitutes at Augsburg in " the peculiar Imperial
grace, gentleness and desire for peace," which suspended
the penalties unanimously imposed at Worms in 1521.
Charles had shown himself the man of circumstance,
always listening, always learning, living from day to day,
yet never forgetting, nor losing sight of the future amid
the necessities of the present and the memories of the
past.

At Augsburg Charles had pressed privately upon the
Electors the choice of Ferdinand as King of the Romans.
In view of the policy which formed the chief interest of
his closing years it may be wondered that he wished
thus to set aside the direct succession of his own, the
elder, line. It would almost seem that Charles had
succumbed to the charms of the newly-found brother
whom he had previously only met in the heated atmosphere of his first Spanish visit. His warm expressions
of love for Ferdinand at this period fall strangely from
the usually cold lips. His very marriage seemed a subject of regret, because it deprived his brother of the
whole Habsburg heritage. Apart from this, Charles had
an overwhelming sense of the nearness of death, which,

if his health and the circumstances of his own inheritance be considered, is not surprising. Should he die, a
disputed succession to the Empire would bring to the
ground the fabric of Habsburg power. He was soon to
start on his campaign against the Turks; four years ago
a similar campaign had cost the life of his own brother-
in-law Louis of Hungary. Charles was now a crowned
Emperor and not, as Maximilian, mere Emperor Elect;
the election of a King of the Romans was therefore
natural and probably constitutional. He might cherish
the hope—the shadow of a hope—that the dignity would
add to the strength of his brother's administration
during his own absence.

The Electors for various considerations gave a somewhat unexpected assent at the beginning of 1531. The
Saxon Elector, followed in this by his successor John
Frederick, protested against the action of his colleagues,
less perhaps from personal or even religious considerations than from a laudable, if crabbed, constitutionalism
which was the hereditary quality of the Ernestine line
of Saxony. Even Luther at last advised his new master
that opposition for the sake of principle had its limits.
Fortunately for Ferdinand the dukes of Bavaria had no
vote, but his election again envenomed the relations
between the two chief Catholic powers. Had the
Bavarians remembered the last Emperor of their house,
or seen in the crystal of the future their eighteenth
century representative on the Imperial throne, they
might have allayed their ambition and tempered their
resentment.

For the next two years Charles was in Germany
or the neighbouring Netherlands. He now knew the
persons and the problems with whom or which he had
to deal. His critics—German and Flemish, Catholic

and Protestant — might complain that his advisers were Spaniards and Burgundians, who neither knew nor cared for Germany. On their side Flemings and Germans did not realise the Emperor's European difficulties; they could not fully understand how directly religious and constitutional disputes in Germany were affected by the enmity of France, of the Pope and the Sultan, by the widening breach with Henry VIII., by the claims of Spain and Italy, by the effort to bring the Scandinavian kingdoms again within the sphere of Habsburg influence. It was only natural that in these two years Charles's slowness, his irresolution, his lack of original conception and decisive action, were most obvious. Circumstances conspired to develop inborn characteristics. Gattinara had been the boldest of all the Imperial advisers. The Burgundian Granvelle and the Spanish Cobos were henceforth the most influential ministers. Both were industrious and cautious rather than adventurous. Neither occupied the place of Chièvres or even of Gattinara. Even before the latter's death the confessor Loaysa had advised Charles never to give him a successor. Loaysa, much to his disgust, had been left behind at Rome. On July 6, 1530 he wrote to beg Charles to be in future his own Grand Chancellor, and to let the result of his own deliberations pass through the hands of Granvelle and Cobos : "If you do not get through more work in a month than you have hitherto done in two, let your Majesty inflict on me an ample penance, although I do not know what greater there can be than to keep me exiled from my country and from the eyes of my prince."[1]

---

[1] Loaysa's letters from Rome at this period are of much interest. *Cartas al Emperador Cárlos V. escritas en los años de 1530-1532 por su confesor*, 1848.

Cobos survived the reign of Charles, while Granvelle quite towards its close was succeeded by his son,
then known as the Bishop of Arras. Both were good
friends of the confessor's, and as the object of his
letter was to persuade his master not to give them
excessive influence, his praise is not subject to the
discount to be deducted from panegyric. Cobos, wrote
Loaysa, was clever at covering his master's fits of
carelessness, contenting the parties concerned and
taking the blame off his lord's shoulders : his devotion and prudence were consummate : he did not
split one's brain by cleverness and subtle sayings like
some other men : he never complained of his master,
and was the best-liked man in the north. The confessor had always held that Cobos was the trunk
wherein Charles kept his honour and his secrets.
Granvelle was an elegant man of letters and a good
Latinist : his tongue was well under control, his
personality carried weight : he was a careful Christian,
faithful, secret, experienced in state affairs, befriending
the good and abhorring the bad : he was not so sweet-
tempered in conversation as Cobos, but as he was wide-
awake he would, on taking an office which required
patience, suffer importunities up to the necessary point.
    While Cobos was confined mainly to the interests
of his Spanish kingdoms, Charles made Granvelle his
chief adviser in the great international relations of
Central Europe. It is noticeable that all the Emperor's
great ministers come from the small French-speaking
states along the Franco-Imperial border-line, and thus
represented a very small portion of the population
of his possessions. Chièvres was Walloon, Gattinara,
though Piedmontese by birth, was trained in the
Savoyard Chancery before he was imported to the

Netherlands, Granvelle and his son were natives of Franche-Comté. Among others of the Emperor's intimate associates de Praet and the members of the House of Orange-Nassau may be classed in the same category. This was thoroughly Burgundian; it had been the practice of Charles the Bold. The smaller the national interests of the minister, the greater would be his unity to the ruler of the heterogeneous aggregate.

Not only Gattinara but Margaret had died. Charles with much difficulty persuaded his sister Mary, the widowed queen of Hungary, to undertake the government of the Netherlands. She was only twenty-five, but was, perhaps, already the cleverest of the Habsburgs, combining tender sentiment with hard commonsense, intellectual alertness, and solid capacity for business details. Her leanings towards Lutheranism had caused Ferdinand grave alarm. She had not, however, as her sister the Queen of Denmark, professed Luther's doctrines, and at her brother's instance she ceased to read Luther's books. To Charles she frankly stated her suspected religious opinions as an obstacle to her new position. He tenderly assured her of his complete confidence; he would never entrust the office to any as to whose orthodoxy he had the least suspicion. The young widow made an absolute stipulation that she should not be annoyed by matrimonial offers, and then accepted the regency. Had Charles not made so admirable a choice there is little question that the tragedy of Philip's reign would have been rehearsed in his.

The year 1530 draws a very strong dividing line through the reign of Charles. His coronation marked the fulfilment of his Imperial ambitions. The settlement of Italy at Bologna was the real conclusion of the first

series of French wars. His aunt and guardian Margaret
and his veteran councillor were gone. Henceforth he
must rely on his own experience. It had been well
for him if the diet of Augsburg had settled the religious
troubles of Germany, even as the congress of Bologna
had decided the political fate of Italy. But in Germany the fateful year was to be rather a beginning
than an ending. The diet might seem a drawn battle,
or a slight success : it was in fact the Emperor's first
real check. He must review the forces at his disposal
for a fresh phase of the conflict. He was, as usual
slow, and the enemy were before him, for on the last
day of the year was formed the Protestant League of
Schmalkalde.

The Emperor's adoption of a suspensory attitude
at Augsburg should have convinced the keen-sighted
that the danger to the Lutherans was infinitesimal.
Charles had intended to bring some 3000 reliable
troops to Germany, but he had not possessed the
wherewithal to pay them. The Lutherans at the
most were more frightened than hurt by the resolution
of the diet. Even for fright they had little reason.
Joachim I. of Brandenburg had blustered about force,
but the other Catholic princes, including fighting Henry
of Brunswick, assured their Lutheran colleagues that
religious dissidence in no way lessened their determination that there should be peace in Germany.
Political peace had been the remedy which Luther
had prescribed from Coburg ; political peace was the
specific enjoined by the more sane or less earnest of
the Catholics ; political peace Charles above all others
was forced to accept as a palliative for the disease
which would not bear the knife.

Nevertheless the Lutherans spent in arming the

time accorded for repentance. Lutheran princes and
semi-Zwinglian towns combined in the League of
Schmalkalde the professed object of which was armed
resistance to any attack on their religion. Among
the German Catholics there was no such bond of union.
Bavaria, alienated by Ferdinand's election, was intriguing with every enemy of Charles. The Catholicism
of the Electors of Cologne and Mainz was less than
lukewarm; the latter, said Charles himself, was neither
Catholic nor Lutheran, but pagan. Von Stadion,
Bishop of Augsburg, was certainly nearer to Luther
than to the Pope. The Habsburgs could no longer
rely upon the Suabian League, scored by religious
divisions and shaken by Bavarian intrigues. Ferdinand
was informed that the League would no longer guarantee
his possession of Württemberg, unless the balance of
the debt, due since the sale of the duchy, were paid.
Least of all was there any unity between German
Catholics and the Curia, for all the hopes of the
former, all the fears of the latter, were centred in a
Council.

The dreaded day of April, which was to usher in
the downfall of heresy, proved a veritable All Fools'
day. Instead of executing the recess Charles must
convince Ferdinand that peace with the Protestants
must at all costs be maintained. The Council, he
wrote, was hopeless; Francis I., to please the Pope
and the English king, would take no part in this nor
in resistance to the Turk. Ferdinand was warned
to make terms, not only with the Lutherans, but with
Zapolya; he must, if need be, surrender Hungary to
avert the Turk's advance; negotiations for a Council
might continue, but only as a blind, to beguile the
Lutherans to compromise.

Ferdinand was still the speculative, adventurous
partner in the Habsburg firm. He was eager for
religion, keen for power, hating compromise with
Lutherans or surrender to his Hungarian rival. Events
seemed to justify his courage, for in October 1531
occurred the unexpected defeat and death of Zwingli.
The rural Catholic cantons, now victorious, had in their
danger been forced to look to their old Habsburg
master for support, while Zwingli was the ally of
France and Hesse. The hour had come when the
Habsburgs might regain their hold upon their lost
Swiss territories, and crush South German dissent,
which stood with its back to the Zwinglian Swiss
cantons. The Swiss, wrote Ferdinand to Charles, were
the backbone of reform in Germany : let him with
the Catholic cantons overpower the Zwinglians, and
Germany was at his feet. Charles was cautious and
calculating ; he had not 2000 men at his command ;
he dared not use Spanish or Italian troops for fear
of offending Germany, nor Germans for fear of a
Lutheran onslaught on his rear ; he was conscious
that Francis I. would not tolerate his intervention in
Switzerland. While the Catholic princes were divided
and unarmed, and could not even trust their subjects,
the Protestants had long been arming. The professed
objects of the League of Schmalkalde were, indeed,
religious and defensive. The towns were probably
honest in these professions, but not so Luther's master
and his princely colleagues. They were in league on
the one hand with Catholic France, and on the other
with Catholic Bavaria for offensive action against
Ferdinand, whose best energies must be devoted to ward-
ing off the Turk from Germany. The Sultan himself
relied upon Protestant hostility to the Emperor, for

when Ferdinand's ambassador assured him that Charles
enjoyed the love and obedience of his subjects, Solyman
sarcastically asked if he had yet made peace with Luther.
Did not Lutherans openly assert that they would sooner
that Germany were Turkish than Catholic? Had not
Luther taught that the Turk was a divinely appointed
scourge whom it would be sinful to resist? The action of
the princely members of the League of Schmalkalde was
really directed to a revolt of the territorial princes, aided
directly by France and indirectly by the Porte, against
Imperial authority. That they deceived themselves
into believing that they had religious motives made them
none the less dangerous to the peace and unity—nay, to
the very existence of their nation.

From every quarter clouds were gathering round
Charles. Solyman was marching on Vienna. The
breach with Henry VIII. now seemed irreparable, and
Francis irreconcilable. Christian of Denmark's last
cast for fortune had ended in his capture, and this
entailed the Protestantism and Anti-Imperialism of
Scandinavia. The Netherlands, with their teeming
population, inclined to violent, if indefinite, dissent,
were hemmed in by powers religiously or politically
hostile to the Habsburgs, while in Italy the Pope was
always ready to conspire against their rule. To the
present day it is doubted whether Ferdinand was not
right, whether Charles did not miss once more his August
day. It is just possible that, with the aid of the
Catholic cantons, he might have broken up the League
of Schmalkalde before Francis or the Sultan were upon
him. Yet he probably judged correctly that Germany
would not tolerate Spaniards and Italians tramping
through her very heart to Saxony or Hesse. Even as
it was, he had to listen in the coming diet to much

plain speaking on his employment of foreign ministers. Ferdinand had a narrower horizon than had Charles, whose eyes scanned the limits of the European world.

Once more then Charles would temporise and suspend. At Regensburg and the adjourned diet at Nuremberg (1532) he was for the Lutherans all patience and conciliation; his outbursts were reserved for the Catholic Estates, which, led by the Bavarian Chancellor and stimulated by Hesse, demanded a General Council with or without the Pope's consent, or failing this a national synod. Charles's independence of the Papacy had never yet gone as far as this, and he indignantly rejected proposals so schismatic. The Lutheran demands were equally preposterous, for the more poltical and aggressive section now realised its strength and the Emperor's weakness. The leaders demanded an extension of the proposed indemnity to all future adherents, and toleration for Lutherans in Catholic states—a toleration which was not intended to be reciprocal.

Such terms meant for the Habsburgs abdication, not only of their Imperial, but of their territorial power. In his dire distress Charles found a staunch ally in his capital enemy. Luther's conservative common-sense and his German patriotism saved the Emperor's cause, and perhaps that of Christianity. He drew the Saxon Elector away from the unscrupulous foreign policy of Hesse. He was at this moment subject to his passion for authority, believing that under so gentle and generous a lord as Kaiser Karl there was no need of guarantees for Lutherans as yet unborn or unconverted. Luther was now no violent propagandist; he had, perhaps, an instinct that propagandism would bear dangerous fruit. Declaring himself against one-sided toleration, he urged that one should do as one would be done by. Dualism of religion was fatal to the vitality of the territorial power, on which he had now pinned his faith.[1]

The result of the diet of Nuremberg was not heroic : it was, perhaps, humiliating both to Emperor and to Protestants. Yet it was a pleasant episode in the tangled tale of Charles and Luther. The Emperor agreed to a further extension of the amnesty to the Elector of Saxony and its allies : no estate should be harassed with prosecution by the Imperial Chamber for religion's sake. The Catholic majority rejected the agreement, and it was not embodied in the recess; it rested on a private understanding between Charles and the Protestant leaders; no copy even was in their hands, so entirely did Luther rely on the Emperor's loyalty.

For this agreement both Charles and Luther have been blamed. Protestant writers have charged Luther with want of courage, of political insight, of party loyalty. But Protestantism rested on moral opinion ; it is doubtful if at this time it could have survived a practical alliance with French and Turks. Luther was deceived in his opinion of Charles's natural mildness, but he was, in spite of temporary lapses, a patriotic German. To bear the back to the scourge divine was no longer an article of faith. He now taught that the Turk must be withstood, and saw that command must be conferred not, as in religion, upon a territorial prince, but upon a higher power. Luther was a practical man rather than a political philosopher, and when he was forced to formulate his conception of sovereignty, he was fairly puzzled.

[1] See O. Winckelmann, *Der schmalkaldische Bund, 1530-32, und der Nürnberger Religionsfriede*, 1892.

In accord, for once, with Luther was his old arch-enemy Aleander, who was now in Germany. He warned his Roman correspondent that the Turkish peril and the French intrigues of the German princes were thwarting the Emperor's orthodox intentions, and that the Papacy, while not endorsing, must shut its eyes to concessions as dangerous as they were unavoidable. Aleander was a man of the world; his enemies even accused him of being a Jew, for could he not write Hebrew? Charles himself had probed him on this questionable accomplishment, receiving the skilful answer that he had acquired it from a Spanish lodger in his father's house.

The Emperor had a more unexceptional adviser in his late confessor. In July 1530, long before the political difficulties reached their full development, Loaysa had written to his master recommending force as the true rhubarb for German as for Spanish heresy. In his very next letter, however, he advised his master to wink at German heresy, to grant the minimum of such concessions as would content the heretics, and induce them to aid in the defence of Germany and Hungary, and in Ferdinand's election; in such a way Charles would fulfil his duty, it would be no fault of his if there were harm which he could not remedy, or good that he could not do; he would at least make his exit from Germany in honour, power and peace.

By the summer of 1532 the confessor's elastic conscience had stretched yet further. In a letter of June 8 he advised either a truce between Lutherans and Catholics, which would leave each party to believe as they pleased, or else an agreement that until the future Council they should all live under their respective rites without molesting one another: if, by fault of the

Pope, the Council should not meet within three years, henceforth the Lutherans might live freely, and continue in their own form of belief without hindrance from princes or diets : all this Charles might grant without blame on the sole condition that they saved him against the common enemy. "Let Your Majesty," continued Loaysa, "have no scruples in making use of them, heretics as they may be, for if your heart is free from sin, their errors will not disturb your own good fortune."

This advice from a Spanish Cardinal is a remarkable apology for the subordination of religious uniformity to political necessity. It clearly faced the possibility of a permanent toleration—a point at which Charles himself never quite arrived. It is highly probable that the letter determined the policy adopted by the Emperor in the following month, though his own mind must have been instinctively passing through the phases which the Cardinal's conscience so rapidly underwent. However dangerous the concessions to heresy, Catholics have small reason to complain of Charles. "God be thanked," wrote Aleander, "for giving us so Catholic a prince, for if in these most evil times we had had for Emperor a Frederick Barbarossa, a Louis of Bavaria, a Henry IV. or the like, we Catholics would soon have little or nothing of a great part of Christendom."

The Emperor's action was certainly remarkable. The compromise was not the result of a constitutional fight with the recognised elements of the German state. To Charles this would have brought no humiliation as it would to a French king ; he had a legal mind, and could recognise constitutional forms and constitutional opposition, although he might do his utmost to drive a coach and four through both. But this was a hole-and-corner compromise made through the medium of two Electors, with a league which had no official basis, and whose only bond of union was a religion, which Charles and the constitutional authority of the Empire had proscribed. Charles had absolutely consented to hold back the hand of the Imperial Chamber, the one existent relic of the constitution, which after his own election had been so pompously inaugurated. And all this was done in secret, embodied in no recess; it was an informal promise of Charles to the Lutherans, a personal instruction to the Imperial Chamber. He did, indeed, stop short of recognising territorial independence, which would have been the upshot of the earlier Lutheran proposals; he bowed to a manifestation of practical power, but would not admit an unconstitutional principle.

There is no reason to charge the Emperor with deceit. His political sympathies were at this time with the more conservative Lutherans. The Imperial Chamber, a hotbed of cantankerous Catholicism, was ordered to respect the terms granted at Nuremberg, and not to proceed in cases relating to religion. The lawyers naturally asked what were the terms of the truce, and what was the Emperor's definition of religious cases. Charles roughly replied that the first question was impertinent, and that the second was for them to answer. He was disheartened and disgusted by the champions of his own religion. Living from hand to mouth he must conciliate the Lutherans who would feed the army which was to fight the Turks. The Protestants justified his confidence; no Estates showed more zeal than the South German towns which had already rejected the treasonable overtures of Philip of Hesse and the temptations of the King of France.

Charles had now brought his Spanish and Italian

veterans to Vienna; he at length found himself at the
head of a respectable army. He longed to have done
with diets, and to meet the leader of the infidels in the
field. The Habsburg brothers, wrote a contemporary,
were eager for a "jolly battle" between Neustadt and
Vienna. But Solyman had no heart to face his rival.
The little fortress of Güns had given the Turks their fill
of fighting, and scarcely less ruinous was the siege of
Gran. The Grand Vizier's forces had been cut to pieces
in the Vienna forest; Andrea Doria had captured post
after post in the Ionian Isles and Western Greece. The
Sultan's great army sullenly retreated. Ferdinand
would fain have crushed resistance in Hungary, which
now would have been easy; but the German princes
had no interest in winning Hungary for their rival, and
no taste for pursuing the Sultan with the chances of
another defeat of Varna at the end. The season was
unhealthy, the winter was at hand. Spain and Italy
were clamouring for Charles's presence and for defence
against the Barbaresques.

Charles left Germany much as he had found it. He
gained his pressing and immediate needs, the election of
Ferdinand and the beating back of the Turk; he could
with decency return to Italy and Spain, further absence
from which might have been highly dangerous. It was
the impossibility of being everywhere at once that again
baffled the Emperor's success. Aleander had been very
sanguine, for he had found Germany far less rabid on
reform than at the time of his previous visit eleven
years ago. He believed that there was every hope of
reunion, if only Charles could stay, but his departure
would gravely prejudice all his friends' fair plans. From
the Roman cardinal in Germany, as from the communes
in Spain and the captains in Italy, arose the recurring

plaint against the absenteeism of the ruler who could not be omnipresent.

Though Charles had made the best of his possibilities, it was clear to Germany and to Europe, that his Imperial power was shadowy and unsubstantial. The King of the Romans had a title without authority; no territorial prince, Catholic or Protestant, had been won or humbled; there was no central authority, no national army that could be employed outside German frontiers: each German prince at his own wayward will was the ally or tool of France, or England, or the Hungarian pretender. Elsewhere successful all along the line, Charles had failed in Germany. He was fully conscious of this, and yet scarcely seemed to resent it. Nor was this mere seeming: notwithstanding the brave expressions of the coronation ceremony, he had little idea of changing the national system. He might shape it to his ends at this moment or at that, but he had none of the acute consciousness of failure, nor the bitter disillusion of a creative genius which is prevented from creating. The opposition of Germany wrecked all his European schemes, but he tolerated this because, though annoying, it was not unnatural: it was part and parcel of the incoherent patchwork which he had inherited.

CHAPTER XI

Charles forms a defensive Italian league—Francesco Sforza at Milan—
The restoration of the Medici—The Italian republics—Elements of
opposition to Charles in Italy—Attitude of Clement VII.—Marriage
of Catherine de' Medici—Death of Clement VII.—Accession of
Cardinal Farnese as Paul III.—Condition of the Spanish possessions
in North Africa in the reign of Ferdinand—Defeat of Ugo Moncada
at Algiers—Settlement of the Knights of St. John at Malta and
Tripoli—The power of Barbarossa—Expedition of Charles against
Goletta and Tunis—His visit to Sicily—Death of Francesco Sforza
—Francis I. reopens the question of the Milanese succession—His
refusal of the Emperor's proposals—French invasion of Savoy—
Charles challenges the French King before Pope and Cardinals.

FROM the coronation of Charles at Bologna to the
death of Clement VII. in September 1534 there are few
marked events in Imperial-Italian history, with the
exception of the settlement of Florence, which was but
the aftermath of the previous period. This very absence
of incident is valuable as showing the Emperor's
natural inclinations, had he been left undisturbed by
France. Throughout these years his policy was purely
defensive. His aim was the preservation of peace in Italy
by closing the peninsula to France, his means a federation
of Italian states bound to himself by interests largely
personal. There was no attempt at centralised government, no ambition for annexation of territory for
territory's sake. The defensive league of Italian states
which Charles personally contrived in 1533, after his

return from Germany, is probably the truest index of his policy, and should therefore receive due weight. It is the very system which he would gladly have applied to Germany in later years, and which, subject to some deductions, would best have suited the political instincts and traditions of either nation.

This Italian league comprised the Aragonese possessions, the Papacy, the states of Milan, Florence, Ferrara and Mantua, and the republics of Genoa, Siena and Lucca. It is of interest to notice how nearly Charles avoided the errors ascribed to Louis XII. in the celebrated criticism of his policy by Machiavelli. Charles did his very utmost to prevent the entry of a rival foreign power ; he took precautions that the strong states within Italy, Venice and the Papacy, should grow no stronger ; he fortified himself by friendly combination with the weaker states. He could not indeed live there in person, nor did he plant colonies, but he did systematically adopt an expedient lying between the two, by planting out his own near relations in Italian courts. Just as Spain, Austria, and the Netherlands were ruled by the family federation of Charles, Ferdinand and Mary, so should each state in Italy be, as far as possible, a link of the family ring.

The all-important problem was the settlement of Milan, the duchy being the first objective of French attack. Francesco Sforza had owed his state to Charles and had then betrayed him. The obvious penalty was forfeiture, and Charles was strongly advised to annex the duchy. He refused, however, to alarm public feeling in Italy and without, and thus not only forgave and restored its duke, but admitted him to the Habsburg circle, by giving him his niece Christina of Denmark. It may be that hope of issue was slight, and Mary

certainly implored her brother not to sacrifice the young
girl, but Charles with somewhat unusual brutality
replied that it was worth the chance.   His optimism was,
perhaps, explained by the Duke's numerous recoveries :
"The Duke of Milan is very ill," wrote Salinas from
Mantua on April 8, 1530, "the attack is extremely
severe, but he has had others of the same sort, and has
seven lives like a cat."

The neighbouring state of Savoy-Piedmont had of
old had French traditions ; its duke was nearly related to
Francis I. ; the French armies had walked over Savoyard
territory as over their own land.   The Emperor, however, had lured away Charles III. through the influence
of his sister-in-law, Beatrice of Portugal.   The duke was
a ruler of little practical capacity ; he ultimately met his
end by knocking his head against the wall in an attempt
to get out of bed on the wrong side.   Beatrice was
clever, beautiful, ambitious, and above all devoted to
the Emperor.   Thus Savoy also was now within the
family federation, and Milan was covered by a large
buffer state, which closed the Alps against a French
advance.

The Medici had been restored to Florence, but they
could only exist there by the continuance of Imperial
aid, while its geographical position and the present
relation to the Papacy rendered it doubly important to
make sure of this city, with its notorious French
sympathies.   To effect this object Charles created the
disreputable Alessandro Duke of Florence, and engaged
him to his natural daughter Margaret.   As Clement VII.
was Medici before he was Pope, the Emperor might well
hope to bind him by this chain alone.   But he had done
much more : he had restored the older Papal possessions
in full, giving up the fortresses ceded as a guarantee

after the Sack of Rome, forcing the Venetians to disgorge Ravenna and Cervia, which during the troubles
they had reoccupied.

Mantua was of the utmost importance to the
Emperor's defensive scheme.   It was an eminently
military state, and its impregnable capital, with the
command of the Mincio and the Po, made it the natural
bulwark against Venice, while no very wide stretch of
territory divided it from Ferdinand's Tyrolese dominions.   The house of Gonzaga had Imperial traditions
and these Charles encouraged by every means.   He
erected the marquisate into a duchy, and allowed its
ruler to marry the heiress of Montferrat.   When the lord
of Montferrat died (1533), Charles invested Gonzaga with
the marquisate, in spite of his brother Ferdinand's
eagerness to possess it.   The little state, wedged in
between Milan and Piedmont, with its strong fortress of
Casale, might prove very valuable in friendly hands.
The heir to Mantua was linked to the Habsburgs by
marriage with Ferdinand's daughter, while Charles
heaped benefits upon the duke's brother, Ferrante
Gonzaga, his foremost general and personal friend, who
in 1535 became viceroy of Sicily.   If Mantua was
Imperialist by tradition, Ferrara, a Papal fief, was ever
French in sympathy—more French than the French, as
Pius II. had said in the fifteenth century.   Moreover
the duke married Renée of France, daughter of Louis
XII.   Nevertheless he was bound to Charles by
gratitude, for Charles alone had saved for him the
Imperial fiefs of Modena and Reggio, and perhaps
Ferrara also, from the Pope.

Of the republics Genoa was tied to Charles by the
gift of freedom and by the interests of Doria.   Dorian
and Imperial influence were interdependent—they must

stand or fall together. As Ferrante Gonzaga was
Charles's general, so was Andrea Doria his admiral.
But, in addition to this, much of the trade of Spain and
Sicily was in Genoese hands, while Genoa formed the
water-gate of Spain in Italy, essential to her communication with Milan and with the Habsburg's Austrian
dominions. Lucca was insignificant, but the state of
Siena was important as lying between Florence and
Rome. In spite of Ghibelline Imperialist tradition the
city was a natural resort for Florentine anti-Medicean
exiles, her coast towns for French or Turkish squadrons.
The turbulence of her chronic factions was a constant
source of peril in this republic, from of old "more madly
administered than any town in Italy," as Commines had
said. Charles tried at first a system resembling that of
Genoa. He established the influence of a Sienese
noble, Piccolomini, Duke of Amalfi, giving him a very
small Spanish garrison, sufficient merely for duties of
police.

Venice was still too powerful and too independent to
be brought within the Imperial system. She had herself
aimed at being the predominant power in Italy, and
could not easily forgive her more fortunate rival. Even
apart from old Guelphic interests, she would look to a
revival of French influence in Italy, which might at
least restore a balance and avert the danger of a single
paramount foreign power. Nevertheless Venice since
the events of 1529 must pursue a cautious, timid policy,
Charles alone could protect her from the attentions of
the more acquisitive Ferdinand, while the ripening
friendship between the Porte and France must sooner or
later drive her to his arms.

This scheme of ruling Italy through her old native
families had many merits but some drawbacks. The

continuity of local independence entailed the survival of local feuds. Every government in Italy had its traditional enemies, and these by force of circumstances became an anti-Imperial and therefore a French party. In many cases French sympathies were of long standing. The Neapolitan baronage had always been Angevin, if only for the reason that the Angevins were not in possession. If the Emperor gave high command to the Ghibelline Colonna, the Guelphic Orsini from pure rivalry were always at the disposal of his enemy, and this division was not only of importance in the Roman Campagna, but in the kingdom of Naples, where either family had extensive fiefs.

At Florence the old Savonarolist party had not been entirely crushed; it retained its devotion to France, and the convent of San Marco might once more prove a focus of disaffection to the Medici. More than this, the great Florentine families, even those comprised in the "Medicean ring"—nay, even the younger branches of the Medici themselves—resented the development of monarchy : their ideal was a syndicate of houses of which the Medici should be at most the ornamental head. The oligarchical opposition to the Medici was by no means in sentiment necessarily anti-Imperial, but the Imperial support given to the Medici compelled it to look towards France, and thus at Florence both extremes, the oligarchs and the democrats, were in this, if in this only, united. Similarly at Genoa the populace which disliked the rule of all old noble families, and the old noble Fieschi who for centuries had hated the rival Doria, equally resented the sway of the Imperial *condottiere*. To the Sforza in Lombardy there had always been the potentiality of a Guelphic opposition, which might attach itself either to Venice or to France. If at Siena one *Monte* or faction enjoyed Imperial favour, this was sufficient to alienate the other.

The forces of discontent, some of them eminently artificial and entirely external to the Emperor's policy, were naturally fed by the general ill-feeling created by the presence of foreign soldiery, and the heavy taxation which the defence of Italy entailed. The discontent would perhaps have been dormant, had it not from time to time been galvanised by the Curia. The Papacy was not strong enough to unite Italy, but it could always head a league to oppose any prince who aimed at the monarchy of the peninsula. The Pope at this period was almost necessarily at variance with the Emperor. As head of the threatened Church he would dislike either the very existence of a General Council, or at all events its objects and methods. As a territorial power he would on the negative side be opposed to Imperial predominance in Italy, or resist being dragged into war with France, while he would have the positive desire for the territorial aggrandisement of the Church or of his own relations, and, if the Emperor would not satisfy this, he would turn to France.

Even the uneventful years which preceded the death of Clement VII. could prove that Charles had neither sufficiently humbled nor propitiated the Pope. Apart from his political position, the personal character of Clement made him an unstable ally. Directly he had made solemn engagements with one of his rivals, he had an inveterate inclination towards intrigue with the other. His horror of a Council has been ascribed to the fear of his own deposition on the ground that the election of a bastard to the Holy See was uncanonical. More probably it was due to the dislike of a prelate of the old diplomatic, Italian school to straightforward, drastic, foreign methods,—to inquiries which would shake the financial foundations of the Curia to their very base. A rude attack, whether from Germany or Spain, on the complicated pecuniary machinery of the Papal Court would be more permanently ruinous than the Sack of Rome. Reform, whether in the German or the Spanish sense, would assume a national character—would result in withdrawing national revenues from the immediate control of Rome, and, in Italian eyes, especially the eyes of such as Clement, the very existence of the Papal polity depended on the cosmopolitan drainage which flowed to Rome as the universal reservoir.

The French Crown had made its Concordat with the Pope, and both parties were satisfied therewith. France alone of the powers had no interest in the Council; France would oppose a Council, if only because the Emperor pressed it. And the Emperor, who up to his coronation had merely urged it in a formal, perfunctory manner, was, since his visit to Germany, convinced of its necessity. France, therefore, on ecclesiastical and temporal grounds, was more than ever the natural ally of Rome, and to France Clement inevitably turned. That Clement in his old age travelled to Marseilles for a personal interview with Francis was much : that he married his young cousin Catherine to the French king's second son was more. There was wild talk as to what her dowry should ultimately be, but the very mention of her claims to Florence and Urbino was intended to give the French king a lien upon Central Italy. It may be true that in his last moments, when personal and family interests were fading, Clement VII. once more turned his eyes towards Charles as to the true protector of the Church, imploring him to watch over her safety, but this was too late to save the unity of the Catholic Faith.

Lutheranism owed its political existence as much to Clement VII. as to the French and the Turks. His weak and crooked policy, strong and consistent only in opposition to ecclesiastical reform, had given it time, and time is the requisite of revolution. The German Reformation had not only both extended and consolidated its political forces, but had defined its doctrines, and moderated them into a working possibility, shaking off the odium of violent extremes, socialist or anarchist. More than this—Clement had lamed the enterprise and, perhaps, injured the character of the most honourable champion of the Church. Charles had been at first straightforward in his attitude towards the religious revolution. He had given Luther a hearing and then frankly declared war in defence of the Church. But the later hostility of Clement, combining with that of Francis I., had driven him into subterfuge and concession—into an attitude of toleration inconsistent with his real convictions. The natural irresolution of his character had found nourishment in the difficulties placed in his way by Clement.

Charles after all was only thirty-four when Alessandro Farnese succeeded to the Papacy as Paul III. There was yet time for genuine reconciliation between Pope and Emperor; the situation might yet be saved, especially when Charles returned to Italy with all the prestige of his Tunisian victory, and all the fervour of crusading exaltation. The Cardinal Farnese had been scrupulously neutral; he came to the throne committed to neither political party. His pontificate, with that of his inferior successor, Julius III., forms a moment of transition between the Papacy of the Renaissance and that of the Counter-Reformation. There was already a party in the Curia zealous for reform of abuses and definition of

doctrine, and this in no illiberal spirit. On this side
apparently lay Paul's sympathies and friendships. The
early promotions fell mainly on this class—on men alike
cultivated and earnest—the modern champions of Catholicism. The Pope himself had given evidence of desire
for reform, and of willingness to compass this by a
Council. On the other hand Paul was linked to the bad
old times. He owed his Cardinalate, said gossip, to the
favour which his beautiful sister Giulia had won with
Alexander VI.; his own life had been far from stainless;
he had bastards whom he recognised. He was to follow
a policy of advancement almost as unscrupulously as the
Borgia, and with more permanent success; until forty
years ago his descendants reigned in the state in which
he established his *nipoti.*

Charles had left Italy before Clement paid his fateful
visit to Marseilles. He reached Spain in April 1533,
and ever since had given his main attention to the
North African problem which he had hitherto almost set
aside, but which imperatively claimed an immediate
solution. At the beginning of Charles V.'s reign the
North African possessions of Spain comprised a series
of posts dotted along the shore from Melilla on the West
to recently conquered Tripoli on the East. Their connection was broken, not only by long stretches of territory, tenanted, if at all, by the native population, but
westwards by the new pirate state of Algiers, and eastwards by the fairly consolidated native state of Tunis.
Cardinal Jiménez had contemplated the conquest and
conversion of North Africa. This was the bolder, but
perhaps the wiser plan. If the energies of Spain, before
the sea-power of the Porte had grown, had for ten years
been devoted to this task, it might have been completed.
This policy would have severed, or rendered innocuous,

the close communication between the Moors of Africa and their kin in Spain, which had long been recognised as a source of danger, and was to form a recurrent nightmare during two centuries to come. Such a conquest, moreover, would have prevented the establishment of the corsair state at Algiers, which became perfect in its military and naval organisation and in its power of attack, possessing perhaps the most mobile fighting force that the world has seen. Algiers offered a refuge to the adventurers, the criminals, the renegades of the Mediterranean basin, from the Straits of Gibraltar to the mainland of Asia Minor, and acted as a rallying-point for the undisciplined fanaticism of North Africa.

A connected Spanish province, paying its own way and drawing its own supplies from the interior, could have offered a far more effective resistance to the westward advance of the Turk than the broken chain of military garrisons. It is often forgotten that the African coast round Tunis lies north of Southern Sicily, and the distance between the two is so slight that the Western Mediterranean at least might have been closed, while aid could have been given to the outposts of Christianity farther east, to the Knights of St John at Rhodes, to the Venetian settlements in the Morea and the Archipelago, in Crete and Cyprus.

The alternative scheme which the Spanish government actually adopted courted disaster from the first. Ferdinand had little sentiment about North Africa; he regarded the conquests of Jiménez mainly as a convenient pretext for massing troops unobserved, which could at need be thrown upon the shores of Italy. Thus the Spaniards retained only isolated posts with no intercommunication, and with no territory in their *hinterland.* They were scarcely trading ports, though

Bugia had in the past a great commercial history; they were military stations, where service was often regarded as a punishment or disgrace, where the garrisons were ill-fed, and corrupted by indolence and a trying climate. Desertion, not only from the Spanish Crown, but from the Cross was common; the *élite* of the Algerine forces contained no inconsiderable number of Spanish renegades. These posts invited surprise; the enemy could close upon them without observation; the garrisons were dependent for supplies, sometimes even for water, on Spain, and thus when once blockaded could be starved into surrender. Even apart from the two expensive expeditions of Charles V., the wear and tear of life and treasure during the sixteenth century appreciably contributed to the bankruptcy of Spain's prosperity, while there was little or no countervailing gain. The policy inaugurated by Ferdinand, and in later years resumed by Philip II., was purely defensive, and defensive warfare in unsupported advanced posts must inevitably end in defeat or ruinous expenditure.

It is to Charles's credit that he strove to change all this—that in Africa he advocated a forward policy —a continuation of that of Jiménez. There is little question that but for the French hounds who, instead of helping the champion of Christendom, clung to his haunches, he would have driven back the danger from North-west Africa. The policy of Charles in fact on the Mediterranean was offensive, even as on the Danube it was defensive; Ferdinand was the shield and Charles the sword against the infidel.

The reign opened with success followed by disaster. The elder Barbarossa, the founder of the Algerine state, was defeated and killed owing to the promptitude with which the governor of Oran, strongly reinforced from

Spain on Charles's orders, sent aid to the native dynasty
of Tlemcen (1518). This was the one bright spot in the
young king's gloomy first visit to Castile. Barbarossa's
younger brother, however, then accepted the suzerainty
of the Porte, was created Bey, and received the aid of
Janissaries in reorganising his power at Algiers. Ugo
de Moncada, an old officer of Cæsar Borgia and of Louis
XII., who knew much of military and more of naval
affairs, and whose enterprises were nevertheless dogged
by misfortune until his death in the celebrated naval
action off Salerno (1528), was then sent to attack the
corsair city. His signal failure was a rehearsal of the
later tragedy in which Charles himself replaced Moncada
in the leading part. The Spanish general occupied the
high ground to the south of Algiers; Algerines inter-
rupted his communication with his fleet, and in attempting to reopen this his force was roughly handled. The
troops were no sooner embarked than a storm sent a
dozen ships and over 2000 soldiers to the bottom (August
1518). Moncada's occupation of Gelves was slight
compensation for this defeat. This island was but
another death-trap; it had been and was to be the
cemetery of Spanish soldiery.

The scene shifts for the moment to the East. The
rivalry between Charles and Francis gave the stirring
young Sultan Solyman his opportunity. Attacking on
the two lines of Turkish advance, the Danube and the
Eastern Mediterranean, his right hand seized Belgrad,
while with his left he ejected the Hospitallers from
Rhodes after a famous six months' siege (December
1522). Charles turned this latter disaster to Christianity
to account by settling the knights at Tripoli and Malta.
Hitherto at Rhodes they had been the advance-guard of
the Cross in the Eastern Mediterranean; driven back-

wards they were now to become its outpost on the
Western basin.   The majority of the knights were
French.   As France had been the Crusading power when
the fight with the Moslem was fought in the East, so
was Spain the Crusading power in the Western Mediterranean, and the Knights of Malta became the forlorn
hope of the Spanish monarchy.   The practical autonomy
of the Hospitallers under their Grand Master corre-
sponded very closely to the syndicate of pirate captains
under the Bey of Algiers.   The knights lived for and by
war.   Their power was eminently mobile ; their galleys
scoured the Syrian and Egyptian coasts, endangering
Turkish commerce, stocking their arsenals and rowing-
benches with Turkish slaves, forming an intelligence
department with nimble fingers and searching eyes in
the very council chambers of the Porte.   The service
of the Knights of Malta became the resource of gallant
soldiers who longed for active employ, and the refuge of
adventurers who would mend broken fortunes or hide
dishonoured heads.   It is small wonder if war between
the Maltese galleys and the growing Turkish squadrons
was unceasing and internecine.   For the protection of
his own dominions the Emperor's scheme seemed yet
more valuable.   Defence was now concentrated in the
narrow seas between Sicily and North Africa.   With his
knightly garrisons at Tripoli and Malta, Charles appeared
to have locked the gate of the westward Mediterranean
in the face of the inquisitive Turk.

Meanwhile Barbarossa took advantage of the Franco-
Imperial conflict in Italy to create a strong North
African territory with Algiers as its capital.   It was
just at the close of the second Italian war that he
wrested Peñon from the small Spanish garrison.   This
rocky island had served as a watch-tower fronting the

port of Algiers ; Barbarossa by connecting it with the
mainland doubled the strength of his defences. His
next move was yet more important. Availing himself of
palace crimes in the weak native dynasty of Tunis under
pretext of aiding the dispossessed king, he conquered the
town, strongly fortified the territory, and, as at Algiers,
extended his power far into the interior (1533). The
danger of this to Naples and Sicily was manifest ; with
their weak naval defences and scanty store of galleys
they were at the mercy of corsair squadrons from
Goletta, Bona, Biserta. Tripoli was now " in the air."
In Tunis Barbarossa had the master-key to keep open
his communication with the Porte, whose Capudan
Pasha he had lately been created.

No feat could be more welcome to Charles's Spanish
and Italian subjects than a crusade for the conquest of
Tunis, and upon this the Emperor therefore set his heart.
For this he suffered the humiliating loss of Württemberg ; for this he even advised Ferdinand to abandon,
if necessary, Hungary to Zapolya. It was no mere
quixotism. A blow against the power of the Barbaresques had become a national and political necessity.
The coasts of Naples, Sicily and Spain were being swept
bare of their population, while the Algerine territories
were being peopled by the migration of Spanish Moors,
who carried across the straits their industrial enterprise
and their hereditary hate. Charles could not for ever
close his ears to the cry of Southern Spain and Sicily ;
he knew that war with France could not long be
delayed ; he thought that he had just time to conquer
Tunis, and he was right.

Charles sailed from Barcelona on May 30, 1535.
All Spain in its enthusiasm seemed to converge upon
the Catalonian port ; all classes, and both sexes, strove

to get aboard the ships. Beneath the great banner of
the Crucified Christ Charles sailed for Cagliari, the
general rendezvous. Hither came Doria from Genoa
with German and Italian troops, and the galleys from
South Italy and Sicily; hither also the squadron of the
Hospitallers and the ocean-going caravels from Portugal.
The united fleet put to shore at Carthage. It was
resolved first to take Goletta, and so clear the way
along the lagoon to Tunis. The defence of the strong
fortress was determined; the garrison made desperate
sorties, while the covering force inflicted serious losses
on the besiegers before it was driven off. At length
Goletta was stormed, and the whole fleet of eighty-two
galleys fell into the victors' hands. After much debate
it was then decided to re-embark, as the attack on Tunis
seemed too perilous, and the corsair state had been
crippled for offensive purposes by the capture of its
fleet. Charles disliked the decision, but, as this was his
first campaign, he would not impose his will on the
experts. At the last moment it was resolved to give
fortune a trial. The army was formed into advance-
guard and rearguard only, with the baggage between
them, and started on its dreaded march.[1]

Tunis was twelve miles from Goletta, and at eight
miles' distance lay the wells. The line of march lay
between the canalised lagoon and olive groves, with a
front of 1000 paces at the most. Barbarossa moved
out to defend the wells, and advanced, under cover
of the olive groves, with a view to enveloping Charles's
right flank and rear. The Spaniards had no transport,
and the very guns were all dragged by hand; the army

---

[1] Perhaps the most graphic of the contemporary accounts is that contained in
an appendix to vol. iii. of the memoirs of Cerezeda already mentioned. Reference may be made to E. Cat, *De Caroli Quinti in Africa rebus gestis*, 1891, and
to *Documentos Ineditos*, vol. i.

was provisioned for five days only, and a check would probably have meant annihilation. The heat was terrific, and when the wells were reached some preferred to die by them rather than rejoin the ranks; others steeped their shirts in the trampled mud and sucked them. Barbarossa's two attacks proved that a well-led European army had little to fear from Turks and Moors. On his second onslaught he worked round to the Emperor's rear, but the Spaniards were well kept in hand, and the clouds of horsemen did not dare face their fire. The enemy's first flight was a feint, but the second was genuine enough. Barbarossa could not re-enter the castle of Tunis, because the Christian slaves rose and held it against him. The town was captured, and Charles was in high good humour; he wrote that he had fallen from his horse and had got the gout, but that God had sent him a good plaster for all his maladies. Andrea Doria reconnoitred the coast and easily occupied Bona. Charles was anxious to attack Algiers, whither Barbarossa retreated with a few galleys, but the troops were suffering from disease and heat, and the season was dangerously advanced; when, indeed, the fleet attempted the town of Africa (Mehedia), it was driven off by heavy weather.

Charles restored Tunis to its dispossessed ruler, Muley Hassan, who had joined him before the march on the capital, but the Spaniards retained Goletta, Bona and Biserta. It would probably have been wise to avoid this system of semi-independent kingdoms, but the Spaniards did not know how easy it is to hold these large Oriental towns. The local danger came really not from these but from the wild dust-storms of fanaticism which rise suddenly in the desert, and then expend their energy upon the fringe of civilisation on the coast.

Although Barbarossa was soon at sea again and harrying even the Balearic islands, the capture of Tunis was really a rude blow struck at him and at the Porte, whose admiral he was. Charles gained much personal prestige ; all Southern Europe looked upon him as its saviour. Hitherto he had always arrived when fighting was over, but now he had proved himself a seasoned soldier in a peculiarly trying campaign. Henceforth he loved a fight and usually led his armies ; he was never so well, so happy, and so genial as when in the field.

The Tunisian expedition had been better timed than perhaps even the Emperor fully knew. He had been in reality racing both Solyman and Francis. Hitherto little more than diplomatic amenities had resulted from the French embassies to the Porte in 1525 and 1528. If France had encouraged, as is possible, the two invasions of Hungary which closely followed these missions, she had learnt that there was no better method than this to reconcile the Germans with the Emperor. The union of Germany and the ill-success of Solyman in 1532 had driven this lesson home. Henceforth French diplomacy sought its path upon the sea rather than on the Danube : its object was to divert the Turkish power from Eastern Europe to the Western Mediterranean, where it could be brought into direct connection with French armaments. The spread of Barbarossa's power along the North African coast and his appointment to the command of the Turkish fleet made him a far more practical ally than the distant Turkish army.[1]

[1] See J. Ursu, *La politique orientale de François I. 1515-1547*, 1909. L. Bourrilly, " L'ambassade de la Forest et de Marillac à Constantinople," 1535-38 (*Revue historique*, July and August 1901). Also J. Zeller, *Quæ primæ fuerint legationes a Francisco I. in Orientem missæ 1524-38*, 1881. The Franco-Turkish negotiations may be followed up in P. de Vaissière, *Charles de Marillac*, 1896. J.

When Clement VII. visited Marseilles, it was known
that an emissary from Barbarossa was present, and the
Imperial government was warned then and afterwards
that mischief was brewing. In February 1535 La
Forest received elaborate instructions as envoy to
Barbarossa and the Porte. He was ordered to suggest
that the former should fall on Corsica, whilst Francis,
marching through Savoy, should attack Genoa by land.
With the Porte the envoy was instructed to treat for a
general peace. Into this the Emperor might, indeed, be
admitted if he ceded Milan, Genoa and Asti, recognised
French suzerainty over Flanders and Artois, and left
Zapolya in peaceful possession of Hungary. It took
La Forest some time to reach Constantinople, and the
Sultan did not return from Persia until the close of
1535. A Franco-Turkish treaty was then concluded
which took effect hereafter; but meanwhile Tunis had
fallen, and Charles's promptitude had forestalled the
dangerous combination. Thus the Tunisian campaign
and the conflict of Francis and Solyman with Charles in
1536-37 may almost be regarded as sections of the self-
same war, which might well have opened by a Franco-
Turkish attack on Genoa.

On his return from Tunis Charles paid his first
and last visit to his kingdom of Sicily. Here he was
welcomed as the deliverer from the scourge which had
so terribly lashed the exposed shore-line of the island.
Landing at Trapani, he held his Parliament and received
his subsidy at Palermo. Thence he travelled through
the heart of Sicily to Taormina, concluding his progress

Zeller, *La diplomatie française vers le milieu du XVIe siècle d'après la correspondance de Guillaume Pellicier ambassadeur de François I. à Venise 1539-42*,
1880. Tausserat-Radel, *Correspondance politique de Guillaume Pellicier 1540-42*,
1899. Indispensable for documents is Charrière's *Négociations de la France dans
le Levant*, vol. i. 1848.

at Messina. On November 1, two days before Charles crossed the straits to Calabria, the Duke of Milan died. This was a momentous crisis in the history of the Emperor's relations to Italy, and therefore to the Pope and France. The compromise which had satisfied Italy, if not France, was at an end. It would have been well for every one if the feeble duke and his pretty Danish wife had left an heir. Milan, governed by a native prince related to the Emperor, would have sufficiently secured him against the ambition not only of Francis but of Paul III., who cast his roving eyes on Milan with the idea that the investiture of his bastard might prove a compromise between the pretensions of France and Spain. The Swiss, whose material comfort depended on commercial friendship with Milan, would probably have protected a Sforza against French attack. Above all Milan would have been saved from virtual incorporation with Spain, and this would have removed the chief cause of French hostility towards the Spanish Crown. But it was no age for miracles, and the necessary son was never born.

Charles had no intention of annexing Milan. He promised the Pope that he would not confer the duchy upon either himself or Ferdinand. Pescara's nephew del Guasto was appointed as a mere military governor to meet military contingencies, but negotiations were at once opened for the continued existence of a buffer state. Ferdinand would gladly have been duke, but Charles had no wish to create another Württemberg on Italian soil. His thoughts turned to Portugal; the investiture of an Infant would have strengthened the family ring, and brought Milan into peculiarly close connection with Savoy. It seemed wiser, however, to compromise the French claim which Francis I. had at once raised, and thus the negotiations for a Valois-Habsburg state began their dreary course of ten long years.

Francis I. had now three sons. Charles would grant Milan to the youngest, provided that he was at once placed under his own care, and that he should marry either his niece, the widowed duchess Christina, or his natural daughter Margaret, now promised to Alessandro de' Medici. He further required that the prince should remain under his guardianship until he was twenty-five and had male heirs, while the chief Lombard fortresses should receive Imperial garrisons. Such a scheme had its merits. French sensitiveness received satisfaction ; on the other hand the French prince, married to a Habsburg and having Italian interests, would readily fall into the family federation. The Duke of Angoulême, seated young upon an Italian throne, might well have given birth to a national Italian dynasty, as the lines of Anjou and Aragon before him, and more than one Spanish-Bourbon line hereafter.

Charles was often just, but rarely generous. He spoiled his reasonable proposal by adding onerous conditions. He required Francis to lend his fleet for the capture of Algiers, to aid him against the infidel, to force Henry VIII. to do justice to Catherine, to support Ferdinand in his Hungarian claims, and the Count Palatine Frederick and Charles's niece Dorothea in their forlorn quest of Denmark, to employ French influence in favour of a Council. The claims of Francis I. were equally exacting. He demanded the immediate usufruct of Milan for himself, and the investiture not of his third but of his second son. This made all the difference. One poor Valois life lay between the succession to the throne and the Duke of Orleans, who became, indeed,

Dauphin before long. Orleans had already on his wife's behalf claimed Florence and boasted the Medici pretensions to Urbino. He had no connection with the Habsburgs, to whom he remained throughout his life consistently hostile. Francis had French as well as Italian reasons for insistence. If Orleans received Milan, he would surrender his claims as second son to Brittany, and so avert the separation of this fief, with all its racial traditions of independence, from the direct authority of the Crown. Charles naturally wished not to contribute to the removal of this Breton bone of contention. Apart from this, he never could have suffered the establishment of French influence at once in the valleys of the Po and Arno. He rightly urged that if Francis received Milan, he would ask for more, that there was no limit to his gluttony, that each fresh slice did but stimulate the appetite.

Neither Charles nor Francis was anxious to begin an Italian war ; each receded from his extreme pretensions, but the question of the investiture of the third or second French prince proved fundamental. Francis then provoked the war, not on a Lombard, but on a Savoyard issue. The feeble Duke of Savoy was, as has been said, drawn from the French to the Imperial side by his masterful and attractive wife. Francis now claimed, on pleas each more preposterous than the last, the duchy of Savoy, the counties of Nice and Asti, the territories of Vercelli and Faucigni. To the claim to the inheritance of the duchy through his mother he added the incompatible pretensions of past Counts of Provence and Dukes of Milan. The Parliament of Paris, scouting its grand traditions, became the pander to the caprices of its worst monarch :—" The King will have it," was the clinching argument of the President, Guillaume du Poyet, in

answer to the Savoyard protests. The onslaught upon
Savoy was a palpable pretence ; it was a mere variation of
the earlier scheme which intended Genoa, the Emperor's
other North Italian ally, to be the objective of an attack
which should drag him into war.

The duke was on the point of establishing his supremacy over the free city of Geneva, the traditional ambition of his house, and an aim now as desirable from
religious as from territorial motives. In December 1535
the Bernese suddenly declared war on Savoy ; in February 1536 they relieved Geneva, and annexed the Pays
de Vaud. At this juncture Francis declared his intention of incorporating the duke's territories. With little
difficulty he conquered Savoy, and, crossing the Alps,
occupied Turin and the greater part of Piedmont.
Charles, when reproached with the abandonment of his
ally, replied with reason that the action of the Bernese
and the French was so sudden that he had no means of
staying it. But his prestige was gone if he did not arm
on the duke's behalf, and war was now inevitable.

Charles was deeply moved by what he regarded as
his rival's treachery in making this unprovoked onslaught
when he himself was resting from his services on behalf
of Christianity. He was now at Rome, and in the presence of Pope and Cardinals he broke out into one of
his rare fits of passion, and renewed his personal challenge to the French king.[1] We have from his own letter
to Hannart, his ambassador in France, an account of his
justification before the Curia. If Francis, he cried,
would not have peace, he, Charles, would be forced to
stake all for all, and Francis also : whichever rival won
would buy victory too dearly, and the Turk, if God did

[1] A detailed description of Charles's reception in Rome is given in Cerezeda's
Memoirs.

not intervene, would be master of all Europe, for man could not prevent it : rather than bring another war on Christendom, Charles would fight Francis man to man, staking Milan against Burgundy, though the latter was also his by right : whichever was conquered should give his whole assistance to the other for war against the infidel. On the following day the Emperor's fit of temper had cooled down, for when the French ambassador reproached him with having challenged his master, he replied that it was no challenge, but merely a proof of his extreme desire for peace. Peace, however, was not to be, nor yet a duel in close field between shirted Emperor and king. However personal and dynastic claims and counterclaims might seem, great nations were really the parties in the suit. The pity was that whether plaintiff or defendant won, the estate over which they quarrelled must pay the costs.[1]

---

[1] For the negotiations see L. Cardauns, *Paul III., Karl V. und Franz I., 1535-6*, in *Quellen und Forschungen aus italienischen Archiven und Bibliotheken*, xi. 1908. The writer continues the subject in his articles *Zur Geschichte Karls V. in den Jahren 1536-8, ibid.* xii. 1909.

CHAPTER XII

Charles at Rome and Siena—His journey to North Italy—The French war of 1536—The Emperor's invasion of Provence—Reasons for his retreat—Indecisive results of the campaigns of 1537—The truce of Nice—Effects of the war upon Charles's position in Italy—Cosimo becomes Duke of Florence—Hostility of the Strozzi to Cosimo and Charles—Marriage of Ottavio Farnese with the Emperor's natural daughter Margaret—Meeting between Charles and Francis at Aigues Mortes, and their subsequent alliance—Death of the Empress—Schemes for permanent friendship with France—The Emperor's journey through France—The revolt of Ghent—Punishment of the city by Charles—Rupture of the negotiations with France—The question of the Emperor's insincerity.

THE war which Charles had so greatly dreaded and so long averted had come at last. His one wish was to have done with it, and that quickly. Notwithstanding his outburst against the French king, he was in high good humour in these days. His entrance to Rome on April 5 must have been a trying moment both for himself and for the Romans who had so grievously suffered at his hands. Doubtless the poet Tebaldeo, grumbler as he was, was not the only citizen who barred doors and windows that he might not see the passing of the unjust Emperor who had not avenged the wrongs of Rome, of which he declared himself innocent, on the scoundrels who had perpetrated them. Yet the majority could not fail to be impressed when they saw the conqueror of the Moslem kneel before the Pope in front of St. Peter's door, and follow him to the High Altar to give thanks. If Charles stayed as the Pope's state guest in the Vatican, he wandered without a guard to see the sights of Rome, and this friendly confidence delighted the Romans high and low.

The Emperor, however, must hurry northwards. He passed to the Imperial city of Siena, by Viterbo, Bolsena, Pienza, full of substantial memories of Pius II., by Monte-Oliveto and Buonconvento, where Henry VII. of Luxemburg had died of poison, as was said, administered with the sacrament by a scurvy priest. At Siena he was at his very best.[1] On entering the Sienese territory he had cried, " We are now at home, let every one march as he likes." Up to this point his force had advanced with all the discipline usual on foreign soil, as though surprise might be expected at every turn. The sudden change was a pretty, friendly touch well calculated to warm the hearts of the impressionable Sienese. As he rode up to the city from the south he was met by processions of its clergy, its children and its gentry. He would not take the keys from the magistrates at the gate, saying that they were in good keeping with magistrates most faithful to the Holy Roman Empire. Charles on entering was radiant with smiles; he would rein in his horse, and joke now with one citizen and now another. Spying a little Piccolomini, a very pretty child, carried in a servant's arms, he called him up, looked earnestly on the child's face and kissed him. The entrance to Siena is none too wide for festal purposes, for the city was more used to guarding against its exiles. Charles would not let the troopers of his escort move until the children had made their bows, for fear that the horses might kick them. He fully earned the genuine cries of

---

[1] See *Carlo Quinto in Siena nell' Aprile del 1536, relazione di un contemporaneo,* edited by P. Vigo, Bologna, 1884.

" Welcome, welcome, Emperor Charles." The Emperor saw all Siena's sights. He trod the pavement of the Cathedral pictured with the Sibyls; he witnessed the games in the sloping brick-paved *piazza*. His visit was only too short, although there was an aftermath of pleasure in the arrival of two dromedaries, fresh from Tunis, which had failed to catch him up. There are few sadder contrasts in history than that between this momentary joyous friendship of the Emperor with his Italian town and the loss of liberty and permanent material ruin which, in his enforced absence from Italy, his unsympathetic Spanish agents were to inflict—the very last tragedy of his reign.

From Siena Charles went to Florence, where, after his visit to the Cathedral which he usually made his first object, he was sumptuously lodged in the palace of Duke Alessandro de' Medici. He was never to see his ill-fated son-in-law again, nor, indeed, Florence, nor Siena, nor yet Rome. The comfortable oligarchy of Lucca set him on his way between the sea and the mountains to where the well-worn track from Central to Northern Italy climbed the valley of the Magra to Pontremoli, and descended from the watershed down the Taro to Fornovo, whence the road across the rolling hills brought him out on the wide Via Æmilia at Borgo San Donnino. Along this ancient route, the Via Romea as it was and is still called, he was following absolutely in the track of another Charles, the eighth of his name in France, who, good-natured, feeble-minded, big-headed, weak-legged, had by this self-same journey caused all the subsequent wars of Europe, had been the unwitting and posthumous author, however indirectly, of his Habsburg namesake's birth, of the Emperor's internecine hostility with France, and of this enjoyable Italian tour which he was now

making for the first and only time. Like Charles VIII.
the Emperor hurried from Borgo San Donnino to Asti,
but thence, unlike him, he was not to retreat into France
but to invade her.

In the summer of 1536 Charles took the offensive
by marching into Provence in person, while Henry of
Nassau attacked Picardy. The aim was not on this
occasion conquest. Charles intended rather to draw
the French troops from Savoyard territory, and force
Francis to a decisive action, of which the result should
be an immediate peace. Thus only could he regain
liberty to renew his operations against the infidel, which
was now his dearest wish. Francis had, however, lost
the fever of fight, which had, on the other hand,
infected Charles. The invasion of Provence was facilitated by the desertion of the Marquis of Saluzzo from
the French cause, which enabled the Emperor to march
southwards from Piedmont by the well-worn track over
the Col di Tenda upon Nice. No armed opposition was
offered to the advance through Provence, and Charles
occupied Aix, the capital of the county. Here his
success ended, and we know from his letter of September
14 the motives of the retreat on which he had determined. The country had been systematically devastated
in front of the advancing force. All mills had been
burnt, all peasants compelled to desert their homes.
The troops were for several days without bread and meat.
No supplies were voluntarily given, for the people
remembered the chastisement inflicted on those who had
supported Bourbon's army. The Imperial force was
weakened by the necessity of detaching large foraging
parties to scour the country far and wide. Doria's
fleet was unable to maintain its communication with the
shore. While Charles lay starving at Aix, the Constable

Montmorenci had gathered a force at Avignon, and
Francis in person was hard by at Valence. Marseilles,
Arles and the fords of the Rhone were strongly guarded.
Meanwhile the French party in Italy was on the move,
and before the Emperor had despatched his letter, he
heard that Guido Rangone with the Fregosi and the
Strozzi had attacked Genoa, an attempt which they
might well repeat.

Such were Charles's own reasons for the abandonment
of his enterprise. He made a feint upon Marseilles, but
only to divert attention from his retreat. His losses
were heavy from famine and disease; de Leyva, the
last Spanish general of the older school, had died from
the hardships of the campaign. Meanwhile in Picardy,
Nassau had been baffled by the strong fortress of
Peronne. The year's fighting had ended with distinct
advantage to the French; Charles could only console
himself with the reflection that he had forced his enemy
to feed four armies on the soil of France. Returning
unmolested to Genoa, he adjudged Montferrat to the
Marquis of Mantua, that he might at least have one
faithful ally in Italy, and then in November sailed for
Spain. His troubles were not yet over. The gales of
early winter swept away the oars of the Imperial galley.
The little fleet was forced to take shelter under the lee
of the islands fronting Cannes. Outside raged a sea
which Andrea Doria refused to face; to westward lurked
a strong French squadron in Marseilles; on board
supplies were running perilously short. But time, the
healer, brought clearer skies, and a three days' run
landed the Emperor safe and sound at Palamos.

A second year of fighting brought both combatants
to a standstill. The war in Piedmont reduced itself to
sieges and skirmishes in which neither side gained clear

advantage. Francis invaded the Netherlands in force,
but his advance was checked, and his retreat followed
by a counter-blow. Barbarossa, now the avowed ally
of France, raided the Apulian coasts, but found the
towns well fortified, and disregarding the protests of the
French, sailed off to attack Corfu. The disastrous defeat
of Ferdinand's troops at Essek by the Turks, contributed
to the compromise with Zapolya, long desired by
Charles, which left the Woivode as king of part of
Hungary for his life with reversion to Ferdinand. In
the north the Count Palatine and Dorothea had vainly
tried to make good their claim to Denmark. Charles
had given them his sympathy, but no effectual aid ; he
now bent to facts, and recognised the elected king,
Christian III. The Pope still clung to his neutrality as
between Charles and Francis, but entered a league with
the two Habsburgs and Venice against the Turk. This
aided to influence public opinion against the coalition
of Francis and the infidel, and to set the moral sense of
Europe on the Emperor's side.

Uneventful and indecisive as were the operations of
the last two years, they admirably illustrate the difficulties of the Emperor's position. The war in North
Italy and Southern France was but the axis of a wheel
whose spokes extended to the rim of Europe and
beyond. The Netherland provinces were engaged in
their devastating conflict with France, but they were also
interested in the Scandinavian succession war, and this
connected itself with Lübeck on the one side and
London on the other. There was rough fighting on the
Danube, while Cross and Crescent were at blows on sea
and shore from Malta to Gibraltar. Spain herself was
braced to resist a French invasion of Catalonia, while
the American colonies were draining her of her most

adventurous spirits, and sending in return the precious metals which failed to rivet the Emperor's ever-leaking jar.

Charles was probably the only man who believed in the possibility of continuing the war. His sister Mary represented that the Netherlands could and would fight no more, and was authorised to negotiate a separate truce as on her own personal instance. Even towards the close of 1536 Charles's Council had earnestly advised peace. Peace would bring in its train a General Council, the pacification of Germany, the restoration of the Faith : it would lead to the recovery of Denmark and Hungary, to security in the matter of Guelders, to the conquest of Algiers, to a crusade of united Christendom : the Duke of Savoy would be restored to his dominions, and Charles could return to Spain in safety, as his subjects so much desired. Spain, Naples and Sicily, urged the Council, were exhausted : there were no skilled generals left to command the ill-disciplined German, Italian and Netherland troops. War would cause eternal enmity with France and trouble Christianity for all time : Francis would bring the Turk against the Emperor and his brother by land and sea : by war the Lutherans would be the gainers. Charles was assured that he had satisfied his honour, for he had invaded France, and the king had feared to meet him : it must be possible to frame conditions under which Milan could be granted to Angoulême, who now by the Dauphin's death had become the French king's second son.

After the campaign of 1537 Charles at length yielded to financial exhaustion, and to his desire to renew operations against the Barbary states. Francis was in scarcely better plight; he had gained little

from his unpopular relations with the Porte. The Pope
at length pressed his mediation with success. Paul
journeyed to Nice, and the two rivals, though refusing
to meet, personally laid their respective cases before
him. It was found impossible to draft a treaty of
peace, for Francis would not surrender his claim to
Milan, nor Charles withdraw his demand for the Duke
of Savoy's restoration. A truce, however, was concluded for ten years on the basis of the *status quo*
(June 17, 1538). The Duke of Savoy's churlish refusal
to admit the Pope within the walls of Nice, for fear that
the Spaniards might surprise the town, made Charles
the less unwilling temporarily to neglect his interests.
Nice was, indeed, the only possession which still remained to the luckless Duke, who had, moreover, lost
by the death of his clever wife his most valuable asset.
The truce was made chiefly at his expense, for such
towns in Piedmont as were not in French possession,
were from obvious necessity occupied by the Imperialists
to prevent their seizure.

The war had sensibly weakened the hold of Charles
upon Northern Italy. The covering state of Savoy-
Piedmont was now mainly in French hands : it was
small consolation that the remaining Piedmontese
fortresses were under the Emperor's direct control.
The family federation had virtually lost a member. It
might seem a paltry matter that the truce recognised
the French protectorate of Mirandola, but this revived
French influence in neighbouring Ferrara, and from
Ferrara it was a short cry to Venice. Henceforth
exiles, adventurers and spies made Mirandola their
rendezvous, while French agents slipped backwards and
forwards through the Grisons and Venetian territory,
escorted over the latter by Venetian troops, and

conveyed to and from the Porte by Venetian or Ragusan ships. The French embassy at Venice became at once a watch-tower, a conspiracy bureau, and a half-way house of call. This was not, perhaps, the worst. The defence of Lombardy against its French neighbours drained every ducat that Charles could raise. Increasing taxation and the presence of a large foreign force added infinitely to the unpopularity of Imperial rule, not only in Lombardy, but in the semi-independent states which were called upon to contribute. It is small wonder if the Emperor's thoughts perpetually reverted towards compromising the French claim to Milan.

In Central Italy Charles had good fortune which could not have been foreseen. His worthless son-in-law Alessandro had been in 1537 murdered by Lorenzino de' Medici. The assassin might vapour of his patriotic tyrannicide, but all the world knew that it was an affair, not of politics, but of paramours. Charles might reasonably have brought Florence under his immediate rule, but, steadfastly pursuing his previous policy, he conferred it upon a member of the junior line of Medici, Cosimo, son of the distinguished soldier Giovanni of the Black Bands, and grandson of the no less martial Caterina Sforza. Thus Florence was held by one who was the very embodiment of the old alliance between Medici and Sforza, and who, indeed, combined some of the qualities of both houses. Little was known of Cosimo, but he was to prove one of the most capable rulers of his age, and, in spite of much temptation and irritation, the surest prop of Charles's power in Italy. Cosimo would gladly have succeeded to Alessandro's widow as well as to his state, but Charles shrank from such extravagance, believing that he could put his daughter to better use: the Florentine duke must be content with Eleanor of Toledo, the daughter of the faithful viceroy of Naples.

Cosimo had a very early opportunity of showing his quality. The Strozzi were a noble family, shouldered out of political office by the *bourgeoisie*, and for a time exiled by the Medici. Restored by Lorenzo the Magnificent, the head of the house smothered political jealousy in personal friendship, and his son Filippo married the daughter of Piero II. after her father's death. In the Medicean restoration of 1512, and again in 1530, Filippo had appeared as a thorough-going supporter of the house, distinguishing himself on the latter occasion by his violence against the republican party. He may, however, have later developed liberal instincts ; he certainly nursed the resentment of an oligarch against a monarchy ; he owed no gratitude to the junior line of Medici, which now supplanted his own connections in the elder branch. It was natural enough that he should strike an attitude as the champion of republican liberty against a renewal of the monarchy, that he should become the ally of France against the Imperialist Cosimo. Filippo in 1537 carried the war into Tuscan territory, only to be taken at Montemurlo and die a mysterious death in a Florentine prison. His fate had a very direct connection with Charles's fortunes, for his son Piero, ascribing it to the Emperor's connivance, became his most dangerous and untiring enemy, lavishing his large revenues on revenge, stimulating now Venice, now France, and now the German Lutherans to war.

Cosimo de' Medici was not the only native ruler through whose agency Charles hoped to secure his hold upon Central Italy. He had refused him his natural daughter Margaret, because he intended her to be the link between Habsburgs and Farnesi. He therefore married her to Ottavio, the Pope's grandson, while he invested Paul III.'s son Pierluigi with Novara. The ambitions of the Farnesi were, however, destined to be the solvent of the conglomerate which Charles had framed as a breakwater against external aggression.

Within a month of the truce of Nice the world heard with wonder that the two enemies, who had found it impossible to conclude a peace, had met and made friends in the harbour of Aigues Mortes, that Francis had paid a two hours' visit to the Emperor's galley, that Charles had for the first time touched French soil in friendship, and slept thereon as the French king's guest, that the reconciliation had every appearance of being lasting and sincere. The Venetian envoy Mocenigo hastened to inform the Doge of all the details of the meeting. The Imperial galley, after being in collision in a fog, had put into Aigues Mortes where she was boarded by the French king. For long Charles and Francis sat together on the poop in close converse. Next day Charles landed, and they dined together. At the dance which followed they would stand, now arm in arm, now hand in hand, bandying jokes and repartee with this lady and with that : never had Charles been seen to laugh so heartily. When Francis, after escorting his guest to his galley, had taken leave, the Emperor called Mocenigo, and with face all joyous told him of the French king's assurances which left nothing to be desired, of his promises to make every effort in the cause of Christendom, when once the eight months of his truce with the Sultan had expired. " In truth," concluded Charles, " I am full of joy, for I hope that the fortunes of Christianity and of my friends will go right well."

What more, indeed, could Charles desire ? Francis had given him a diamond ring, and said that therewith

he betrothed him for a brother; he had sworn upon his
honour that he would never again attack him, that he
not only wished to be his friend, but friend of his friends
and foe of his foes, and this because he realised that His
Cæsarean Majesty was the wisest among living Christian
princes. A few days later Charles convinced Mocenigo
of his belief in the certainty of permanent peace, for he
and Francis had tried to harm each other and not succeeded—they had merely brought ruin upon their subjects,
and so now had recognised their error, and intended to be
wiser, and by mutual friendship to gain much pleasure.

Charles may have had interested motives in his con-
fidences to the Venetian envoy, because his friendliness
with France would remove the hesitation of the Republic
as to the wisdom of a Turkish war. It would appear,
however, from a letter to his sister Mary that he genuinely believed in his new friendship. He assured her
that the numerous political antagonisms which had
hitherto made peace impossible would become mere details which the Imperial and royal ministers might or
might not arrange. The Emperor's wish was probably
father to his thought. His constant aims were resistance to the infidel and the restoration of Catholic unity :
he had proved conclusively that neither could be realised
in the teeth of French hostility. The ostentatious reconciliation with his rival served at all events to cover the
disrepute which the war had brought upon the Imperial
arms. For the first time a contest had ended in favour
of Francis. He had annexed Savoy and most of Piedmont ; French garrisons were within striking distance of
the Lombard capital. But even if Charles had yielded
somewhat in Italy, the friendship of France was ample
compensation, for it would convince Turk and Lutheran
that his power was unimpaired.

Venice had wished the Emperor to visit Italy and organise a crusade. He replied that his presence in Spain was essential to the reawakening of her crusading zeal, to the levy of men and money for the spring campaign. The spring came, but, instead of heading a crusade in the Levant, Charles was meditating a journey to the Netherlands to suppress revolt in his native town of Ghent. Francis pressed him to prove his friendship by passing through France on his way to Flanders. Charles hesitated, but was unable to refuse. A cold fit had followed his enthusiastic hopes. He assured his anxious sister that he would obtain guarantees in writing, that he would travel fast, and conclude no state business on the soil of France. He took the precaution of instructing his ministers to secure, on the pretext of covering their own responsibility, letters of invitation from the king and queen, the Dauphin and his brother, the Constable and the Cardinal of Lorraine. They all affectionately pressed Charles to pass through France, and so avoid the dangers of the sea ; they engaged that he should not be troubled with state affairs, nor be detained beyond his wish.

Among state affairs was included a project of the French government for which Charles expressed great repugnance. On May 1, 1539, the Empress had died. This loss was in the eyes of her husband irreparable, but for others it was an irresistible opportunity for ingenious matrimonial combinations, for the Emperor was only thirty-nine. Queen Eleanor early pressed remarriage upon her brother, and in the French court the idea soon took a definite shape. Francis was eager for an Imperial son-in-law. To Granvelle he greatly praised his daughter Margaret, who was just twenty years hereafter to marry the Duke of Savoy. She was, exclaimed the father, a rose among thorns, an angel among devils : if Charles were wishing to remarry, he could not in this world make a better choice. The paternal panegyric was not unmerited, but the coveted bridegroom insisted that on his journey there must be no talk of a second marriage. The Emperor's sorrow was slow of healing. When later the proposal was renewed, he curtly wrote : " We pray the king to renounce the project of which there has been question since our journey through France. We have no intention of marrying again, and we are, moreover, too old for Madame Marguerite."

The boy Philip was left as governor of Spain, and to him Charles gave a paper of instructions which contains the clearest evidence of his intentions at that moment. It had been arranged between Emperor and king that Charles should grant to Angoulême, now Duke of Orleans, either Milan as the dower of Ferdinand's daughter, or his Burgundian possessions with the hand of the eldest Infanta. The agreement was as yet only personal and provisional, but Philip was advised, in the event of his father's death, to carry it to completion, as being essential to the welfare of his states. This was not all —Charles desired yet further to bind Habsburg and Valois by ties of common interest. If Orleans married the Infanta, Milan should be granted to the French princess Margaret and Ferdinand's second son, while Philip should marry Jeanne d'Albret, titular heiress of Navarre, and buy her rights over Lower Navarre and Béarn. All possible subjects of dispute might thus be compromised.

Charles entered France on December 12, 1539. At Loches he was met by his sister Eleanor and the king. On New Year's Day he rode into Paris, which even then was a hostess unequalled in the art of entertaining royal guests. In three weeks more he reached the Netherlands, having been fêted " as though he were God fallen from Paradise." Between that date and the close of April, by way of grim contrast, the fate of his native town was sealed, and the sentence against her issued.

The rebellion of Ghent was the most violent episode of the reign of Charles in the Netherlands.[1] The conflicts and compromises between local and central govern ment, which form the essential features of his rule in these provinces, will be elsewhere treated in their general bearings. This revolt, however, affected to such a degree his personal plans and movements that it is convenient to detach it from the more impersonal survey of his policy and difficulties, and to place it in its chronological connection. It may be premised that the rebellion was the supreme manifestation of resistance to taxation of which there were lesser examples at several periods and in many places.

When the French invaded Artois in 1537, Mary had called on the Estates General for a subsidy wherewith to support 30,000 men for six months. The moment was so critical that she personally attended the session, surrounded by all the magnates of the land. Brabant took the lead in assent, and was followed by the other provinces with the exception of Flanders whose deputies referred the proposal to their constituencies. Three of the four members or quarters of Flanders, Bruges, Ypres and the Franc consented to their quota. Ghent alone refused, and refusal soon led to revolution.

Three classes had a share in the municipal constitution, the Patricians or Poorters, whose livelihood was

---

[1] The classical authority for the rebellion of Ghent is *Relation des troubles de Ghent sous Charles Quint, par un anonyme*, edited by L. P. Gachard, in *Collection de chroniques belges*, 1846.

derived from landed or invested property, the Guild of
Weavers, divided into seventeen wards, and the fifty-two
Lesser Guilds.   The most absolute resistance came at
first from the Poorters, for the two lower bodies, although
refusing the subsidy, offered to send the town militia to
the army and support it, and this proposal was ultimately
carried.   Mary regarded an untrained militia as useless
to resist the French armies, but offered as a compromise
to accept half the subsidy.   When this was rudely refused, she arrested the inhabitants of Ghent who happened
to be at Brussels and Antwerp, on the principle that
private citizens were responsible for their city's debt.
She took the high line that both written law and natural
reason were on her side, as the subsidy was intended for
the defence of the country : that the vote of the majority
should be regarded as binding the whole province,
according to the precedents of 1525 and 1535.   The
contribution was levied in the rural districts of Ghent,
and the inhabitants flying into the town added fuel to
the flames.   When the city petitioned for the prisoners'
release and the cessation of the levy, Mary replied that
the town must pay its quota first, and then appeal to
the Court of Malines or the Privy Council, and that, if
the appeal were successful, she would repay.

Failing to impress Mary, the city appealed to Charles,
and received a long letter written at Barcelona on
January 31, 1538.   He expressed his astonishment that
they had refused Mary's offer, and that they not only
exempted themselves from payment, but prevented the
inhabitants of their quarter from paying, as if these were
their subjects and not his, and could give nothing without their consent.   "We had," he continued, "always
had this idea and hope concerning you, that in our
absence you would take more pains to aid, assist, and

serve us than any others, because we ourselves are of
Ghent, and were brought to birth in the city of Ghent."
Charles concluded by reiterating Mary's advice that the
town should pay, and then appeal to the Council : he
could not take the matter into consideration away from the
country, and the date of his return was quite uncertain.

The dispute simmered on until the summer of 1539,
and the revolution actually broke out on the election
of the new guildmasters.   Before this the people had
refused their magistrates' proposal to join the other
provinces in condoling with the Emperor on his wife's
death, and they had suspended the customary measures
for farming the city taxes for the coming year.   They
now refused to submit a list of three candidates for the
mastership of the guilds to the aldermen for selection,
and demanded the punishment of the late aldermen for
failing to execute the town-council's decrees.   Most of
these fled, but some were arrested.   The democracy now
got the upper hand, seized the gates, and inaugurated
an era of imprisonment and confiscation.   It then
became bloodthirsty, torturing and slaughtering a late
magistrate for selling to Charles a document which only
existed in its wild imagination.

Had the town government been resolute it might
have put down the revolution with the aid of the
Poorters and the Weavers, to whom it now appeared
socially perilous.   But it was cowardly, and actually
effected the formal breach with Charles by yielding to
the compulsion of the trades, for it publicly tore the
celebrated Calf-skin in pieces, distributing the shreds
among the mob, who wore them in their hats.   The next
step was to order the construction of new fortifications,
to overhaul the town artillery, to force contributions
from the religious houses, to organise the people into

companies under captains devoted to the cause. Ghent was well fortified, she was rich, her guilds were well armed, she had memories of glorious fights against Counts of Flanders and forgetfulness of discreditable collapses, her territory stretched for miles around the city. The movement had spread to Alost, Oudenaarde, and Courtrai, while the other members of Flanders, though not disloyal, were tentative and timid. The revolutionists fondly imagined that they could carry all Flanders with them, and then, perhaps, with the aid of France and the German Protestants throw off the sovereignty of Charles.

Mary was absolutely powerless. She sent the President of the Court of Malines and another high official to negotiate, and then to save their lives was forced to yield to the rebels' demands that their aldermen should be deposed, and that the magistrates in future should take an oath dictated by the populace. Beneath the seal of the new commission she wrote the words : *Par force et pour éviter plus grand mal ay consenty ceste commission. Marie.*

The guilds were not yet content; they would in future elect their own guildmasters without the intervention of the aldermen ; they ordered the other cities of Flanders to admit no governmental troops; they commanded Mary to recall all soldiers from the quarter of Ghent, and to surrender the citizens who had taken refuge with her. They offered, it is said, to put themselves under French obedience; it is certain that they sent deputies to Paris. Mary, direct as ever, wrote to her brother, that it was now a question of being master or varlet, that he must either leave Flanders to a communal form of government or must show himself to be prince (September 27, 1539).

Charles at length made up his mind. From Madrid he sent the Count of Rœulx to tell the rebellious city that he was coming. The Poorters and Weavers were now thoroughly alarmed, but the people laughed at the count's threats, believing that French and Lutherans and Turks would keep Charles busy. In the revolution there was now a strong religious and socialist element : it is said that a day was fixed for the plunder of the rich, the monasteries and the churches; the Count of Rœulx's life was in extreme peril. There was every reason to fear that the religious and social fermentation might infect other towns, where the condition of the lower classes was very similar.

Charles was at length upon his way. Hurrying through France, he met Mary at Valenciennes on January 21, 1540. Here he told a deputation from Ghent that he had come in great haste and at much inconvenience in the dead of winter, and that he meant to make an example of the city. His anger was none the less for having been long suppressed. He had ascribed the failure of the siege of Terouenne to the refusal of the town's subsidy ; he regarded the tearing of the Calf-skin as an impudent act of high treason ; he was deeply moved by the menace to the Catholic religion. In this temper he left Brussels on February 9 with his household, his guards and a crowd of magnates on his way to Ghent.

There was no shadow of resistance. The democracy of Ghent, now as in the following reign, was braver at constitution-making, at plundering and murdering, than it was at fighting. It meekly laid its head on the block for Charles, as it afterwards did for Parma. Not a shot was fired from its newly burnished guns, not a stone was knocked from its ostentatious bastions, not a man of its fire-eating citizen militia risked his skin,

Charles entered on February 14, and the dreams, if such
there really were, of an evangelical republic under
French protection vanished.   The Emperor knew well
the political power of pageantry.   He had been joined
by the king his brother, the queen his sister, the Duchess
of Milan his niece, by princes, bishops and ambassadors.
The flower of the Netherland nobility, the bands of
Netherland regular horse, his 3000 German *landsknechts*
held the town with a grip of steel.   The chief legal
functionaries of the provinces were summoned to consult
with the Council of State, the Privy Council and the
Knights of the Golden Fleece on the measures which it
were right to take.   The leaders of the movement were
netted, and nine of them were executed on the spot
where the first judicial murder had been committed by
the city.   The first stone of the fortress which was to
curb the rebellious populace was now laid.   On April
29, Charles, sitting on his throne with the doors of the
palace open that all might hear and see, passed sentence
on the aldermen, guildmasters, and other representatives
of the town.

Ghent was declared guilty of disloyalty, disobedience,
infraction of treaties, sedition, rebellion and high
treason.   Her privileges, rights and franchises were
forfeit; her property, movable and immovable, her
artillery and munitions, were confiscated.   She must
pay her share of the subsidy of 1537, and an indemnity
of 150,000 gulden and a yearly fine of 6000 more.   On
a day and at an hour to be fixed the magistrates and
their staff with thirty notable burgesses must appear
before the Emperor, bareheaded, clad in black and girt
with cords.   Fifty members of the Guild of Weavers, six
of each of the fifty-three lesser guilds, and fifty of the
revolutionary party named *Creesers* (criers) must in their

shirts and with ropes around their necks pray the
Emperor and the queen for mercy. An ordinance of the
same date abolished the constitution founded on the
trades, substituting an aristocracy under the immediate
influence of the prince. It deprived, moreover, the
city of its jurisdiction and pre-eminence over the towns
and districts of the quarter of Ghent. The name of
Carolina given to the new constitution preserved the
memory of the triumph of the Crown. On May 3 the
humiliation was completed. The black-robed or white-
shirted suppliants begged for mercy. Charles seemed
to hesitate ; then Mary prayed for forgiveness for the
city of his birth, and the prayer was heard.

Charles had not proved himself vindictive and inhuman, considering the provocation. Little blood was
shed in comparison with the violence of the revolution.
The number of executions is not quite certain, but the
evidence of Charles himself limits it to nine. The indemnity of 150,000 gulden with the annual fine were commuted for 78,000 gulden, which cannot have defrayed the
bare expenses. Not only had the danger been very real,
and the interruption to the Emperor's programme very
serious, but the revolution gave him the chance of
thrusting aside the local privilege, which everywhere
was an obstacle to his conception of rational administration and common defence against the aggression of
Solyman or Francis. For once he made the utmost of
his opportunity. At Ghent on that May morning he
recovered somewhat of that long-lost Autumn day.
After 1540 government in the Netherlands was easier,
in spite of foreign complications to west and south.
Yet Charles studiously advertised his intention that the
offences of the quarter of Ghent should not be visited
upon loyal, if lukewarm, provinces. He had proved

that, distant as he might be, he was a lord indeed who could not forget, and found it difficult to forgive.

Charles was always happier in action than in resolution. He now had the pain of deciding which of the two alternative brides he should grant to Orleans. He pleaded for delay : his promise had been conditional on Ferdinand's approval, and he could not, he said, get the project into his brother's head. Ferdinand was naturally unwilling to abandon the marriage of his heir with the Infanta, between whom and the Spanish crown stood only a somewhat weakly boy. The Netherland nobility agreed with him in resisting the alienation of the magnificent Burgundian heritage, which was the alternative towards which Charles was clearly leaning.

The question was decided by the French king's refusal to accept any of the conditions which Charles suggested. He would not surrender his claim to Milan, nor relinquish Savoy : he would not pledge himself to aid the cause of Catholicism against his whilom allies, Turk or Lutheran. The possession of the Netherlands, he cried, was but a shadow, which would vanish if the Infanta died childless : he would in that case have abandoned Savoy and Milan without equivalent : it would pay him better to leave matters as they were. "Be it so," replied the Emperor, "if the French king thinks it good, I also hold it for the best."

The immediate result of the rupture of negotiations was the close alliance of Francis with the Emperor's enemy the Duke of Cleves, to whom he married the child Jeanne d'Albret against the wish of her parents, who would fain recover Navarre for their house by the more brilliant union with the heir of Spain. This was in July 1540, and Charles, more leisurely, retaliated by investing Philip with Milan in October, leaving the

ultimate disposal of the Netherlands to be decided by
the future interests of his house.

Charles, like most men to whom decision is difficult,
was, perhaps, not ill-pleased that Francis had saved him
from the necessity of making up his mind. Yet it
would not seem, as has often been assumed, that he was
insincere in his proposals, although Granvelle confessed
to the Papal nuncio,—" We shall take good care to
give nothing that is ours." Charles had already determined on his expedition against Algiers, for which the
friendship or neutrality of France was indispensable.
The events which had followed the death of the Duke of
Guelders in June 1538 were endangering Catholicism
in Lower Germany and the Netherlands. The election
of the heir of Cleves, Juliers and Berg by the Estates
of Guelders, in defiance of the treaty with the late duke,
which secured the reversion to Charles, had created a
powerful and hostile state in the *hinterland* of the Low
Countries. William of Cleves, who almost immediately
succeeded to his father's possessions, was in close alliance
with the Lutheran princes : towards the end of 1539
his sister married Henry VIII., and there were schemes
for his own marriage with Mary Tudor. Whatever the
duke's religious antecedents or preferences might be, it
was certain that he would gravitate towards the League
of Schmalkalde. Only by alliance with France did it
seem possible for Charles to parry this fresh blow, for
the Habsburg marriage would make it the interest and
duty of France to recover Guelders for the French
prince's state. It was not unnatural that Charles
should seek to convert the Netherlands into a distinct
state under a resident ruler allied to France. He may
well have foreseen the future troubles in the provinces,
of which the revolt of Ghent was but one of several

symptoms. That he later returned to his proposals after a victorious campaign in France would show that this project of buffer states between the Valois and the Habsburg was a serious and constant factor in his policy. Hesitation was due less to insincerity than to irresolution. But it must be conceded that irresolution is equally exasperating with insincerity to one of the temperament of Francis, who must have everything he wanted, and that upon the moment.

CHAPTER XIII

German history since 1532—The loss of Württemberg—Anabaptism at
Münster—The revolution at Lübeck and the Danish war—Decline
of Catholicism—Hostility of German Catholics to the Papacy—New
religious policy of Charles—The truce of Frankfurt—Death of
George of Saxony—Advance of Protestantism—Bigamy of Philip
of Hesse—Religious conference of Regensburg—Causes of its failure
—Intrigues of France—Moderation of Charles—His ill-humour
against Bavaria—His reconciliation with Philip of Hesse.

When Charles had made the Netherlands secure, he
passed into Germany in January 1541. This visit was
long overdue, for the Emperor's second absence of nearly
nine years had produced nearly as great a change as the
corresponding period which closed with his arrival at
Augsburg in 1530. Imperial authority had sensibly
shrunk, while Lutheranism had visibly expanded. Ferdinand, busied with Hungary and Bohemia, could exercise
no adequate supervision; he had almost as little weight
in Germany as Charles. The tide seemed setting steadily
against the Habsburgs.

Württemberg was the most vulnerable point in the
German possessions of the house of Habsburg, and here
in May 1534 the long-threatened blow had fallen. The
attack was due to a coalition of Philip of Hesse with
the Bavarian dukes and Francis I., who, though nominally at peace with Charles, made little secret of his
hostility. Ferdinand foresaw the danger, and warned

his brother that the Landgrave, under pretence of
quelling the Anabaptist disturbances which had broken
out at Münster early in the year, was really arming
against Württemberg, and that France and England,
perhaps even the Pope, were his paymasters. He
implored Charles for help, if only on the ground that
the struggle would be in truth a religious war. The
Emperor gave cold comfort to his excited brother,
urging him to stand strictly on the defensive, and avoid,
at least for the current year, any cause of offence which
might drive the Protestant party into the arms of
France.[1]

At the last moment the Bavarians and the Landgrave quarrelled over Württemberg. The dukes supported the claim of their nephew Christopher, for he had
been brought up a Catholic, and had none of his father's
villainous antecedents. Philip, on the other hand, insisted on the restoration of Ulrich, who would protestantise his duchy with the zeal of a convert and the savagery
of a tyrant. The dukes drew off, and the Landgrave
single-handed overthrew the Habsburg rule. Ferdinand
had turned to the Suabian League, but this once
formidable weapon of his grandfather's forging lay
broken in his hand, split by the flaw which was rending
the solidity of all Germany. The skirmish of Lauffen
decided the fate of the wealthy duchy. The acquisition
of Württemberg had been the most notable success of
the Imperial dynasty in recent times. Now after
fifteen years of Charles's empire it had needed only a
second-rate power to restore the territorial prince whom
an Imperial decree had ousted. The restored exile
dared in the face of the recess of Augsburg to exclude

---

[1] See J. Wille, *Philipp der Grossmütige von Hessen und die Restitution Ulrichs
von Wirtemberg, 1526-35.* 1882.

the Catholic religion from his duchy. Lutheranism seemed likely to become as predominant in Southern Germany as in the north.

On the loss of Württemberg followed the final dissolution of the Suabian League. Bavarian and French influence contributed to the decision not to renew it when the current term expired. There was, in fact, no use as yet for a league the object of which was to promote political and social order; those only could succeed which stimulated or stereotyped religious disagreement. The Suabian League, however, had so long been regarded as the cleverest stroke of Habsburg diplomacy that its collapse might well portend disaster to the dynasty. At this moment Charles and Ferdinand seemed weaker than their grandfather Maximilian.

The dark hour was followed by the proverbial dawning. Since the loss of Württemberg there were symptoms of reaction. As Zwingli's death turned to the Protestants' advantage, by forcing the Zwinglian towns to seek the shelter of the Lutheran princes, so did the Württemberg misfortune bring its compensation to the Habsburgs. The Bavarian dukes drew nearer to them. They were offended by Ulrich's restoration, for not only had he wreaked his physical violence upon their sister, but he was exercising his religious outburst upon the orthodoxy of South Germany. Ferdinand's unexpected readiness to compromise detached Philip of Hesse from the side of France. The treaty of Cadan, which closed the little war, was eminently reasonable. Much to Ulrich's disgust his allies conceded that Württemberg should remain an Austrian fief, though with a seat in the College of Princes, but the informal promises made to the Lutherans at Nuremberg were now more formally confirmed. Philip paid a friendly visit to

Ferdinand, and confessed to his own sister that he should like to be out of the religious league, and make his peace with the Habsburgs.

There was some chance that the League of Schmalkalde might expire at the close of its first term in 1537. The alliance of towns and princes was due only to immediate emergency. Moreover several cities, as not subscribing to the Confession of Augsburg, were excluded from the benefits of the truce of Nuremberg. Many had never belonged to the League of Schmalkalde. There was a general feeling that a union of Hesse, Württemberg and the South German towns would be sufficiently powerful to resist the Catholics, while it would safeguard their more advanced opinions against the tyranny of Saxon formalism. Such a union would necessarily have been Zwinglian, and the political results of its inevitable antagonism to Lutheranism are not easy to calculate. On the other side the Saxon Elector also paid a visit to Vienna. Although Ferdinand refused to Lutheranism the wide concessions of time and space which he demanded, and although therefore the Elector declined to give formal recognition to Ferdinand's title, yet the personal relations were far more friendly. Had Charles been in Germany, he might have made himself master of the situation. As it was he skilfully affected to make light of the Württemberg affair, dissembling his knowledge of the French king's aid, and pushing off the inevitable French war until the Tunisian campaign was ended.

In these days two ominous disturbances in Germany diverted the attention of the Protestant princes from the absent Emperor to the more immediately troublesome democracy which the Reformation itself had engendered. The Anabaptist movement at Münster and the exploits

of the militant democracy of Lübeck have only an
indirect connection with the biography of Charles, but
their importance to German and to Netherland history
makes it impossible to omit all notice of them.

Anabaptism, crushed in the country on the defeat of
Münzer, had crawled sore and maimed into the towns,
where tradesmen and artisans gave hospitable shelter to
any form of doctrine which their superiors had reason to
dislike. The extreme ferocity of the legislation against
the sect would have provoked reprisals, even if violence
were not a necessary consequence of its original programme. Strassburg had been selected as the site of
the New Jerusalem, but circumstances somewhat
accidental led to the establishment of the kingdom of
Sion at Münster. This was nominally an episcopal, but
practically a free city, and was mainly Lutheran, though
one of the Lutheran leaders, Rothmann, had passed
through the medium of Zwinglism to Anabaptism. The
latter sect became so strong that the patrician families,
Lutheran or Catholic, were dislodged from the municipal
government by an Anabaptist democracy. Münster
then became the refuge for Anabaptists from all quarters,
especially from the Netherlands, where they were probably most numerous. The two new leaders of the sect
were successively Mattys, the prophet from Haarlem, and
John of Leyden, who, upon his master's death, set up his
theocratic monarchy, which an organised system of communism and polygamy rendered all the more attractive.

The Bishop entirely failed to force an entrance into
his city in spite of aid from Philip of Hesse and other
neighbours. Upper-class Germany became alarmed, for
the Anabaptists sent forth apostles to spread their doctrines, and made every effort to win large episcopal cities
such as Cologne, Liège and Utrecht. The slightest

success might have caused the recrudescence of the Peasant Revolt of 1525 in an urban and more dangerous shape. Hence the two neighbouring circles undertook the reduction of the city, this being the first important occasion on which this new organisation was called into activity. The circles proved as powerless as the Bishop, and then at the diet of 1535 the Empire was forced to put forth its strength. After desperate resistance the famished town was surprised and stormed at the end of June 1535 ; the siege had lasted some eighteen months.

Münster was the first important German town which had been taken by storm for a century or more. The Bishop was restored, and his garrison overawed the city, which forfeited its freedom. Victory had once again declared for the territorial princes. The German towns had recognised this danger. Lübeck, under the influence of the demagogue Wullenweber, had offered mediation, but Lübeck itself was suspected of Anabaptism. The South German cities, above suspicion on this score, sent a deputation to urge " King John " to treat for terms, but he scorned any dealings with the priests. The victory of territorialism did not contribute to good feeling between towns and princes. From the very first Catholics and Protestants had combined against a movement which threatened social and political as well as religious revolution. The settlement was, however, one of the scanty gains of Catholicism. Although the Bishop with Philip of Hesse's aid would have been glad enough to protestantise his see with a view to making it an hereditary principality, both the neighbouring circles and the diet, under the influence of Catholic majorities, had made the restoration of Catholic worship and property a condition of their assistance. Thus a Lutheran town once again became Catholic.

The regent of the Netherlands had watched the siege with much anxiety, for many of the defenders were Charles's subjects, and a chance spark might set his adjoining province on fire.   Mary herself had to suppress Anabaptist revolt in Friesland, while Amsterdam was within an ace of sharing the fate of Münster.   She offered aid to the Bishop, but the history of Liège and Utrecht convinced him that Burgundian assistance to Bishops in distress was not disinterested.   The temper of the circles was shown by their stipulation that the town should not be handed over to any foreigner, and by this term the German princes meant their Emperor.

The revolution at Lübeck is of far wider interest than that of the Anabaptist fanatics.   Its leader Wullenweber possessed real political force and a brilliant imagination. Germans of the colonial party still honour him as one who would have recovered the sea-power for his nation, though to his own vision the nation took the microscopic form of Lübeck city.   The reformation at Lübeck had taken a violent political complexion, and had led to the overthrow of the old aristocratic constitution and the expulsion of many patrician families.   Wullenweber with two of his colleagues, the lawyer Oldendorp and the *landsknecht* Meyer, conceived the adventurous idea of using the new motive force of democracy for reviving Lübeck's moribund naval and commercial power.   The Baltic cities, the so-called Wendish section of the Hanseatic League, had lost their prosperity, partly owing to the action of the absolutist rulers of Denmark, who made the most of their control of the Sound for their own and their people's profit, partly to the competition of the Netherland cities, which under the rule of the house of Burgundy had outstripped their Baltic rivals.

When Christian II., returning from Augsburg, had

attempted his restoration, he had received somewhat
grudging and lukewarm support from Charles's Netherland government.   Mary, indeed, afterwards professed
that he had marched through the provinces because she
had no means of stopping him ; her main desire was to
rid the country of his presence.   Protestant Lübeck
naturally supported Frederick of Holstein, the elected
king of Denmark, who had not only the merit of
Lutheran proclivities but the power to confer commercial
privilege.   Christian's capture was followed by a general
peace between Frederick, the Hanse towns and the
Netherlands, which, however, Wullenweber and his
associates resented.

In April 1533 Frederick died.   The kingdom of
Denmark was elective, but the late king's heirs enjoyed
a traditional precedence.   While Frederick left two sons,
his imprisoned predecessor had two daughters.   The
exiled Archbishop of Lund urged that Habsburg influence might be revived by the marriage of one of the
princesses to her first cousin the Infant Philip.   Before
long Dorothea was in point of fact engaged to the Count
Palatine Frederick, the whilom lover of her aunt Eleanor,
and he became a candidate for the throne.   The Danish
nobles favoured Frederick of Holstein's eldest son
Christian, a zealous Lutheran, while the bishops preferred the younger brother, who might be coaxed into
Catholicism.   Candidature was not confined to Danish
princes and princesses.   Francis I., following and anticipating the policy of other French kings, coveted Denmark as a point of vantage in the North Sea and Baltic
against his Burgundian and Imperial rival.   He therefore canvassed for himself or for his brother-in-law the
King of Navarre, promising large gratuities to the
electors, and engaging to support Lübeck against the

Emperor, if she would place herself under a French protectorate for a term of years.

Electoral rights in Denmark were confined to nobles and bishops, but popular suffrage would have given the crown to the imprisoned king, because in the day of his might he had done his utmost by fair means, or preferably foul, to exterminate the nobles. On his side were the burgomasters of the semi-German towns, Copenhagen and Malmö. In the sympathy of peasants and artisans for Christian II. Wullenweber saw his opportunity. He persuaded Copenhagen and Malmö to enter the Hanseatic League, and to take up arms for Christian, who would protestantise the kingdom, close the Sound to Netherland ships, and destroy noble and ecclesiastical privilege. Lübeck hoped once again to control the commerce and succession of the Scandinavian kingdoms : Denmark at least should become a monarchical *annexe* to her own democratic government. Not content with Denmark, the Lübeck triumvirate resolved also to oust Gustavus of Sweden, because he had cancelled the monopolies which he had previously granted.

The democratic wave swept the Baltic from end to end, from Stockholm to Copenhagen, to Riga and Revel, throwing down the breakwaters of race which divided German from Scandinavian or Finn. Here and there other Hanse towns stood out as islands, fearing the propagandism of Lübeck or her dangerous foreign policy. In compensation there was no lack of adventurous nobles to serve democracy for three months' pay and a possible bonus of a Scandinavian crown. John of Hoya attacked his brother-in-law Gustavus of Sweden, while Christopher of Oldenburg sailed for Copenhagen, and roused the popular agitation over Seeland, Funen and Jutland.

The question of Danish succession and the supremacy of Lübeck had already passed far beyond the Baltic shores. Marcus Meyer, knighted by Henry VIII., persuaded the Tudor tyrant to unite with the Lübeck demagogues against the abuses of Rome and the prosperity of the Netherlands. Henry was tempted by promises of the protectorate of the Danish-Hanseatic combination, even by a prospect of the Danish crown. While the exiled aristocracies of the Baltic towns joined the nobility of Denmark and Holstein, and appealed for redress to the Imperial Chamber, Lübeck invoked the aid of the League of Schmalkalde, of which she was a member. Philip of Hesse, however, sent his troops to Christian III., who had been elected by the Danish nobles; Albert of Prussia and the Luneburg princes also threw their weight on the side of nobility. The new king had little of Wullenweber's ambition or imagination, but admirable capacity for the adaptation of means to ends. Neglecting the loss of Denmark and the attacks on Holstein, he marched straight on Lübeck, cut the city off from the sea, and starved it into a partial restoration of the old constitution and an agreement to limit the war to Denmark.

Wullenweber was not yet beaten; his fertile imagination still found resources. By promises of the crown of Sweden and the reversion of Denmark upon Christian II.'s death he won the restless, feckless Catholic prince, Albert of Mecklenburg, uncle of Philip of Hesse. Religion apart, Albert was a strong candidate; his family had held the Scandinavian thrones; his wife was a niece of Christian II.; his house, if not Scandinavian, was at least not German. Henry VIII. was still sufficiently inspired by the vision of Baltic suzerainty to send ships towards Copenhagen.

The war went badly for Lübeck. Her forces were defeated by land and sea. Meyer was killed and Copenhagen was starving. The pretentious shadow of Henry gave no substantial shelter; the fiery Mecklenburger proved but a flash in the pan. Yet Wullenweber's inventiveness or impudence was inexhaustible. He turned for aid to Charles V. himself, supporting the candidature of Frederick Count Palatine, now the husband of Dorothea. Copenhagen throughout the terrible starvation of the winter of 1535-36 looked in vain for Burgundian succour, forgetting that the mainspring of the war had been the wish to boycott Burgundian commerce. The end had come. The Imperial Chamber decreed the restoration of the expelled members of the old *régime* at Lübeck; the Hanseatic diet, wearied by her harassing activity, declared against her policy. As a consequence Wullenweber was removed under honourable pretexts. The people, to save its religion, for which it chiefly cared, threw overboard the democratic principles and the political ambitions which had well-nigh sunk the city in the Baltic which she had aspired to ride. For all his enemies or rivals Christian III. built graceful bridges of retreat. By the peace of Hamburg he was recognised as king, restoring to Lübeck her ancient privileges. Copenhagen capitulated in July 1536; in October Catholicism was formally suppressed.

Although Charles was not actively concerned in the Baltic conflict, every stage of it was anxiously watched. He could not intervene, because his energies were fully occupied with the Tunisian expedition and the ensuing French war. But the interests involved were large, no less than much of the trade and therefore of the loyalty of the Netherlands. It seemed quite possible, as the Archbishop of Lund warned Charles, that either France or England might establish her influence in the Danish peninsula, and hence act upon Netherland discontent or Lutheran hostility. Denmark had originally been included in the fascinating scheme of a family confederacy, and although Charles had long lost faith in Christian II., it was not easy to abandon the dynastic alliance which protected the flank of the Netherlands, and gave the entry to the Baltic. Charles therefore must have some sympathy for the attempt to restore Christian II., and more for the proposal to raise his personal friend the Count Palatine and his own niece Dorothea to the throne. On the other hand Lübeck, the originator of these schemes, had flagrantly violated the recent peace ; her original motive had been the exclusion of Netherland commerce ; she was in alliance with Henry VIII. ; she was ultra-democratic and ultra-Lutheran, if not Anabaptist ; the exclusion of Catholicism from Denmark must be the result of her victory.

The favour of the Netherlands was with Christian of Holstein, because Lübeck was the common enemy of both. But then Christian was the incarnation of Charles's most dangerous foe, capable territorialism ; his chief allies were Philip of Hesse and Albert of Prussia ; he was a zealous Lutheran and sang hymns as lustily as any smug tradesman of an Imperial town. The problem then was really difficult. Mary, for once more adventurous than Charles, encouraged Albert of Mecklenburg to continue his resistance throughout the winter of 1535-36. Charles has been credited with influencing the Imperial Chamber against Lübeck. However this may be, he must have known well that Denmark was lost to him whatever happened. He was wise in not intervening ; the utmost he could do was not to irritate the winning party, whichever that might be. For long the Emperor's diplomatists amused themselves with the claims of Frederick and Dorothea, but his support of his niece was as academic as that previously given to his aunt Catherine. The ultimate solution was not unfortunate. The main desire of Christian III., in spite of French alliances and Lutheran friendships, was to be left alone, and this was becoming the one ideal of Charles.

During these years the policy of Charles and Ferdinand in Germany took new directions. There was no more talk of coercion, and gradually the agitation for a Council died away. The one aim was to propitiate the Lutherans, and prevent their union with France in the war which closed in 1538. Protestantism spread almost unhindered. Princes and towns, aware that Charles could not fight, wrought havoc with ecclesiastical property as yet unplundered, in defiance of the peace of Nuremberg. Charles in his remonstrances took his stand upon this treaty, but the Lutheran divines never lacked scriptural arguments for spoliation. Lutheranism was, moreover, internally consolidated by the *Concordia* of Wittenberg in May 1536, which concealed, if it did not entirely close, the doctrinal rents of the Saxon and South German parties.

Equally noticeable with the consolidation of Protestantism was the disintegration of Catholicism in the states which passed for orthodox. The Catholic priesthood seemed likely to expire through inanition. Among the Austrian sees, the Bishop of Passau only ordained five priests in four years, he of Laibach seventeen in eight years. The nuncio Vergerio could find no candidates in Bohemia save a few paupers who could not pay the fees ; the old Catholic stronghold Breslau in Silesia was now entirely Protestant. Faber, Bishop of Vienna,

said that but for himself and Ferdinand the whole town
would be heretic.   The lapse into Lutheranism, Zwinglism or Anabaptism, even among the gentry, was of
such daily occurrence that it was scarcely noticed, much
less punished.   In Catholic states there were often more
monasteries than monks.   Regensburg was one of the
more conservative cities, but her beautiful monasteries
had only one or two inmates apiece, and the splendid
Cathedral only some twenty worshippers.   Nuremberg
would not call herself Lutheran, and was loyal to the
Emperor, but the town council changed the mass,
abolished festivals, introduced marriage of the clergy
and communion in both kinds, and all by lay authority.
Augsburg, more violent, persecuted her bishop and white-
washed her churches.

In 1535 Joachim I. of Brandenburg, a most stubborn
supporter of the Church, died, and Joachim II. was from
the first suspected of unorthodox leanings.   Louis, Elector
Palatine, was nominally Catholic, but was always either
drunk or hunting, and his capital of Heidelberg with
its University was described as the most Lutheran town
in Germany.

The feeling among German Catholics was strongly
hostile to the Papacy.   Clement VII. had shrunk from
the very mention of a Council, and although Paul III.
professed his eagerness and actually summoned a
Council to Mantua, it was soon obvious that it was a
sham.   The King of France was the ally of Lutherans,
and therefore Clement's visit to Marseilles, and the
marriage of his young cousin, Catherine de' Medici, to
the French prince had caused bitter resentment among
Catholics.   Vergerio warned the Pope that people in
Italy did not sufficiently realise the hostility of Germany :
a high authority—presumably Ferdinand—had told him

that it only wanted a hint, and the whole of Germany—
men, women and children—would rush greedily on the
Church and pour into Italy, craving, as their sole
reward, the overthrow of the Pope and all adherents
and dependents. Ferdinand was furious at the Pope's
refusal to aid in the defence of Württemberg, and
Charles at his partiality towards France and his rejection of a Council.

Honest German Catholics who loved their religion
and their country were equally indignant. " If the
Church," wrote George of Saxony, " were robbed of
10,000 ducats it would be a matter for anathema, for
raising an army, for calling all Christendom to the
rescue; but when 100,000 souls are being lost by
devilish artifices the shepherd takes counsel of him who
has always striven to destroy the sheep and subject
them to himself." The duke, with his usual simplicity,
added the nuncio, had copies of this letter distributed
to all who wanted them. The prospects of improvement
under Paul III. were soon clouded. Ferdinand said
plainly that he was even more wrapped up in his
family's advancement than was Clement; that the tithes
which he granted to the French king would be used as
subsidies to the Turks in their attack upon himself and
Charles; that the Pope's lukewarmness would be the
ruin of the world. The German Catholics, despairing of
a Council, were being forced to the alternative of a
national settlement by means of a diet, an Imperial
convention, as they termed it. This, repeated nuncio
after nuncio, would imply the separation of all Germany
from the Church. The Catholic princes, to save their
states and even their lives, would have to make large
concessions : the ecclesiastical princes were being tempted
by the bait of hereditary thrones, and many of them

were wavering : the Lutherans, abandoning their more extreme dogmas, were directing all their venom against Rome, thinking that the Catholics would prefer domestic peace and old friendships to the interests of the Holy See, for which already the ecclesiastical princes cared not a jot : German Catholics were reading and re-reading a speech of Henry VIII. on national independence, and Imperial agents muttered that an Imperial settlement was the only remedy.

This suggestion of a national settlement Charles, in his slow, deliberate way, was now beginning to assimilate, although he had once indignantly denounced it as schismatic. In 1536 he sent his agent Held to Germany to consult Ferdinand on the subject. If, he wrote, Paul III. continued in his cool indifference towards Germany, might it not be well to summon a Council without the Pope or France, or if this did not commend itself to the majority of Germans, it might be possible to adopt some other means of securing either an eternal peace on the lines of the truce of Nuremberg, or else a settlement by a national synod in which concessions might be made in matters not essential to the faith : in no other way did it seem possible that Imperial authority could be preserved. Held did not utilise the proposals, but they are none the less important in the development of the Emperor's views, for the one contained the germ of the Interim, the other of the Religious Peace of Augsburg. The suspensory method was giving place to that of comprehension, or of a permanent agreement to differ. Charles and Ferdinand were being driven towards reconciliation with the Protestants by their common hostility to the Pope. Their own orthodoxy was unimpeachable, although Morone described that of Ferdinand as consisting mainly of externals, of works of

charity and regular attendance at Mass. On the other
hand Ferdinand's advisers were almost openly Lutheran,
while those of Charles were Erasmian or indifferent.
Already Ferdinand was insisting that the Pope must
allow marriage of clergy, grant the cup to the laity, and
modify the doctrine on the punishment of mortal sin.
He was infected by the general hostility to the Papacy;
he argued hotly with Morone that it was due to the
evil example of the Curia that he could not find a
confessor who was not a fornicator, a drunkard or
an ignoramus. He actually expressed the view that
Charles should make peace with France, in person settle
the religious troubles of Germany by a compromise, and
so buy its support against the Turks.

Another remedy was also tried in these troubled
years. The policy of the Lutherans was imitated, and
an attempt made to form a Catholic league on the model
of that of Schmalkalde. George of Saxony and Henry
of Brunswick eagerly threw themselves into the Imperial
plans. But the Rhenish Electors held aloof, and
Bavaria would only enter on condition that the league
should exclude all other than religious aims. On these
terms the Catholic League of Nuremberg was formed,
but it did little more than prove how weak and divided
the party was in face of the more energetic, more
united Protestants. Catholicism in fact, with the Pope's
supposed desertion to the Franco-Turkish cause, lost
its central principle : it is creditable to the remaining
Catholics that in spite of dangers and temptations they
clung to their faith so long.

The success of Charles at Tunis inspired considerable
respect in Germany, and when once he was at war with
France, the Lutherans felt that they had nothing to fear
—that, in Bucer's words, they were as little likely to be

attacked by the Emperor as by the King of Calicut.
They were, indeed, so secure that they could afford to
be patriotic. Since 1536 French agents ceaselessly
tempted them to alliance, insinuating that Francis I.
was only outwardly a Catholic, and begging them to
send their theologians to Paris with a view to religious
union. Philip of Hesse would gladly have entered into
such a scheme, but John Frederick of Saxony sternly
forbade the visit which Melanchthon eagerly wished to
pay.

When the war with France was over, the Lutherans
were suddenly seized with fear. Francis I. had refused
at Aigues Mortes to join Charles in any but peaceful and
mediatory measures, but the Emperor spared no pains
to let Germany believe that the alliance was directed
against all his enemies, whether Turk or heretic. Thus
at length John Frederick, Philip, Ulrich and Christian
III. of Denmark formulated a treaty with the King of
France, who, as they believed, had saved them from a
Council and an hereditary monarchy. The towns, however, rejected all overtures for alliance with the power
which persecuted true Christians and was in open alliance with the infidel. Neither Emperor nor Lutherans
had any mind to fight, and thanks to the mediation of
the Elector Palatine, a moderate Catholic, and Joachim
II., a moderate Protestant, although as yet undeclared,
the two parties came to terms. The Lutherans made
exorbitant demands, the Emperor clung obstinately to
the *status quo*, and once again he had his way to all
appearance, although in reality the Lutherans were so
strong that for immediate security they could afford
to relinquish permanent guarantees. The defection of
Philip of Hesse probably turned the scale; his health
incapacitated him from undertaking a campaign, and

once more he was under the glamour of Habsburg smiles.

The truce of Frankfurt (April 1539) was the last of the purely suspensory agreements; it was limited to six months, but protected all existing Lutheran states. The lawyers of the Chamber were once more befooled. These industrious officials were regularly insulted and irregularly paid. Their main function was the protection of vested ecclesiastical interests, by no means all of them abuses, against the greed of princes and municipalities, who could only meet the expense and extravagance of modern life at the cost of the pious founder. In the compact of Frankfurt the German Catholics and the League of Nuremberg were treated as non-existent, and they were righteously indignant. George of Saxony spoke his mind, as always, with justice and with emphasis. If Charles and Ferdinand, he said, left the Catholics in the lurch, the latter must look for peace and quiet elsewhere : if Lutherans escaped the decisions of the Imperial Chamber, Catholics would not be bound by them : if the Lutherans had gained their aim by refusing a subsidy against the Turks, the Catholics could follow suit. No terms, he added, could bind the Lutherans : no engagements had prevented their enlisting fresh recruits : the Catholics must enter on counter propagandism.

This last appeal was that of a dying man. In April died the most honest and consistent character of all that age. At once loyal and patriotic, moral and religious, prudent and courageous, he had never disguised the necessity of reform, and always denounced the ruinous consequences of dissent. None had a higher ideal of what the clergy of a German territory ought to be, and yet none was more loyal to the ancient Church. While performing to the full, and with much autocratic inde-

pendence, his duties as a territorial prince, he still retained his devotion to the unity of the Empire and the
German nation. The Habsburgs never replaced his loss ;
he was the true son of his father, who would rather that
the whole house of Saxony should beg its bread than
that the Habsburgs should come to ruin, who had
pointed to the Order of the Golden Fleece and said,
" This is the lamb that I cherish in my heart and wear
ever on my breast." True to the last to the Imperial
house and the Catholic religion, he bequeathed his
dominions to the Habsburgs, if his brother and successor
decided for Lutheranism. George of Saxony has rarely
had his full deserts in history ; he spoke too plainly
both of Pope and Protestants.

It might have been thought that the close friendship
between Charles and Francis, and the ease with which
the Emperor conquered Ghent, would encourage him to
attempt a religious reaction in Germany. But it was
soon apparent that the truce of Nice would expire in
early infancy, and that Ferdinand must face another
Turkish invasion. Charles himself believed that before
the war with France broke out he would just have time
to destroy the hornets' nest in Algiers. All success,
however, depended upon peace in Germany. During
the five years from 1539 to the peace of Crépy Charles
entered upon a fresh stage of policy. On the one hand
he inaugurated the national conferences between the
representatives of the two religions, on the other he
exercised his attractive power on the more military and
more dangerous of the Lutheran leaders. Neither
scheme was entirely new, but both were now definitely
and continuously adopted *pari passu*.

Lutheranism in 1539 received notable accessions.
George of Saxony was succeeded by his brother Henry,

a pronounced Lutheran, and he in 1541 by his son
Maurice, who married the daughter of Philip of Hesse.
To 1539 is usually ascribed Joachim II. of Brandenburg's
open change of faith. He reformed his Electorate in the
following year, although on conservative and episcopal
lines ; following the example of the Tudor king he would
be *pontifex maximus* within his territory. Joachim
was not, however, yet officially recognised as belonging
to the Protestant party. Even more important than the
defection of the Hohenzollern Elector from Catholicism
was the imminent admission of William of Cleves into
the League of Schmalkalde. Already elective duke of
Guelders, he had now succeeded to his father's dominions,
and thus become one of the most powerful princes of
North Germany, far more dangerous to the Emperor
than his old foe Charles of Egmont. Looking around for
aid William turned to his two brothers-in-law of Saxony
and England, to Francis I., uncle of his child-bride
Jeanne d'Albret, to the king of Denmark, and above all
to the Lutheran league.

For this rapid advance of Lutheranism there was
some compensation. Religion seemed so secure that in
each territory the political current was apt to turn back
into its old channels. On the Catholic side community
of religion had never yet produced unity of policy. Now
that Protestantism was no longer on the defensive, when
it was nearing its second generation and had become a
matter of course, it was doubtful how long it would retain its binding power in general politics. Charles had
for some years past given instructions to his agents to
win the fighting Lutherans, Ulrich of Württemberg,
William of Fürstenberg, the great recruiting sergeant
who had led thousands of *landsknechts* into French
service, but above all Philip of Hesse.

In the scandals of the ablest Protestant leader's private life Charles found his opportunity. Philip was a remarkable example of the intermingling of genuine religious feeling and loose moral practice characteristic of periods of religious strife. Confessing that since 1525 he had never been for three weeks faithful to his wife, he yet could not reconcile his conscience to receiving communion. Luther had always thundered against divorce, and thus Philip fell back on bigamy as the only available palliative for his constitutional immorality. He gained the grudging consent of his wife and of her near relation the Saxon Elector. The leading divines, Luther, Melanchthon, and Bucer, could prove that bigamy was scriptural. All, however, made the condition that the bigamous marriage should be a profound secret, and Luther was opposed to any matrimonial ceremony. Philip was too proud of his success to keep the secret. The Lutheran leaders were heartily ashamed, and shame made them quarrelsome. John Frederick and Ulrich refused to protect Philip from the consequences of his offence, for which the legal penalty was death. Melanchthon nearly died of remorse. Luther, as he himself confessed, was more thick-skinned, and saw in so good a cause no evil in a stark official lie.[1]

Scandals, it is fair to remember, were not confined to Lutheran circles. Ferdinand of Austria and George of Saxony were, indeed, models of propriety, but of the other two most devoted Catholics, Joachim I. had been unable to attend a diet without his mistress in the incognito of masculine attire, while Henry of Brunswick, to silence the voice of scandal, buried his paramour in effigy, and concealed the original in his hunting-box.

---

[1] This unsavoury story has always been the subject of controversy. For a fair and common-sense review of the more recent literature see W. Köhler, *Die Doppelehe des Landgraf Philipps von Hessen* in *Historische Zeitschrift*, No. 85, 1905.

The Papacy had before now given dispensation for what plain-speaking men might term bigamy and incest. But the Protestants laid claim to a higher code of morals, and Philip could base no excuse on the evils of a disputed succession, for his wife had given him eight children. The private sin was a public calamity to the Protestant cause, and the reformed religion paid dearly then and thereafter for the lapse of its theologians.

Philip was angry with himself and furious with his friends. He swore that he would turn to the Pope for divorce and dispensation in due form, and not look too closely at the few thousand ducats that it might cost. When in this frame of mind he was approached by Granvelle on the Emperor's behalf during the Conferences of Hagenau and Worms. These to outward appearance were resultless, but in reality not only was Philip detached from his late friends, but a scheme of religious comprehension was arrived at between the Imperial and Hessian theologians. This agreement was all the more remarkable inasmuch as the latter were virtually Zwinglians, and, therefore, farther removed from Catholicism than the more conservative Lutherans.[1]

The two parallel schemes for dividing the Lutheran party and for preparing the way for a general reunion had already met with palpable success. With regard to the conferences there can be little doubt that Charles was in earnest, although Lutherans denied it. His chief aim at this time was to avail himself of the united strength of Germany, or at least to withdraw Protestant aid from France. He knew that searching reforms were needed, and that even on the test doctrinal question,

---

[1] For these conferences see R. Moses, *Die Religionsverhandlungen in Hagenau und Worms*, 1889. W. Friedensburg uses important unpublished reports by Granvelle in his article, *Zur Geschichte des Wormser Konvents*, in *Zeitschrift für Kirchengeschichte*, 1900-1.

Justification by Faith, undoubted Catholics were divided ;
he believed that, without abandoning essentials, a temporary working agreement might be framed ; he would
stretch the circle of the Church as far as possible, so that
its circumference might give sufficient range to divergence of opinion.   The conferences were professedly held
with a view to a future Council ; they were to establish
a general basis of agreement, leaving for the decision of
the Council the few points still disputed.   Charles must
have felt that the prospects of a Council, whose verdict
both Catholics and Lutherans would accept, were in the
extreme indefinite, but meanwhile a successful conference
might establish at least a more satisfactory truce than
the previous method of suspension.

That Charles in person attended the conference of
Regensburg in April 1541 proves his deep interest in the
expedient, although the nuncio Morone, no unfavourable
witness, was doubtless right in his assertion that he probably understood little of doctrine, and was in this dependent on his ministers.   Even for the theologian these
conferences have but an academic value, because in the
light of later events it is obvious that agreement was
impossible.   Nevertheless, to outward appearance, since
the great schism had begun, Catholicism and Protestantism never approached so near as now at Regensburg.
Charles had begged the Pope that a legate might attend,
and had let him know that none would be more welcome
than Gasparo Contarini.   No great Churchman had the
cause of peace so truly at heart, none was more conscious
of the abuses of the old faith, none could so acutely
appreciate the doctrinal difficulties and subtleties of his
opponents.   Perfect gentleman as the Venetian was, he
could with equal grace reprove the intemperate zeal of
the ultra-Catholic Dr. Eck, converse on indifferent topics

with Hessian preachers and Strassburg envoys, and warn
the Emperor to his face against the sufferance of false
doctrine.

The presidents of the conference were Granvelle and
the Count Palatine Frederick, both eager for peace,
neither of them susceptible to theological polemic. Of
the three Catholic divines whom Charles selected, Eck,
Gropper and Pflug, the two latter were known to be
studiously moderate, if not Erasmian; the zealous
Catholic, Vice-Chancellor Held, regarded Granvelle,
Pflug and Naves as the "three evil spirits" among his
colleagues in Imperial service. The sole fighting man,
Dr. Eck, had shortly to withdraw from illness. On the
Protestant side the presence of Melanchthon seemed a
guarantee for a spirit of compromise, while the Hessian
ministers, Bucer and Pistorius, must follow the new
direction of their master's policy. Before this body
Charles himself laid the so-called *Book of Regensburg*
as a basis for discussion. This was a provisional draft of
a compromise on the main points of divergence, and had
been in fact compiled by Gropper and Veltwyck acting
for the Emperor, and Bucer and Capito as the representatives of Hesse; it was the theological outcome of
the Conference of Worms. The book was previously
shown by Charles to Contarini, who made some twenty
emendations, which were graciously accepted. Dr. Eck,
who brought against it a string of objections of a purely
academic character, received, at Granvelle's instance, a
severe lecture from the legate.[1]

The conference lasted nearly a month, from April 27
to May 22. The committee agreed upon a fair propor-

---

[1] For the conference of Regensburg see J. P. Vetter, *Die Religionsverhandlungen auf dem Reichstage zu Regensburg*, 1899; L. Pastor, *Correspondenz Contarinis, 1541*, 1880.

tion of the less contentious clauses; it even evolved a
formula of Justification which convinced each party
that its own doctrine had been accepted. This was,
indeed, a hopeful presage of peace. Contarini was
jubilant, and Granvelle gleefully committed the article
to paper with his own hand. Here success practically
ended. There could be no agreement on the Authority
of the Church, when the Lutherans denied the infallibility not only of the Pope, but of a General Council.
Still less was compromise possible on Confession and
Absolution, on private Masses and the invocation of
Saints, and on the Eucharist. Melanchthon's outbreak
on the hierarchical organisation of the Church virtually
closed the discussion. Even before this the tone of
Contarini's letters to Rome had completely changed;
he evidently despaired of conciliation; he could only
recommend on the one hand the strengthening of the
Catholic League, on the other the reform of the episcopate, the grant of the cup to the laity, and the
reorganisation of preaching and education, in which
successive nuncios admitted the Protestants to be infinitely superior.

For the failure of the conference neither one side nor
the other can be blamed; the chasm which had cleft
Germany was too wide for a fatigue party of theologians
to bridge. The controlling forces lay quite outside the
conference. Had an agreement on the basis of the
Book of Regensburg been framed, it would never have
been passed by the majority in the College of Princes.
Even the compromise on Justification was formally
rejected at Rome, and Wittenberg only accepted it on
the condition that Melanchthon should make no more
concessions. Luther and his master set spies to watch
the intercourse of Melanchthon with the Catholics; they

sharply rebuked the slightest symptom of surrender. In point of fact Melanchthon was now much more in awe of the Elector than of the Emperor. If in nothing else, he agreed with Dr. Eck in a policy of resistance and obstruction, while the Hessian divines, on the contrary, following their master's lead, worked in harmony with Pflug and Gropper.

The opposition both of Catholics and Lutherans to the conciliatory measures of the Emperor was fully as much political as it was religious. The Bavarian dukes had attributed the progress of Protestantism to the weakness of Charles, whom Granvelle was bribed to lead astray. But when they recommended neither conference nor Council but force, the real object of their attack was not the Saxon but the Habsburg. Contarini was well aware of their interested intentions. "There is scarcely a man," he wrote, " or very few who serve God with honest heart. These dukes, seeing that Philip of Hesse and the Saxon Elector have become great by their leadership of the Lutherans, want to be heads of the Catholics, and without having a penny of their own would make war at the expense of the Pope and the ecclesiastical princes." Contarini had to expostulate against their wish to plunge Germany into war, which would give the impression that the Catholics shunned the light of reason.

On the Lutheran side it was not now Philip of Hesse but John Frederick who urged a political alliance of both creeds against Charles, and this to enable the Duke of Cleves to retain his hold on Guelders. The Elector refused to be present at Regensburg, and instructed his representative to reject any peace with "murderous, idolatrous princes." Luther had discovered that it was lawful to disobey the Emperor, because

not Charles but the "devil of Mainz," the Archbishop
Albert, was really Emperor; he warned Philip against
Charles as a false, lying man who had forgotten his
German morals, and held the papistical, cardinalistical,
Italian and Saracenic faith. Yet Luther and his master
were ready enough to further the interests of France,
and therefore indirectly of the Turk. Many Catholics,
wrote Morone, had private leagues with Lutherans, and
every one sought his individual interest.

Even before the conference began, the German
princes were intriguing with France against reunion.
Dandino, the nuncio at the French Court, assured
Contarini in March that the French did not wish the
religious differences healed, and that the German princes
had promised not to agree to the Emperor's proposals
for reunion, for fear that he should then turn his
strength against them. Religious disunion had, indeed,
become inextricably intertwined with territorial independence. Charles desired religious union if only
because it would render common action against the
foreigner possible. The princes widened the religious
breach for fear that reunion would bring with it
Imperial consolidation. In defence of their cherished
particularism Protestants and Catholics alike would
further the interests of French or Turks, or Papists or
English, or any enemy that Germany and the Emperor
might have. French policy was at this moment under-
going a curious change. At Hagenau the French envoy
Baif, especially invited by the Emperor to be present,
had used his opportunity to attempt the seduction of
the Protestants. A Lutheran embassy to France was,
indeed, promised, but in spite of the aid of Sleidan, the
official historian of the party, Baif met with no positive
results. At Regensburg French agents were accredited

to each of the religious parties. With the Lutherans here again success was negative, although Calvin, who accompanied the Strassburg delegates, made use of his logic and his eloquence on behalf of the persecutor of his creed. The failure was due to the absence of Luther's master, who was, as has been seen, eager at this moment for French alliance. The ultramontane Catholics offered a more fruitful field. The Bavarians were always ready for a promising intrigue. Albert of Mainz, forgetful of his earlier pagan indifference or Erasmian tolerance, had personally suffered from Protestant interference with his sovereignty at Halle : he threatened Charles with deposition if he departed but a hair's-breadth from the Faith. The French king contemplated a protectorate of the Catholic League of Nuremberg, which Dr. Egelhaaf has compared to Philip II.'s patronage of the League of Paris.

Nevertheless French intervention was more interesting than it was important. To it has been ascribed the wreck of the most promising scheme for German religious and political reunion. This is a gross exaggeration, due, it must be confessed, in part to the vanity of the French diplomatists who, at Regensburg as in England, in Venice or at Rome, were more ingenious than effective. German Catholics and Protestants only contrived their secret assignations with the French temptress as a consolation or excuse for the rejection of the legitimate union. Had every French diplomatist concentrated his cash and eloquence on Scotland or Mirandola the result of the conference of Regensburg would have been unaltered.

It is more than time to return to Charles, for his disappointment at Regensburg is, perhaps, the most enlightening event in his theological career. There is

reason for believing that he was at this crisis much
under Granvelle's influence, though it is fully possible
that the relation might be reversed, and that the
minister was mainly the official spokesman.   Before the
conference opened Granvelle expressed his belief that,
if a remedy were not found, all Germany, Italy, the
Netherlands and even France, already deeply affected,
would join the schism.   No one, therefore, had a keener
interest than Charles in the search for this remedy.
During the conference he protested strongly to the
Saxon envoys against the statement made by Luther's
friend, Amsdorf, that he was not in earnest, calling God
to witness that he would, with the help of the Estates,
set reform in hand even without the Pope's consent.
When agreement seemed hopeless, Contarini implored
Charles to use his authority to bring the heretics back
from their errors.   The reply was chilling.   The
Emperor confessed that he was no theologian, but he
understood that the quarrel on the Sacrament was only
over the word Transubstantiation, and that the Protestants were willing to reintroduce Confession : it seemed
to him better to win the Protestants as far as possible,
and at the conclusion to examine the articles still disputed, and make the requisite precautions.   His final
sentence emphasised his meaning,—it was easy enough
to break off the whole negotiations : this could be done
any minute, but very much depended on such a breach.
No sooner had the conference failed than Charles proposed that the articles agreed upon should be regarded
as binding both parties, and that there should be mutual
tolerance upon the others until a final œcumenical or
national settlement.   However great were the practical
concessions made hereafter, never before or again did he
so definitely suggest the principle of tolerance.   This is

an isolated moment in the history of his ecclesiastical attitude. His motive was, he assured the legate, to avoid the inconvenience—nay, the impossibility, of war, to check the "rush" of heresy by accepting such gains as were at the moment possible. Contarini denounced such weakness, which would only widen schism, if Pope and Emperor should recognise or even keep silence on false doctrine: if it were necessary to have peace in Germany, it was also necessary that every one should know that Catholics and Protestants were doctrinally severed, and that not only should there be no agreement with the latter, but that there should be no stint nor stay in their reprobation, though this with gentleness and without the clang of war. Such was the view of the most moderate of Roman theologians.

With Luther Charles had equally poor success. His attitude towards his chief antagonist had been throughout significant. Before the conference he had had the agreement of Worms privately laid before him. During the session Contarini states that Charles was disposed to allow Luther to appear by proxy. Now at the close the toleration proposal was submitted to him by friendly princes. Luther veiled refusal in the demand that the Emperor should in every state cause the accepted articles to be "purely and clearly preached,"— that is, interpreted in the Lutheran sense. Impudent as the answer was, it was full of satirical good sense, for the agreement was a mere fog of phrases which only momentarily concealed the bridgeless gulf.

The Emperor's ill-humour was vented not against Luther but against Catholic Bavaria, whose political hostility was wrecking his schemes for religious union. The Bavarian Chancellor was, indeed, playing a disreputable, reckless game, urging Charles to suppress

heresy by force, and intriguing with the Lutheran
princes for a league on behalf of German liberty under
a French protectorate. When Contarini urged Charles
to join the Catholic League, he replied that he would
make no league with so-called Catholics, who in divers
ways never ceased to spoil the Church : he would not
always be entangled in wars for their personal interests :
his duty was to fight the Turk, and in this he found no
support : if every one else only sought his own advantage,
he must do the same. Five days later he assured the
legate that, if the Bavarians did not mend their ways,
he should come to terms with the Protestants. Charles
flatly told the Bavarian dukes themselves that he had
no money for a war ; and that, if he had, he would not
spend it in Germany to no purpose, for the war would
be all the stiffer with Germans fighting against Germans,
and all the more useless, for the Protestants, even if
beaten, would not abandon their opinions. It had been
well if this sentence had recurred to his memory after
the victory of 1547.

The Pope was nearly as roughly handled as were the
Bavarians. Paul, in furtherance of his dynastic interests,
had utilised the Emperor's embarrassments to attack the
territories of the faithful Colonna. Charles did not
disguise his anger ; he told the legate, moreover, that he
believed the Pope to be plotting with France and Venice,
and complained bitterly of his stinginess. To Contarini's
entreaty to defer his departure he answered that he had
been four months in Germany without doing any good
or receiving any help : he meant now to leave great
enterprises alone and devote himself to small ones,
seeking his own interest as others did : he had no faith
in the Pope's promises,—" When I see the Council I
shall believe it." Charles in fact at this moment dreaded

the Council which Paul had summoned to Vicenza, because it would only accentuate division and lead to religious war.

Baulked in his hopes of comprehension and in his scheme for toleration Charles fell back upon the old method of suspension. Within the space of eighteen months the results of the conference should be laid before a General Council, or, failing that, a national synod, or, as a last alternative, a diet. In the recess the truce of Nuremberg and the edict of Augsburg reappeared side by side, but the restrictions officially imposed upon the Protestants were completely nullified by a private declaration of the Emperor. The possession of Church property, the Christian reformation of sees and convents, and the removal of religious cases from the competence of the Imperial Chamber, received Charles's personal guarantee. The veto on Protestant propagandism was sensibly modified ; the Lutherans were promised seats in the Imperial Chamber ; they were suffered to interpret the accepted articles of the *Book of Regensburg* in the Protestant sense. As the sole ostensible reward Charles received the paltry promise of 12,000 men for three or at most four months. This grant was made on July 29 ; on the same day of August Solyman took Buda-Pesth, and, brushing aside the claims of Zapolya's son, incorporated it with his dominions. The Hungarian cathedral became a Turkish mosque. Just two months before, when the Protestants received solemn warning, they only laughed and answered that they had more faith in Turk than Christian. Meanwhile the more devoted German Catholics were virtually the Turk's allies.

Charles had apparently been beaten all along the line. Nevertheless he had in reality pierced the Protestant left wing, while containing and neutralising the Catholic

right. The ostensible operations at Regensburg were of
less real importance than those which were privily conducted. Here the negotiations opened with Philip of
Hesse at Worms were brought to their conclusion. The
Landgrave was promised indemnity for the past, protection and advancement for the future. In return he
engaged to oppose the admittance of France, England,
or the Duke of Cleves into the League of Schmalkalde,
to recognise Ferdinand upon the Emperor's death, to
reconcile Christian III. of Denmark with the Count
Palatine Frederick and his wife. This was not the only
gain. Philip's son-in-law, Maurice of Saxony, was detached from his father, Duke Henry, who had disliked
the Hessian marriage. Joachim of Brandenburg promised not to enter the Protestant league, in return for
the Emperor's confirmation of the hybrid reformation
which he had imposed upon his Church. Saxony was
virtually isolated and France rendered harmless. This
was in reality the first blow of the campaign, of which
the fight at Mühlberg was the last. During these years
Charles or his ministers would sail very near the wind
of conscience to gain a Lutheran soldier. Granvelle
once suggested to Schärtlin, the best professional captain
in Protestant service, that he should attack France
through Lorraine, and occupy the three bishoprics, Metz,
Toul and Verdun, for his pains. "Then," said Schärtlin,
"I should turn the bishops out." "Do it, if you like,"
replied Granvelle, "but do not talk about it."

Having divided the Lutherans, Charles at once propitiated and hampered the Catholic agitators by joining
the somewhat shadowy League of Nuremberg. The
Papal party had long pressed this, but Ferdinand had
dissuaded it, as it would be the beginning of religious
war. The Emperor, however, only joined on the con-

dition that the union should be defensive.   He had
now secured his rear against a French or Lutheran or
Catholic attack.   The diet of Regensburg, abortive as it
had appeared, enabled him to leave Germany for Algiers.

The Truce of Frankfurt

The Truce of Frankfurt (see p. 334) is so illustrative of Charles's attitude
towards concession in 1539, that it seems to require somewhat fuller treatment.
The Protestant Estates met at Frankfurt in February, and there was much
division of opinion as to the wisdom of forestalling the Emperor's expected
attack, Saxony and Hesse both being at first in favour of the offensive.   Then
appeared as Imperial plenipotentiary, not as before the Strong Catholic Held,
but the moderate Archbishop of Lund.   The Protestants demanded a permanent peace for all who might now or hereafter adhere to the Augsburg Confession, in order that the Gospel might have free course.   They rejected Lund's
requirement that no ecclesiastic should henceforth be deprived of his revenues.
He then tried to exclude all Sacramentarian Estates from the benefits of the
Truce of Nuremberg, and to confine it to Germany proper, thus closing the
door to England, Denmark, Prussia, Riga and Revel.   At this moment Henry
of Brunswick's troops threatened to execute the ban against the Protestant
town of Minden.   This would inevitably have produced a general war but for
Lund's undertaking to disband them, and for the Landgrave's physical condition, which disabled him for active service.   The danger hastened the truce of
April 19.   This was concluded for at all events six months, during which time
no penal proceedings should be taken against the Protestants, while they
should admit no new members to their league, nor withdraw revenues from the
clergy except for the necessary support of pastors, preachers, schools and
hospitals.   Before the close of the truce a national assembly should strive to
effect a religious reconciliation in the presence of the Emperor's and Ferdinand's
plenipotentiaries, but without the intervention of a Papal envoy.   It was
agreed that the truce should extend to fifteen months if Charles would consent
(1) to concede after its expiry the protection of the Truce of Nuremberg to all
present and future adherents of the Augsburg Confession ; (2) to forbid during
its term the enrolment of new members in the Catholic League of Nuremberg.
These conditions Charles refused ; he cared little for the Catholic League, but
much for the limitation of heresy both in space and time.   Thus the truce was
limited to six months.   The Protestants gained this much, that, during that
term, Estates not protected by the Nuremberg truce were safeguarded, and that
the principle of religious settlement by a national assembly was accepted by an
Imperial representative.   Charles, on the other hand, secured himself at a very
critical moment from the admission of Cleves, England or Denmark into the
League of Schmalkalde.   The subject is clearly treated in Dr. Egelhaaf's *Deutsche
Geschichte*, vol. ii. pp. 341-348.

END OF VOL. I

Printed by R. & R. Clark, Limited, *Edinburgh.*